£5

D1349654

AT THE CUTTING EDGE

Also by Sir Fred Catherwood

The Christian in Industrial Society
Britain with the Brakes Off
The Christian Citizen
A Better Way
First Things First
God's Time God's Money
David : Poet, Warrior, King
Pro-Europe?

At the Cutting Edge

Sir Fred Catherwood

Hodder & Stoughton
LONDON   SYDNEY   AUCKLAND

Copyright © Sir Frederick Catherwood

First published in Great Britain in 1995

The right of Sir Frederick Catherwood to be identified as the author
of this work has been asserted by him in accordance with the
Copyright, Designs and Patents Act 1988.

10 9 8 7 6 5 4 3 2 1

All rights reserved. No part of this publication may be
reproduced, stored in a retrieval system, or transmitted
in any form or by any means, without the prior written
permission of the publisher, nor be otherwise circulated
in any form of binding or cover other than that in which
it is published and without a similar condition being
imposed on the subsequent purchaser.

British Library Cataloguing in Publication Data

A record for this title is available from the British Library

ISBN 0 340 64246 7

Typeset by Palimpsest Book Production Limited,
Polmont, Stirlingshire
Printed and bound in Great Britain by
Mackays of Chatham PLC, Chatham, Kent

Hodder and Stoughton
A division of Hodder Headline PLC
338 Euston Road
London NW1 3BH

to Elizabeth
my good companion for most of these adventures

CONTENTS

INTRODUCTION

During a long life in industry, public service and politics I always seemed to be at the heart of the argument about Britain's place in the world. We British were reluctant to move away from the destiny of a great Empire, we took our place late and uneasily in Europe, pulled always by our American ties. Yet on our own, we found it hard to keep our share of world trade, to stabilise our sliding currency and to get off the interminable wage-price spiral. One reason for this book is that I have worked over the years with the most of the key players, close enough to understand what, in the crunch, swayed their decisions for good or ill.

First came the effort to make British industry more professional and more competitive; then the effort to persuade governments accustomed to ruling empires to attend to the industry and commerce on which our strength and future depended; followed by the need to gain equal access to the rapidly expanding European markets and, while baulked of that, to find the resources needed to keep British products up to date. Then, in the EC at last, came the first oil shock. A Labour government dominated by its anti-European left yet supported industry's great effort to take our share of the new market, an effort which was totally destroyed after four successful years by a Conservative government dominated by its Monetarist right with the loss of nearly a quarter of our manufacturing industry and leaving over three million unemployed.

Finally, came the rarest experience of all: fifteen years of trying, against an increasingly anti-European home government, to carry British interests through the much more powerful instrument of the European Community, and to reform that Community and build it into a democratically accountable and lasting Union.

Woven through the last twenty-five years has been the conflict in Ireland where, uniquely, with friends on both sides of the border of that divided island I have shuttled back and forwards, wherever I could see an opening, trying to edge the two insecure minorities, the Catholics in the North and the Protestants in the island of Ireland, to an agreement which would protect them both.

But woven even more deeply in the story is the faith of an active Christian in a society which, for thirty years, has thrown over its thousand-year Christian heritage and is trying to work through the dangerous social experiment of a permissive materialistic society, with great damage to our social stability and great risk to our Christian heritage of freedom and democracy.

Life is not a black and white sketch, and I have tried to make the story reflect the rich and colourful tapestry of people and places. My work has taken me to all five continents, not with the superficial glance of the tourist, but in hard negotiations with politicians, businessmen and civil servants and, at a quite different level, debate and discussion with churches and students. I hope the book comes over as the world came to me with the quick quips which summed up the long arguments and which reflected such different backgrounds and assumptions. I could not have had a more interesting life and I hope you enjoy this brief story as much as I enjoyed writing it.

Chapter One

ULSTER ROOTS

In 1916 there was an Irish nationalist rising in Dublin. It was the beginning of five years of bloodshed all across the island. The British government tried repression, sending in undisciplined ex-servicemen as auxiliary police, the notorious 'black and tans'. Protestant houses were destroyed and the 'black and tans' indulged in indiscriminate reprisals. In 1921 Lloyd George met the provisional Irish government, and a treaty was signed dividing the thirty-two counties into twenty-six for the Irish Free State and six for the Protestant counties in the north-east. Eamon de Valera repudiated the treaty and there was civil war, in which the charismatic government leader, Michael Collins, was killed by the rebels.

Creagh House, where the Catherwoods had farmed for 150 years – and the Courtneys for a hundred years or more before that – was in the six counties, but it was also in Nationalist country.

The Catherwoods had come over to Ulster with the first Jacobean settlement, when William Shakespeare was still writing plays and before the Pilgrim Fathers sailed for America. The big family bible records the family line from 1754.

The only Catherwood to achieve any fame in those days was Frederick, an artist and architect, friend of Keats and Joseph Severn, who did very accurate drawings of Roman and Egyptian ruins, but is best known for the first drawings of the Maya temples in Yucatan, done on expeditions with the American explorer John Stevens in the 1840s.

My great-grandfather William took over the farm in the 1840s, when Henry, my grandfather, was born. But then the terrible potato famine gripped Ireland. William took his elder daughter to America to see whether they and the rest of the family could make a new life there, but he died very shortly afterwards in Arkansas. Not long after that, his wife Catherine died too, leaving Henry to be brought up by his mother's family, the Stewarts.

A remarkable religious revival came to Ulster in 1859 and young Henry and his grandmother, both of whom had been only nominal Presbyterians, became true Christians. Henry went to his minister and told him that he had been converted, was now a committed Christian and wanted to learn more of his new-found faith. His minister told him that he would soon get over it. But someone put him in touch with what we would now call a 'house-group', who took him under their wing. They went on Sundays to a Brethren Assembly in Magherafelt, so he left the Presbyterians and and stayed with the Brethren for the rest of his life.

Henry's Stewart cousins were given a good education and went into the professions, but Henry was neglected and, after the death of his grandmother, he went to live in Moyola Cottage on the Creagh lands with his elder brother John and his uncle Matthew. He also seems to have turned his back on the 'establishment', as represented by his Stewart cousins and the Presbyterian Church, and buried himself in the work of the farm.

When he was thirty-five, he married Elizabeth Irwin, some years younger and by all accounts very beautiful, but also very strong-minded. She bore him eleven children, of whom my father, Stuart, was the tenth, and presided over the house and farm even when in her sixties. She was a formidable lady, and with good cause. When my father, Stuart, and his elder brother Ernest volunteered to fight in 1917, she intercepted the letters from the regiment and tore them up. She told them, 'If you go, who is going to defend us against the Sinn Feiners?'

She had a point. As I have mentioned, Creagh House was in Nationalist country. Her husband was then in his seventies, her youngest son Courtney was lame, the farm hands were all Catholic, and my father and his brother were the only two able-bodied men at hand.

Yet the Catherwoods, though Protestants, were not at all involved in Unionist politics or the quasi-politics of the Orange Order, because the Brethren's strong pietistic tradition kept politics at arm's length, and they lived in peace with their Catholic neighbours and workers.

That neighbourliness was not enough to protect Creagh House when the 1916 rising in Dublin spread to the whole country at the end of the war. But despite two hold-ups for paraffin to burn the Toomebridge police barracks, Creagh House survived. The Irish Treaty was signed and then a further rebellion broke out against the new Irish government which had signed it. The family feeling was, 'If they hadn't started fighting each other, we'd have been done for.'

The faith of Henry and Elizabeth Catherwood burned bright, but, having married late, Henry brought up a family while in his forties, fifties and sixties and he forgot that each child has to find faith for themselves.

Their eldest daughter Edith was married to a solid farmer, William Anderson, and of Aunt Edith's Christian faith I have no doubt. But their eldest son Fred rebelled. He was exceptionally bright and did very well at school. But there was no proper job on the farm and the family restraints irked him.

So in March 1907, aged twenty-three, the pride of his parents, the elder brother of whom all the younger brothers and sisters stood in awe, Fred left for America, sailing from Liverpool on the White Star Liner *Baltic* with three thousand on board. It was a common enough story all over Europe, but the sharp edge of a rebellion on his side and of failure on theirs made it a severe blow to his parents.

I have his photograph, taken at the time, in which he stands in a stiff white collar with a proud and self-assured expression, and the letters he sent back to Edith, his newly married sister. His first job was in the oriental rugs department of Gimbel Brothers in Philadelphia (advertised as 'the biggest store in the world'). In his letters he is torn between amazement at the amount of money he can earn and loneliness at the loss of the lively family circle. He tries to reconcile the two by saying 'a couple of weeks would see me in Ireland'. The family argument flits like a ghost through the letters. He says he wanted to be independent, to make his own decisions about his faith and his future.

In the first few months he still asks whether his father will give him the independence which he wants in a job at home; if not, he will go west. But his father, with three other sons and three unmarried daughters – half still at school – gave no assurances. Fred, on his side, announces that he has quickly been promoted and, enjoying the confidence of a hard and experienced boss, is beginning to realise his own abilities. Now he wants his head even more.

The next letters are from Idaho, where he has found work in the mines. He is living in much rougher conditions, but making a lot more money which he begins to invest in property.

Then the letters stop. One fatal day he was driving an electric railcar down the tunnel into the mine when there was an electrical fault and he was killed. Fred was buried in the Masonic Cemetery in Spokane and the Masons sent his few belongings back home. I still have his penknife with the Masonic insignia.

It was a tragedy from which Henry Catherwood never fully recovered. My father, who was ten, remembers the first Christmas after Fred died and it put him off Christmas celebrations for the rest of his life. Henry felt himself to blame, not realising that, like many sons of the Victorians, Fred was as likely to react against his parents as to follow; that each must answer for themselves.

My father, though a rascal in his youth, dropping out of school at sixteen, worked steadily to develop and mechanise the excavation of Lough Neagh sand and, when in 1924 he married Jean Agnew, the daughter of a neighbouring farmer, his parents approved warmly.

They lived at first in Moyola Cottage, which my father renovated and which stood where the farm bordered the Moyola River as it flowed into Lough Neagh. I was born under its thatch in January 1925, six months before my grandfather died at the good old age of eighty, another Fred and the first grandchild to carry on the family name.

Six months later we moved to Belfast, but Creagh House and the farm remained a central part of my childhood.

One of my earliest memories is riding back from the meadows to the farm, when I was staying during the hay harvest of 1927 on the front of the rickshifter, the low sideless cart which carried the hayrick.

At the farm there were kittens to play with, donkeys to ride, terrifying turkeys as high as I was and which rushed at me down the farmyard; fat pigs giving birth to litters of piglets, cows being milked in the byre. There was a dairy with a big churn which made the butter, dark lofts up steep wooden steps and pumps in the yard, which brought up very cold water.

When all else failed, there were the aunts, Lily, Hilda and Ethel. Aunt Lily was loving and motherly, Aunt Ethel played jokes and Aunt Hilda was tall and dignified. Aunt Lily also kept the farm shop, which had sweets as well as big bins of oatmeal, sugar, tea and lots of other things whose names I didn't know. I felt very important being on the 'inside' of the long wooden counter and Aunt Lily was very generous with the sweets. At night the oil lamps were lit, and threw great frightening shadows on the walls, but there was always a reassuring aunt at hand.

At Creagh House Aunt Lily and Aunt Hilda decided to start a Sunday School and I remember attending one of the first in a back kitchen. Soon the kitchen couldn't hold the number of children, mostly Catholic, pouring in from the lanes around on a Sunday afternoon so the aunts bought an ex-army hut which they filled to overflowing. I remember lessons there in the winter when the windows were shut and the body smell was unforgettable.

They also started a Sunday afternoon meeting, with preachers down from Belfast. In the summer, when the windows were open, there was a constant background of farmyard noises, which country folk never noticed, but it was a sore trial to urban speakers to have their purple passages greeted by prolonged crowing from a nearby cock.

I also remember going to Sunday morning services in local Brethren Assemblies, which would be no more than a tin tabernacle, with the road on one side and a field on the other. They were solemn occasions for the adults but incredibly boring for young children and our attention wandered easily to the animal life outside. My father remembers a cow coming to an open window and trying to pull a green roller blind. Each time it pulled and lost its grip, the blind would spring back, until finally the cow managed to pull the whole blind out of its socket and trail it triumphantly back to the middle of the field, to the silent cheers of all the children.

But what impressed itself most on my childish mind was the sincerity and passion of the speakers. Their words might be uncouth, but how they meant them! I could see that something had happened to them which made their whole attitude to life quite different from the ordinary. And all of human life was there. I remember a big raw-boned policeman, whose wife had died during the week. He did not stay at home silently mourning. He came to the meeting and electrified everyone by his prayer. He spoke to the Lord from his heart, thanking him for the wife he had given him, pouring out his distress in his loss, praying for strength and grace for himself and his children to bear it and assuring the Lord that, whatever happened, he still trusted him.

The Brethren were also in the old pietistic tradition which believed in almost total separation from the social life of the world. This kept my grandfather and father from the identification of their faith with Protestant supremacy. But there was still at Creagh House and at my mother's home, Rockview, the long Calvinist tradition that the Lord had put us here to fulfil our earthly calling and that we should work hard to develop whatever talent we had been given. The insistence on education and hard work, the belief among the brothers, including Fred, that they must develop their talents, all came from the common culture of the Scots and Ulster Scots which traces back through John Knox to John Calvin.

My aunts were in the same tradition. Though Edith was widowed, she made sure that all her children were educated and had a profession. Joseph was a company secretary, Hilda was a nurse and later a much loved matron of Antrim Hospital, Doreen was a secretary, Cather an engineer and Arthur a farmer. When my grandmother died, Aunt Hilda had retired from teaching and she and Aunt Lily were in their sixties. During World War I the air force had turned their farm into an airfield, so they had moved to Northfields in Antrim, where they had a house with a large garden. They could have retired with dignity, but they felt that they should make themselves useful, so they set up a flourishing business in day-old chicks in the garden of their Antrim house which kept them busy for more than ten years until finally their health began to fail.

I understood none of their motivation at the time. I only knew that my parents came from the same tradition, determined that I and my two sisters should have as good an education as we could and that we should make the best of it.

As soon as I was born, it was clear to my father that the farm and sand business could not support his new family, so he decided to start his own business. My mother had inherited some money on the death of her father and they invested it in a bus, which ran initially from Toomebridge, near the Creagh, to Belfast. Buses were, for the first time, as reliable as railways. They were also far cheaper to run and much more flexible, stopping at the side of the road wherever there were passengers; but they needed to be as frequent as the trains. For that, one bus was not enough, and to finance the number of buses for a regular service, it was necessary to run on the busy routes. So within a short time Father switched to the main Belfast, Ballymena and Portrush route, buying a fleet of Leyland buses on hire purchase.

Competition was quite unregulated. Bus owners would buy their rivals' timetables and put their buses on a few minutes ahead. Father aimed to have experienced drivers, courteous conductors, buses which were clean and never broke down, and a regular and frequent service. Then, if a rival bus drew up at the stop, passengers would decide to 'wait a minute or two for the Catherwood bus'.

To buy a whole fleet on hire purchase was a risk; yet those who did not have a regular service were certain to fail. The other competitors, the railways, were vulnerable. They were twice as expensive and people were tired of running for a train and finding the gates slammed in their face.

The bus routes spread to Derry and down to Dublin, duplicating the main lines of rail traffic, and rail freight also began to move to road. The railways were horrified. Since Father had taken away more business than anyone else, they sent an offer to buy him out. With the cheek of youth, he made a return offer to buy them out, adding that he was being specially generous to offer for a rapidly declining industry.

During the summer his cashflow was strong but in the winter he depended on the banks. The railways suggested to the banks that they should call in their loans, but the banks had done their sums and they continued to back Father. The railways then pointed out to the police that a law to prevent overloading of horses limited the number of passengers in a road vehicle and that the legal speed limit was 12 mph. No case was brought on this archaic law but, just to be safe, Father took on ex-police sergeants as travelling ticket inspectors and had no trouble until the law was changed.

The Londonderry City Council asked him to run a bus service for the city and he also found a loophole in Belfast City Council's by-laws which enabled him to put on, unasked, a service from all the tram terminals into the city centre. Since the buses ran for half the tramfare, at twice the speed and twice the comfort, the city trams soon rattled along empty. The City Corporation brought an injunction and the matter was only decided by a settlement across the province on who ran where. Father, being the biggest problem, came out with the best routes, Belfast–Dublin and Belfast–Ballymena–Derry/Portrush.

I was immensely proud of the Catherwood buses, in their Cambridge-blue livery with 'HMS Catherwood' (Harold Matthew Stuart) along the side. I was especially proud of the first double-deckers to be seen in Ireland, which had to be built especially low to go under the Templepatrick railway bridge. The maintenance garage was an old aircraft hangar in Donegall Road. In the summer, and when the RAC Tourist Trophy motor race was held on the Ards Circuit (Dundonald–Newtonards–Comber), all the cars came there to be examined by official scrutineers. I can still see those huge shining Bentleys, in British racing green, the Alfa-Romeos in red, and the Frazer-Nashes, racing Rileys, Aston-Martins and MGs, all with long bonnets, huge instrument dials and the regulation minimum mudguards and headlights (to establish that they were tourers and not racing cars). We were given two free tickets for the grandstand and I went with Father's driver, Eddie Woods. It was the noisiest and most exciting day of the year. We watched the Italian genius Nuvolari in a red Alfa, Freddie Dixon with his own Riley, and the back-marker, E R Hall, with a big heavily handicapped Bentley. There was the roar of the start, the drama of the pit-stops and the special drama at the end as the big cars began to catch up with the small ones, until there were only seconds between the leaders as they came down the straight for the chequered flag.

When I was five, and after the birth of my two sisters, Mary and Elizabeth, we moved from a small 'garden suburb' semi to a bigger house with a large steeply sloping garden – Ballin a Cor – further out on the Antrim Road. At the back the fields ran up to the woods of Belfast's Table Mountain, Cave Hill, and in front we had the most wonderful view along the lough, to the Norman-built Carrickfergus Castle and beyond it, on a good day, to the Scottish coast at Portpatrick.

In those days there was a constant traffic of ships on the lough. The daily ferries to Liverpool, Heysham, Ardrossan and Glasgow, the constant shuttle of little colliers and bigger tramp steamers, the tender to the trans-Atlantic liners and, very occasionally, the new liners from Harland and Wolff, with tugs in attendance, out on their sea trials. The ships, small and large, caught my romantic imagination.

On my sixth birthday, I had pneumonia and hovered in delirium for several days before the crisis passed. It was 1931 and in the height of the slump, Vestey's Blue Star Line had taken a 16,000-ton passenger ship, the *Arandora Star*, off the South American route to a Mediterranean cruise. Father and Mother decided that a sea voyage would do me good and I was in seventh heaven. My first sight of England was the Mersey ferryboat. I remember the huge arch at Euston, the red London buses passing along Euston Road, the big tidy fields and farms of southern England, and the long line of boats laid up by the slump, riding at anchor all the way down Southampton Water.

Through the Bay of Biscay, Father and I were the only people in the dining saloon and I have been grateful ever since then for good sea legs. I made friends with everyone, but especially the Chief Officer, with three gold rings on his sleeve and his own cabin opening on to the main deck. He took me up on the bridge and down to the engine room and, as I had a sailor suit, I was soon given a sailor hat, with 'Arandora Star' on the ribbon. We went ashore at Tangier and Algiers. I remember the huge harbour at Malta with the dusky P&O ships on the India route. Passengers would go from ship to shore in two motor boats and, when the main rush was over, I was allowed to steer one in and out at Susa, Derna, Port Said, Jaffa, Haifa, Beirut and Rhodes. Our last port of call was Palma and my last memory of the Mediterranean was the lights of Gibraltar.

As I got a bit older, I used to go on one of the buses to Portrush to see my cousin Irwin and on a bicycle to Downview Avenue to see Harry, Sidney and Stuart. I remember the bitter cold of Portrush in the winter, but the warmth of Aunt May's welcome. At school my closest friend was Edwin Quekett, whose father was Northern Ireland's Attorney General. They lived in a big house at the top of Cavehill Road. We explored the back of Cave Hill on bicycles and sloshed down the streams in wellington boots. I also learned to ride a pony, which was more common for boys in the days when cars were still a novelty.

Sunday services and Sunday School were a central part of our lives. We attended Victoria Hall, a city-centre Brethren Assembly in a converted music hall in May Street, just off Donegall Square. We had to sit right through the hour-and-a-half Sunday service and sing hymns without piano or organ. It was a working-class church with professional leadership. But in the morning service any male member of the congregation could speak or pray and it was quite impossible for a boy to follow most of them. What impressed me was the love and kindness of the elders. It was clear to me that these were good and wise men, who had something special about them and I was prepared to put up with all the rest for their sakes. At Sunday School, even more working-class than the church, my teachers were the elders' daughters, gentle and kind and simple in their teaching.

From 1930 to 1936 we went to Portballintrae on the North Antrim coast for our holidays and years later I found that I could remember every ridge in the rocks. I used to rush down very early in the morning to go out with the fishermen to raise the lobster pots and through the day the whole place was alive with other children to play with. There was also a children's mission, the CSSM, based in nearby Portrush and led by John Carson, later Moderator of the Presbyterian Church in Ireland. We decorated the pulpit built of sand, from which the university students led us in catchy choruses and gave us simple talks. In the afternoon there were competitions and on one evening a week a special sausage sizzle in the sand dunes across the River Bush. Second only to my mother, the CSSM must have been one of the most formative influences in developing my Christian faith.

In the summer of 1934 there was a big tent mission on a vacant site opposite the Belfast Opera House, with Fred Elliot, a Scottish miner, as the missioner. He was about forty with twinkling eyes, curly black hair and a broken nose. He was the sort of man a boy could believe in, friendly and cheerful as he talked to us afterwards. He would swallow a raw egg to keep his voice from cracking (in the days before good loudspeaker systems). He had earned his living the hard way down the mines and I respected him. So I confessed my misdeeds and asked God's forgiveness. Since that day sixty years ago I have known what it is to have a personal faith, to have a daily personal communication with the God of the bible, through prayer and the answers to prayer which come through the bible itself, through a sharpened conscience and through the events about which I have prayed. I know more now than I did as a nine-year-old, but the personal faith is just the same. There are those who would say that this is all explicable in terms of upbringing, with Christian parents and grandparents, and regular indoctrination in church, Sunday Schools and seaside missions. But the effect on my Uncle Fred had been just the opposite. He, like many another, rebelled against the heavy teaching of family and church. If youthful indoctrination were the golden road to faith, then the twentieth-century churches would never have emptied as they did. In any case, the faith of the boy of nine has lasted for sixty years.

In the same year, I was sent away to a boarding school in England. The Headmaster and some of the teachers were Christians, but some were not and few of the boys had the faith which I had just found. So I was subject to peer pressure from the beginning. But, young though I was, I was quite clear which standard I had to live by.

I was far from perfect. I had a fierce Irish temper and I could, as I grew older and stronger, occasionally hit boys weaker than I was. I doubt whether I worked nearly as hard as I should have done and I was bored to tears by the Brethren service every Sunday morning. We used to divert ourselves by counting up the authors of the hymns to see who had written the most, James G Deck, the most prolific, being disallowed.

Kingsmead School was on Cheshire's Wirral coast, where William of Orange had mustered his troops before embarking for the Irish campaign which resulted in victory over James II at the Battle of the Boyne. The Irish Sea was an impassable barrier which added to the feeling of separation from the family for the three long months of each term.

The great metropolis was Liverpool, then in its heyday as a North Atlantic port. The famous overhead railway ran from one end of the long Mersey docks to the other; the Adelphi Hotel was newly built; Lewis's was the wonder departmental store which sold everything and, shortly after I went there, King George V came to Liverpool to open the new Mersey Tunnel. The huge Anglican cathedral was nearly finished and Liverpool seemed to us to be the essence of urban sophistication, a great treat when parents came on a rare visit, or when, at half-term, another boy's parents took pity on those who lived too far away to go home.

In winter our compulsory Sunday walks took us along the flat, bleak and windy Wirral coast, bounded by endless sandbanks and miles of concrete, a boring contrast to the hills, rocks and beaches of the Ulster coast. After we had endured them, we came back to the Headmaster's wife, Mrs Watts, whose son Leslie Lyall was a missionary in China, and she would tell us, with the aid of a big map of China over the fireplace, all about that war-torn country. It was the time of what we now know as 'the long march', when the Communists under Mao marched from south to west to north to establish themselves nearer to the Soviet Union. On the way they had picked up some missionaries, and each week we would be given the latest news of their fate. Some were martyred, but others survived to tell the tale.

The Headmaster's sons, all in their twenties, were very active Christians. Gordon, the eldest, was training to be a physical training teacher and was muscular Christianity personified. Ian was a rugger blue at Oxford and we were all enormously proud of him, listening to the Oxford matches on the wireless. David, who eventually took over the school, played soccer with us in his bare feet. Fat cheerful Hilbre used to take Crusader class – a sort of Sunday School –

and we asked him all the awkward questions we could think of.

'Sir, God has promised to answer prayer.'

'Yes of course.'

'Well then, if we prayed for a Mars Bar, he should really give us one, shouldn't he?'

We wouldn't have asked Arthur Watts, his father, questions like that. He was a brisk and awesome figure, not to be trifled with. He was a good Christian and a good teacher. He taught mathematics and you learnt to learn. If he caught you reading books inside on a fine day, you would soon be outside without further ceremony. I don't remember newspapers at Kingsmead, but the cook had a wireless and we crowded into the kitchen to hear the abdication speech of Edward VIII.

At that time there seemed to me to be a settled order of government, represented by the Duke of Abercorn, who was the Governor of Northern Ireland, Lord Craigavon, the Prime Minister and Sir Crawford McCullogh, who was the Lord Mayor of Belfast. Only with the abdication did I become conscious that there was a British Prime Minister, Mr Stanley Baldwin. The Duke of Abercorn came to look at the Catherwood buses at the Balmoral Agricultural Show and said that he was very glad that he had sold all his railway shares.

But the railways were to have the last word. In the slump, when people decided that they could no longer pay double for the privilege of travelling by train, the railways running across the sparsely populated island of Ireland were hard hit and made heavy losses. In desperation they went to the two governments and pleaded that they were a strategic asset. Since Ireland had to import coal as well as oil, it is not clear why the railways were more strategic than the roads, but in those days of protectionism, the argument had some resonance. The first to concede was the newly elected Irish government headed by the former rebel, Eamon de Valera. In 1934 all the road transport in the Irish Free State was nationalised. At that time, the Catherwood buses ran on the two trunk routes in the Irish Free State, from Belfast to Dublin and Dublin to Cork, and although the disappearance of that business was a heavy blow, it was not fatal.

The Stormont government took longer. It set up a Commission

of Enquiry and that eventually reported that the road transport of the province should be nationalised. The Northern Ireland Road Transport Board took over the company at the end of 1935, a blow from which my father, then aged thirty-six, took years to recover. Nationalisation was a disastrous failure. The Board made a loss from the start and was reorganised about a dozen times before Ulsterbus and Citybus, chaired by my cousin Sidney, finally made a profit. So maybe the Catherwoods of the Creagh had the last word after all.

Father had put all he had into the buses. From having just one bus in Toomebridge, he had eventually covered all of Ireland. His tours, 'See Ireland first', had given thousands their first sight of their native land. He never had a strike. He never discriminated between Catholic and Protestant. When a driver applied for a job, explaining that, though a Catholic, he was not a very good one, Father said that he would prefer to employ a good Catholic than a bad one, but what most interested him was whether drivers were experienced, safe, sober and reliable. He gave free passes to all clergy, whether rectors, ministers, priests or nuns. He was not only the first to introduce double-deckers in Ireland, but his American Faejal buses were the first to have all-round independent suspension, giving a totally new standard of road-holding and comfort.

Father told me never to put my trust in politicians! And it reinforced his determination that I should have the education he had so foolishly given up at sixteen. He felt that he had been outmanoeuvred by the talking classes; he had had the strongest case, but had not known how to argue it. And, if the worst came to the worst, 'They can take away your business, but they can't take away your education.' So it was to be the best school, the best university and the best profession.

He soon became involved in Christian outreach, joining a committee of Christian businessmen who organised and financed interdenominational evangelistic campaigns, like the tent campaign of Fred Elliot. The Churches seemed unable to reach those outside. So, if people would not come to church, let the Christians – across the denominations – go to the people.

This feeling was reinforced in Northern Ireland by the remarkable revival in the twenties when, under the charismatic leadership of a Presbyterian minister, W P Nicholson, thousands had been converted. It was said that the great shipbuilders, Harland and Wolff, even had to open a special building for the return of stolen tools. The revival died down, but W P Nicholson was still around and Father bought a great tent, which he lent to two Nicholson campaigns in the thirties, one at Downpatrick and the other at Ballynahinch.

I went to some of those meetings. They were unforgettable. The greatest part of the audience were young farm workers and Nicholson gripped them. He preached hell and heaven, sin and salvation, God's one and only way, through the atoning death of Jesus Christ. He left nothing to the imagination. He had no good thing to say about the liberalism of the official Churches, Pharisees and Sadducees all. And those sunburnt, sweating young faces were awestruck. It was their responsibility, they could not escape, they had to decide.

He did not mind embarrassing people. He was asked at the last moment by the Cambridge Inter-Collegiate Christian Union (CICCU) to replace their speaker, who had dropped out at a joint mission. When he was welcomed on Cambridge station by the CICCU executive, he insisted that they knelt down on the station platform at once to pray for the mission. Addressing the opening of the mission from a platform of liberal clergy, he said that all men are sinners, all men needed to repent. 'If you haven't repented, wearing a dog-collar and dressing up in fancy robes will not get you into heaven.'

Word went out that the CICCU had a mad Irishman as their mission speaker and the Nicholson meetings were packed. But he gripped them, just as he gripped the young farm hands of County Down and those who came to mock, stayed to repent.

Father's shattered nerves were finally cured by Professor Kish, a leader of the Brethren in Hungary, whom he met on a visit to Budapest in the spring of 1938. They went from Budapest to Vienna, where the country was in crisis. Chancellor von Schuschnigg had replied with a defiant speech to Hitler's demand for an Anschluss between their two countries. Father and Mother found that von Schuschnigg was staying in their hotel, which was surrounded by police. They went on to St Anton in Arlberg to learn to ski and one morning woke up to find the whole village decked with Nazi flags and their ski-instructors wearing swastika arm-bands. Their train to Switzerland was full of Austrian Jews, leaving while they could.

That summer was my last at Kingsmead. Despite the patchy education it offered, it was a good school for a new Christian. I admired the Watts sons, who were good role-models. The Sunday afternoon sessions on the Church's mission in China opened my eyes to the wider world and to the ultimate loyalty of Christians faced with martyrdom for their faith. And the Christian teaching in the school gave a good basic grounding in the faith, which I was to need in the much more hostile climate ahead.

Chapter Two

AN ENGLISH EDUCATION

Shrewsbury, like any other English public school, was not so much a school as a way of life. The public schools were the training ground for the rulers of the British Empire which, in 1938, still covered the map of the world with red. So the new boy was not just told where to put his belongings, which was his form and what was the timetable. He was inducted into a cultural sub-system, with its own customs, code, discipline and language.

We had top hats and tails for Sundays, we wore boaters for going into the town. New boys wore Eton collars outside their coats; second and third year stiff collars which were rounded; fourth year, stiff collars with a point, and the first elevens and the first eight wore soft collars. First and second year were on call to polish the boots of the prefects, make them toast for tea and go on errands to the school shop. The prefects kept discipline and enforced it with corporal punishment (though fortunately for me, the head of house in my first year did not believe in it). Hierarchy was everything and independent thought and action were severely discouraged.

All the sturdy independence of my Ulster background was against it. We in Ulster did not doff our caps to landowner or parson; our Presbyterian elders were elected by the congregation. And we had a very deeply ingrained sense of personal responsibility which resisted all peer pressure.

Although Shrewsbury was a 'Christian' school with compulsory chapel, public school religion was very different from the committed faith of Arthur Watts. There was a hearty chaplain who shortly disappeared to the navy and his pathetic replacement commanded no respect. The daily chapel service was a pure formality and the Sunday sermons were devoid of any useful content. When the Headmaster preached, there were bets on the number of times he would take off his clip-on glasses. Divinity was a matter of learning the parts of the bible on which it was possible to test our memory and, as we got up the school, of reading the complex rationalisations of liberal clergy, who didn't want to believe more than they could help.

The school's formal Christianity left less than there would be today to differentiate a Christian who took his faith seriously. But there was enough to mark you off. I didn't swear and I read my bible openly. So in my second term I had a rough time from the son of a clergyman who resented my failure to conform. He tried to stir up trouble and, for the first time in my life, I prayed with a desperate urgency. Time and again, I saw my prayers answered. That experience of the immediacy of prayer and response greatly strengthened my faith.

We had one year of peace before the war came. Then we had blackout, rations and corps parades. We started off with World War I uniform, peaked caps and brass buttons. There were boots and buttons to be polished and hours of drill as the sergeant majors tried to form gangling schoolboys into a military machine.

The field days were more fun. We certainly got to know the Shropshire countryside, detraining at places like Leebotwood and marching up the lanes which flanked the Long Mynd or out to Haughmond Hill. Years later I found again a black and white Hall up a lane to the Long Mynd, where the old squire, full of enthusiasm, had given us all apples, told us where the hunt usually came through and how the Manor across the road was an upstart affair, compared with the Hall.

We fought mock battles across Haughmond Hill, breaking step as we marched out across the Kingland suspension bridge, and getting blisters as we marched back again. I eventually graduated into the Intelligence section and mastered the one-inch Ordnance Survey map, which minor skill, years later, helped the family find its way through some of the most beautiful parts of England.

There was none of the jingoism of 1914. We knew all about

the slaughter of the Somme and the low life-expectation of the platoon commanders who led their men over the top. As we marched along the school avenues, the band played inspiring military music and it all seemed worth while, but as the war went on and the sixth form went off to fight, the mood darkened. A freshly retired general addressed the school battalion drawn up on the playing fields and told us that dying for our country was the greatest thing in life. That went down like a lead balloon. He had had his life and we wanted ours.

The sixth form came back in uniform, with wings, one pip or a single naval stripe. Then we would hear that they had been lost in action; Monty Cave, killed on the beaches of Sicily; Mark Scott, drowned in an Arctic convoy; Geoffrey Barr in the Fleet Air Arm drowned when he overran his carrier. Exuberant spirits gone for ever, now just cold names on a war memorial.

After the fall of Malaya, we had a new 'battle-drill' which was meant to inculcate in us the Japanese method of encircling points of resistance, and we started to rush about shooting live ammunition. I volunteered for the mortars, which seemed safest; but we all had to handle live hand-grenades, sweating with fear and praying that we didn't drop it with the pin out.

We also did our bit on the land, cycling out to the farms or having to stand in the back of farm lorries. Hoeing long rows of sugar-beet in the full summer sun was by far the worst. Potato picking in the cool of the autumn was better, but the most satisfactory was felling fir trees for pit props, especially the final thump as the tree came down. Those of us whose parents could not come for speech days – and with permits needed for cross-channel travel, that included all the Irish – could volunteer for a day on a farm instead. I was always glad to escape from the awful formality and fuss.

In our third year we were allowed to go out cycling on Sunday afternoons south of the Severn across the lovely rolling countryside from Lyth Hill to the Long Mynd and, further west, to Pontesford Hill and the Breiddens. Our favourite was the tiny village of Castle Pulverbatch on the north side of the Long Mynd, with a pub which did teas. On Ascension Day we were allowed the whole day off and could go farther. I remember cycling as far as the Stiperstones with Martin Whitworth, probably my closest friend, and dropping loose iron rails down the shaft of an old lead-mine. On the way, they hit the sides with a deepening and very satisfactory bell-like boom!

The rich Shropshire countryside with its warm red-brick buildings, neat farms and park-land was quite different from the bleak Wirral coast or the grey little towns of Northern Ireland, and I grew to love it. The country houses were new to me too. We arrived to work on a farm one day and, since no one was around, went to the front door of the big house. A smiling lady opened the door on a lovely hall with a graceful curved staircase beyond it. I had never seen anything so beautiful. On one Ascension Day, Martin Whitworth, Hugh Stewart and I went to the other side of Welshpool and at the end of a long valley was an eighteenth-century country house, Bryn Mawyr, where some cousins of Martin's lived. They were dear old ladies, rather low on food for hungry cyclists, but they fed us on dry Ryvita and jam.

The other great joy of Shrewsbury was the river. I never had too good an eye for a ball, but I took to the river like a duck to water, especially to sculling. For the fours, as for cricket and football, someone else decided on our likely form but in a single sculling boat, you performed on your own merit and anyhow I enjoyed it. We followed the long horseshoe of the Severn, up beyond the Welsh bridge, back under Kingsland suspension bridge, through the froth of the old brewery, under the English bridge and back again. There was no better way to spend a summer afternoon.

In the winter I took up long-distance running, where, as in sculling, you had to learn to pace yourself, and to last the course, disciplines of endurance which I found of great help all through life.

After Father's buses had been nationalised in 1935, he looked at various other businesses, but his formidable accountant H C Merrett always discouraged him. When the war came he offered his services to the Northern Ireland government, but they had not really wanted this independent character in 1935 and they were equally discouraging four years later.

The following spring he was offered Rosapenna Hotel in County Donegal at a knock-down price by Charles, third Earl of Leitrim, whose bank manager wondered how the hotel – and the overdraft – would survive the war. The hotel had been built in 1893 by the second Earl on the dunes between the Atlantic rollers of Sheep Haven Bay and the long fjord of Mulroy Bay. It is a spectacular site, standing back from the mountains of North Donegal, which ring it round at a respectful distance. The pinewood hotel had been prefabricated in Norway, shipped to the nearby Mulroy Pier and assembled on the site and, though there had been additions and it now held a hundred guests, it kept to the same Norwegian style.

The dunes had been made into an eighteen-hole golf course by Harry Vardon, one of the best professional golfers of the day. There was salmon fishing on the Lackeagh River and trout and sea trout on Glen Lough above it and also, above that, on the Owencarrow River flowing in from Lough Veagh up in the mountains. The hotel had a four-piece orchestra which played at afternoon tea, at dinner and, after dinner, in the ballroom. Dressing for dinner was compulsory.

Father, tired of negative advice from his accountant and of having nothing worthwhile to do, shook the dust of Northern Ireland off his feet and we moved across the border to Rosapenna.

The ambience of Rosapenna was that of the last and most eccentric phase of the Anglo-Irish establishment. Shorn of land and then of political power, those who were left lived on as long as they could in the 'big house' while the world passed them by. Some of them still came to Rosapenna. The fourth Marquess of Headfort had married a London music-hall star, Rosie Boot. She was a sensible and energetic lady and, due to her vigorous management of his affairs, they still lived at Headfort House in County Meath; he had been one of the first Irish Senators. Viscount Powerscourt still lived in Powerscourt in the Wicklow Mountains. Having been taught to eat asparagus with my fingers, I was fascinated to see him using a knife and fork.

I remember another viscount, a sour-looking man with long drooping moustaches and a fat cheerful wife who eventually ran off with the chauffeur. One peer, more eccentric than most, used to come with a friend, who turned to him one evening after staring long and thoughtfully into the peat fire and said suddenly, 'You know, I think our class is finished.'

During the war, when the Royal Navy was in Lough Foyle

and there were scores of RAF airfields across Northern Ireland, a great many officers came to Rosapenna for short leaves, including Lord O'Neill, later killed in action. One day we heard that the Commander-in-Chief, Northern Ireland, was coming. A car drew up and two men got out, one tall, with a striking moustache and strong military bearing, the other small and unassuming – clearly the Commander-in-Chief and his ADC. Not until we saw the tall man changing the wheel next day did we realise that the unassuming little man was the Commander-in-Chief.

General Bucknall became one of the most regular visitors. While the Taoiseach, Eamon de Valera, was denouncing 'the Nazi-Fascist army of occupation in Northern Ireland', the general was, with his agreement, protecting Ireland's shores against invasion by mining the key approaches. When he was due to retire he had a telegram from a grateful Taoiseach: 'Dear Gerry come down to Dublin to say goodbye stop Dev.'

De Valera himself came and I was introduced to him, a tall quiet kind of man, rather like a schoolmaster. When the dining room was empty the waitresses kissed the seat of his chair. He was the father of the nation.

I learnt to play golf at Rosapenna, but it spoilt me for playing golf anywhere else. There were never any queues at the first tee, no dodderers ahead nor impatient players behind, the air was pure and invigorating, the views breathtaking and the turf always dry and springy.

My cousin Joe Anderson taught me to fish for brown trout and sea trout. The hotel had a boat on Glen Lough and an old gillie rowed us to the best corners. I went sailing with my equally inexperienced cousin Irwin in a fishing boat with no keel and we went in among the strong currents, sandbanks and narrow channels of Mulroy Bay. It was a miracle that we got back safely. I never sailed again but Irwin went on to captain Cambridge and to a life behind the sail. My sisters taught me tennis, which was more sociable than fishing, and after tennis we would all go swimming off the rocks, where the rise and fall of the Atlantic tide was a full fifteen feet. We enjoyed a glow of health which, for a few weeks, put us on top of the world.

Then we had to go back to the war and the blackout. Donegal was a big county and a poor one, and the roads were terrible.

Even in a good car, Belfast was a three-and-a-half-hour drive and then beyond that there was the journey back to Heysham on the old ferries, pressed back into wartime service. From there Mary, Elizabeth and I had a long journey on trains crowded with troops, changing at Crewe with three trunks and no porters. At Shrewsbury at last, I handed over my sisters to someone from Acton Reynold School and, though it was only seven miles away, never saw them for another three months.

Academically I was not brilliant, but my house-master, J R Hope-Simpson, pushed me forward and, when I had done School Certificate (modern GCSEs), he suggested that I specialise in History. For the first time I found my form in a subject which I really enjoyed. My only remaining hangup was Latin. Cambridge demanded a credit, which I got on the third attempt.

I tried for Clare College. A friend from Ulster had gone there before me, its first eight was Head of the River and it looked so beautiful, but I had to take its entrance exam. The Headmaster worked out a careful railway timetable and pointed out to me that it was unnecessary and undesirable to go through London. I thanked him politely and took the train straight for London and the Underground to Piccadilly Circus. All the novels I had read centred on London and especially on the West End. I was immensely excited. I ate an indigestible sandwich at a sandwich bar in the Circus and the man beside me propped up a magazine, *The Drummer*. I was shoulder to shoulder with someone playing in a West End band!

London was grey and battered. The big blitz was over, but the whole place was drab. I walked down Lower Regent Street to the Duke of York Steps and two young officers passed me talking in loud voices, walking briskly towards the Horse Guards. There was so much to be seen in London and no time to see it. But I had to get to Cambridge. All Clare's candidates met in a small dining room. The Master of Clare, Henry Thirkhill, passed out some examination papers and then left us alone. We were summoned one by one for an interview. Evidently that was what counted. If he liked you, you were in; if not, you would get a note to say that your paper had not come up to standard. I was accepted and wanted to go to Cambridge at once. I had had enough of Shrewsbury. But the Headmaster was against it

25

and so was Thirkhill. Academically they were right, but I think I was too old to be stuck in a boys' boarding school and those last two terms were a mixed blessing.

They did, however, allow me to justify myself. Martin Whitworth was head of house in my last term and I was made a house monitor. The History Sixth had had no competitive examinations in my two years there and I had been placed bottom on the form-master's judgement. But, in the last term we were to be placed on our Higher Certificate (A level) results and I came top and took the form prize. And on the river I won the school's Senior Sculls.

But I never succumbed to the public school system which turned out district officers for the Empire, officers for the armed services and civil servants to run the country, and which made the sons of northern manufacturers reluctant to follow in their fathers' footsteps.

One counter-influence was a Brethren family, the Nightingales, father, mother and daughter, whom I used to visit for tea once a term. Father and mother were very old – he had been a boy at Shrewsbury in the 1870s, when the school was still in the middle of the town. They were retired missionaries and real living saints, a reminder, in the middle of each term, of another world.

Another of the counter-influences was a friend of the family, a New Zealander, Robert Laidlaw, who was the Chairman and part-owner of the largest mail-order store in New Zealand. At the start of the war, he was in England with his wife and daughter. He sent them home to safety and volunteered as an 'Army Scripture Reader', the Brethren equivalent of an army chaplain.

That decision alone, to stay with the bombs, blackout and rations, was enough to make any boy respect him. But it was his personality which won everyone over. He had absolutely no pride in wealth or achievement. He allowed me to argue with him as an equal – and I was at an argumentative age. He was full of enthusiasm, had an enormous sense of humour and boundless enjoyment in everything he did. We made him tell us one long evening how he had built up his own business from a mail-order list worked out in his spare time, until his own company, Laidlaw Leeds, was challenging New Zealand's reigning mail-order business, the Farmers' Trading Company.

They offered to buy him out and he accepted. He felt later that his faith had failed, that he could and should have gone on alone.

We discussed the hard decisions which had to be made in business and its relation to the Christian faith. Decisions about people were the hardest but you owed it to other employees and to the customers to insist on honesty and competence. But above all, a Christian faith meant that you had to set the highest standards for yourself. In a gentle and humorous way he took apart all my public school pomposities so that they looked rather small and fussy. He told me why he found Darwinism incredible and, even though I was at Darwin's school, I had to agree with him. Beside his strong Christian common sense, all the sermons in the school chapel seemed to be feeble and evasive. He had written a booklet for his staff, 'The reason why I am a Christian', and that, too, did me a power of good. It has sold over a million copies and is still selling.

He was always ready for anything new and one Christmas holiday at Rosapenna, he and I went out with a local friend who was going to shoot wild geese. Their landing place was on the long low bare spit of land reaching out from our Rossgull peninsula to Melmore Head. Three times we crawled a long way up a shallow slope of short turf and three times our friend put his head cautiously over the ridge and three times, he announced, 'They've gone.' We hadn't seen their sentinels, but they had seen us. We knew then why it was called a 'wild goose chase'.

Robert Laidlaw's willingness to go out with a boy on such an escapade, his sharp mind, unvarnished common sense and deep commitment to all his friends were just the antidotes I needed for all my teenage dogma. It helped me to resist the pressure for conformity to the mind-set of an English public school. He left me with a strong sense of the usefulness and excitement of building a business and showed me the difference between the formal soulless Christianity of the school chapel and the living faith which extended to every part of life. I had found a role-model.

My mother insisted on Cambridge because she had heard that it had a very strong Christian Union. I had an invitation to a welcome meeting for freshers from the College Christian Union almost as soon as I arrived, and found myself surrounded at once by a warm and friendly group who made me feel at home straight away.

The pietistic working-class Christianity in which I had found my faith had survived five years of formal public school religion where it had seemed to me that it was hard to be both educated and a committed Christian. But here were intelligent, educated people who held strongly and unapologetically to orthodox Christian beliefs instead of trying to explain them all away.

And though the message in Victoria Hall every Sunday night was evangelistic, no outsiders seemed to be attracted, let alone converted. Yet within weeks of the beginning of term, our College Christian Union was joined by freshers who had gone along to the Sunday-night sermon of the CICCU (Cambridge Inter-Collegiate Christian Union) and had been converted.

The spiritual powerhouse of the CICCU was the daily prayer meeting at the Henry Martyn Hall beside Holy Trinity Church. People came along to pray for the conversion of their friends and then later to thank God for that conversion when it came. I had heard lots of wordy prayers before but had never experienced this gripping expectation that prayer for conversion would be promptly answered.

But to prove it, there were the converts in our own college: John Marsh and, later, David Leggett. A few months ago they had been just like all my friends at school – so they said – and now their faith shone through their eyes and, more convincingly, in their actions.

We met once a week as a college group and I had never known anything before like this intelligent discussion on the meaning of key bible passages, the give and take, the high standard of argument and, above all, its practical helpfulness in setting standards in ordinary life. This group were to include lifelong friends.

At Cambridge I began, for the first time, to carve out my own way of life. Coming from a rowing school, I was asked to join the boat club and soon found myself in the Clare first eight. I also won the Freshers' Sculls, for which I still have the cup. I was reading History and the lecturers were brilliant – Kenneth Pickthorn, the University MP (before Mr Attlee abolished the University franchise), Kitson-Clark on English history, Postan on economic history and, above all, Herbert Butterfield, who very soon became the Regius Professor, on European history. They all made the past come alive and inspired me to read and to argue.

We all had to spend one day a week in the Senior Training Corps. I joined the Gunners, because, brought up on the stories of World War I slaughter of infantry by machine guns, the Gunners seemed safer. But on the first day our colonel told us that in the new war of tanks and aircraft, the Gunners were the most exposed and that officers in observation posts were especially exposed. Gun-drill did have one lasting benefit: it taught the lifetime skill of handling repetitive manual jobs with speed.

Despite the war, the University was fairly full. Military service was suspended for two years for medics, engineers and scientists; arts students were allowed one year. But food rations were limited and cake queues long. Fuel was scarce and my landlady did not allow a fire until November; in college we were limited to two sacks of coal a term. We had to fire-watch one night a week and I slept every Wednesday night, with two others, in the Old Schools on the floor of the room over the gateway. Fortunately there were no raids on Cambridge.

In my first May Races I was in the first eight, which started Head of the River. The boat which starts from last year's order as Head of the River can be challenged from behind by repeated spurts, but it alone has to row the whole course or be bumped. So we needed endurance and a steady nerve. We had a splendid President of Boats, John Garson, and he and another blue, Brian Thwaites (later inventor of the new maths and Principal of Westfield College), kept us going. We survived every attack by Trinity Hall and ended, as we started, Head of the River, for which feat we were allowed to keep our oars – mine still hangs at home.

At the end of the summer term I went to see the Dean. I said that, coming from Ireland, I was not subject to military service, but thought that perhaps I should volunteer and come back for the rest of the course at the end of the war. He was strongly against. The Germans were being driven out of Russia and by the end of the summer would be out of France. I would not see any fighting and, unlike World War I, there was no shortage of manpower. The University would be overwhelmed by returning ex-servicemen and since I did not have to go, he could not guarantee to take me back.

The colonels of the STC seemed to take the same view. There was a final parade, with a general taking the salute on the steps of the Fitzwilliam Museum. I was No 1 on the gun, with my head through the roof of the towing 'quad' and, as we turned the corner of Lensfield Road into Trumpington Street for the salute, I saw with horror that the rest of the crew were deep in their *Daily Mirrors*. I appealed to their better nature and we all did a last 'eyes left'.

That summer I was asked to go to a CSSM beach mission in Bude in Cornwall and on from there to a Varsity and Public Schools Camp at Iwerne Minster in Dorset, both led by the Reverend Eric Nash. I was not too happy at the beach mission. It was the first time I had come across class distinction by Christians. I was told by the old hands that the recreations of middle-class and working-class children were quite different and if we tried to cater for both we would get neither. I'd not been aware of class distinction at Portballintrae and came to the conclusion that England must be different.

At Iwerne Minster the problem was simply solved. The camp was only open to the best public schools. The leader, Eric Nash, affectionately known as Bash, was a unique character. An insurance clerk turned Anglican clergyman, he had a single-minded vision for the establishment of Evangelical chaplains and Christian Unions in the English public schools, and for the conversion of boys at the holiday 'camps' at Clayesmore School. Having suffered for five years under the dead chapel religion at Shrewsbury, who was I to argue? And yet I did argue. I was taken for a long walk by one of the senior officers, a Cambridge blue and later a Headmaster. He heard me out with a worried look and then just said, 'Let's pray together about it.'

Right or wrong, Bash's strategy has been spectacularly successful. Church life is now studded with the products of Bash-Camp and public school Christian Unions – John Stott of All Souls, Langham Place; Dick Lucas of St Helen's, Bishopsgate and Timothy Dudley-Smith, former bishop and perhaps the greatest hymn-writer of our generation; the chaplain at Shrewsbury for many years, Michael Tucker, and Mark Ruston, a much loved vicar of the strategic Round Church at Cambridge, were both senior officers in my time. After the war there were daughter camps as the work spread and fifty years on, the work still flourishes.

The talks in the school library were simple, direct and short. They aimed to convert and to instruct young Christians in the basics of their faith. Each officer had a dormitory and, before lights went out, he commented briefly on a verse and prayed. It was his job to talk to any boy who was interested. Yet I remember being extremely surprised when one boy in my bedroom, Bob Otway, told me that he wanted to become a Christian. We talked and prayed together and he seemed extraordinarily happy. He went on to be an Anglican clergyman. Sadly he died young, but we met his daughters a few years ago when they were in the CICCU.

During the war we spent most of the day working in local farms or on the hills above in the woods owned by Rolf Gardiner, a very successful and articulate farmer. My particular camp duty was to work in the office, first under John Stott and then, after he was ordained, under Philip Tompson, who continued as Secretary of the camp for many years.

The success of Bash-Camp was not an accident. Under Bash's gentle, caring, courteous attitude was an iron will. Each camp, we were asked in turn to a tête-à-tête over eggs and bacon in an old-fashioned cottage in the village, while he probed our souls and our plans, and tried to turn them gently and unobtrusively to his own vision.

He was much against girl-friends, since they tended to lead to marriage which ordinands and chaplains could not afford. He was also much against the 'intellectual' tendencies of the Inter-Varsity Fellowship, to which the CICCU was affiliated, and we were strongly discouraged from going to the IVF Easter conferences, which conflicted with the Easter camps. As a result Bash-Campers were notorious at Oxford and Cambridge for their attitude to women and the hold of Bash-Camp ideas over the Oxford (OICCU) Executive roused a strong deter-mination among the majority that the same should never hap-pen in Cambridge. In IVF circles, Bash-Camp was seen as a

31

kind of sect, commmanding a loyalty altogether too absolute.

There was another down-side to Bash-Camp. The simple message produced genuine conversions like that of Bob Otway, which stood the test of time. But not all conversions were genuine and, even among officers, there were one or two spectacular lapses. Of course the Apostle Paul also records spectacular lapses and it may be unfair to blame Bash-Camp any more than a Church should be blamed for lapses of its members. Bash and the senior officers certainly took great pastoral care. Every boy and every officer had someone responsible for keeping in pastoral touch. But a faith which is based on pietism, which does not discuss problems as well as praying about them and which discounts the need for a firm doctrinal framework for university students, is especially vulnerable to losses.

John Marsh, David Leggett and I had not come through the system as boys, so we sat rather loose to the Bash-Camp dogmas and when we graduated, we all turned to other things. But for two years it did us great good. Whether it was CICCU or Bash-Camp, I was certainly stirred to far greater interest in the bible, and Bash-Camp was extremely helpful in building a genuine devotional life. Unlike the pietism of the Brethren, it really stirred me to action and in the big officers' room, the identity of purpose and the troubles and problems shared created a camaraderie which has lasted a lifetime.

The heart of the work was the boys themselves – the drawling young Etonian who told us that they wondered which of them the Princess Elizabeth would marry, the windswept Marlburians, the intellectually assured Wykehamists – they were fun to be with and, whatever the faults, it was a worthwhile work and did a lot of good. I would not have missed it.

After my first Bash-Camp in the summer of 1944, wartime travel to Ireland being difficult, I spent the week before the long vac term with Martin Whitworth and his parents in an inn in Henley-in-Arden, cycling most days to Stratford-upon-Avon and the Shakespeare Theatre. It was a lovely village and, since there was very little traffic on the roads, very peaceful. Brigadier Whitworth had been posted from India to Birmingham, from the dignity and estate of the Indian Army to a position a good deal inferior to that of the arms manufacturers who used their firm's petrol allowance to drive to the nearby roadhouse for its famous duck suppers. Mrs Whitworth had been a war correspondent during World War I and her views of this change of status were strong and to the point. With the very English beauty of Henley-in-Arden, my first experience of Shakespeare plays and the company of the Whitworths, it was a memorable week.

In my second year I was on the CICCU executive and still rowing. I now had a room in Old Court, which was just by Hall, so I had a lot of callers and it was hard to find time for History. My father had insisted that I had to qualify as a chartered accountant – after which I could do what I liked – and in those days the class of degree didn't matter. So, as the prison gates of the City of London loomed, there was the strongest temptation to get the best out of Cambridge.

The CICCU executive worked hard. I was Vice President under John Batstone of Jesus College. We met once a week, took turns in chairing the daily prayer meeting and the Saturday bible study, had to meet and entertain speakers, to meet with the women's union (CWICCU) – an innovation in our time – and to deal with whatever crises arose.

John Batstone had a term's leave of absence in the summer to look after his mother and family, since his father was dying, and I became acting President, which took up even more of my time just before the History Part I exam. My father meantime advised me to switch from History to Law for my third year. It was good advice, but Law needed a lot more work. The Bash-Camp faction wanted me to succeed John Batstone as President, but the stories from Oxford of the prolonged Bash-Camp Presidency there stirred strong opposition, which prevailed. I also learned that a No 2, responsible for carrying through someone else's agenda, faces formidable obstacles to becoming No 1. I should have quit with the rest of the old executive, but was pressed, for the sake of goodwill, to continue as Vice President into the Michaelmas term when John Marsh took over.

The CICCU was not perfect. There was an enthusiastic peer pressure which is common to all student enterprises and some of it had little to do with Christian teaching. Like everyone else, I wanted my friends to become Christians. But I was impatient, taking an acceptance of the message of an evangelistic sermon at face value and I forgot the parable of the sower, that not all of the seed sown brings fruit. I also asked to sermons those who had not shown the slightest interest.

The person who really wanted help was not a rowing friend, but a neighbour, first in digs and then in Old Court. I didn't even ask him to an evangelistic sermon; he asked me to take him. Afterwards he seemed deeply moved, I was very happy and I felt I had done all that was meant to be done. Then we shared the college fire-watching rota, dossing down on camp beds in the junior common room. I had a strong feeling that I should kneel down and pray by the camp bed, which I did, feeling very self-conscious. Next evening he asked me up to his room. He was sitting at his table in great distress. I suggested that we pray together. So I prayed with him that God would accept his true sorrow for sin, his faith in Christ's redemption, take away the burden of guilt and give him the gift of the Holy Spirit. Then there was a complete change in him and sudden happiness shone through the tears. That, I learnt, was true conversion, the new birth, which, like natural birth, comes through pain. He never looked back.

But CICCU did attract a lot of members whose faith was superficial and which did not survive life beyond Cambridge. Dr Basil Atkinson, Assistant University Librarian and long-time pastor to the CICCU, said that, in his experience, half the members of the CICCU would later drop out of active Christian life. Two of the presidents in my time dropped out and the third became a theological liberal.

The liberal Student Christian Movement (SCM) was still a powerful force in the 1940s and was supported by most college chaplains. The denominational societies were also active and liberal. Against this we stood our ground with fierce dogmatic argument. I was as dogmatic as any, taking on the gentle Charlie Moule, later Regius Professor of Divinity, who was known as a 'liberal Evangelical'. He was most courteous then and entirely forgiving afterwards.

In the CICCU hothouse there was also great pressure to go into full-time Christian service, either in the ministry – which is where Bash's quiet, persuasive and insistent voice tried to steer me – or as an overseas missionary. In those days it was expected that the great mission field of China would be open again after the war, and all over the British Empire, Christian missions were flourishing.

The thought of a rectory with roses round the door was very appealing to the natural man, as was the one hundred per cent devotion to Christian ministry to the spiritual man. I suppose that it was my essential Ulster non-conformity that held me back from the Anglicans and the example of Robert Laidlaw which made me see the role of Christians in a secular world. There was also, I'm bound to say, an old-fashioned respect for my father's views which kept me on course.

It was also made quite clear to me that I was totally unsuitable as a missionary by David Bentley-Taylor, the most enthusiastic missionary I have ever met. At a 'missionary breakfast' in the old Dorothy Café he outlined the qualities needed – good at languages, not queasy about illness, great patience, ability to suffer fools gladly – and as he went on, I realised I had not a single one of these gifts. But the good Lord has answered by giving my wife and me a role in the International Fellowship of Evangelical Students (IFES) which has more than satisfied my urge for foreign mission.

Not only was Bash insistent on the separation of the sexes, but the CICCU too was, unlike the OICCU, all male. In the summer of 1945, while John Batstone was away and I was acting President, the CICCU executive made the first move towards the ending of this absurd segregation by asking the CWICCU President, Margaret Ellis, and her executive to breakfast in my rooms in Clare. Not long afterwards the two unions merged, though not until 1993 did the CICCU have its first woman President.

It may seem odd, in these sex-obsessed days, that we readily accepted the segregation into men's and women's colleges and that we had to be in college behind locked gates by midnight. But before the age of majority was reduced to eighteen we accepted the role of the University as *in loco parentis* and that we were *in statu pupillari*. And, before the 'pill', there were strong practical reasons for protecting the virginity of women students. Nor was there the national obsession with sex which came twenty years later. The girls wanted to get engaged and marry and the men were correspondingly careful before they began to create the climate for lifetime commitment.

The gates were not, of course, the only means of entry. Ted Ford who lived on the ground floor below me had a set of bars on his bedroom window which could be removed from inside; but after the nightly traffic through his bedroom got too heavy, he threatened to have the bars cemented in again. An Iranian friend complained that the temporary wooden gates in St John's Street ruined his dress shirts as he climbed over. And the postgraduate theological college, Ridley Hall, had a row of spikes along the wall, which curled over at the wall's end to stick out horizontally and provided a narrow but convenient ladder.

In Michaelmas term, 1944, I rowed in University Trial Eights, but at ten stone was thought too light for the Goldie or University crews. I stroked the Clare first eight for the 1945 Lent Races, the peak of my rowing career. Then Martin Whitworth, who stroked the University Boat, also asked me to stand in for someone who had dropped out of the Goldie crew, the University second boat. So I rowed for Goldie against Imperial College and we lost by nine lengths!

Law is not a precise science, but it is a lot more precise than History. You either know your cases and statutes or you don't. Even with the help of a long vac term I was struggling, trying to keep up in tutorials with those who had been reading Law for two years. Yet without that preparation in a precise discipline, I should have been lost in the even greater precision of accountancy.

Unbelievably, after six long years, the war was over and the army lorries finally left the shelter of the trees along the Backs. We had the first large intake of ex-servicemen and the maturity of the University rose sharply. But the new Labour government continued with all the wartime austerity and controls. Student opinion, which tends to be against the reigning ideology, moved sharply to the right. I joined the Cambridge University Conservative Association and bought a bust of the great Duke of Wellington – which I still have. But there was no time for active politics.

Immediately after the war, the mood among Evangelicals was expressed by the campaign for 'Revival in our time'. A divine providence had saved the nation from disaster. Now it was over, we had begun to realise what a close-run struggle it had been. A group of businessmen, headed by Lindsay Glegg, rented the Royal Albert Hall for a mass meeting and filled it. The most popular evangelist was Tom Rees, whom we had met while he was on a campaign in Ireland. He continued to fill the Royal Albert Hall meetings on Saturday nights and had a great many professed conversions.

In January 1945 Father bought a house in Hildenborough in Kent where, at the same time, Tom Rees had turned Hildenborough Hall into a conference centre. My sister Elizabeth was at art college in Tunbridge Wells and Mary and I were due to be working in London; so we hoped that Father, who was forty-six, would sell Rosapenna and, with everything starting up again, find a business in or around London.

On my twenty-first birthday we took a box for Tom Rees' meeting at the Royal Albert Hall and, to my great embarrassment, Tom Rees announced this and asked the eight thousand present to sing 'Happy birthday, dear Frederick'. One of the speakers was Dr Martyn Lloyd-Jones of Westminster Chapel, who was shocked at this frivolity and decided that this was the first and last time that he would speak for Tom Rees.

In retrospect, it was the beginning of the end of a long period of Evangelical pietism which had started with the Keswick Convention in the 1870s, gone on through the Moody and Sankey missions of the 1880s and 1890s, but which, for the first time, took the Evangelicals outside the mainstream of national debate so that they failed completely to answer the growth of secular humanism outside the Church and of liberalism within it.

Yet, like Bash-Camp, Tom Rees was successful in what he set out to do. He was also a very thoughtful pastor. I remember his sitting up with me until the small hours in their cottage in the Mendips on my way to Bude and also his coming in from Watford to the Euston Station Hotel the same summer for an hour or so to help to put me right.

His wife Jean, daughter of the Chairman of Carreras Tobacco, was also a great character, just as dynamic as he was and they made a marvellously balanced couple. Their second child, Justyn, was born on the day of my twenty-first birthday party and also got applause in the Royal Albert Hall.

Tom was finally upstaged by rallies which were even bigger and better than his. The Billy Graham crusade of 1955 killed Tom's Albert Hall rallies. But the conference centre went on, moving to Frinton in the early sixties and then to the downs above Otford in Kent. And he went on campaigning, dying in the saddle on a campaign in New York.

All these Christian leaders had their place. W P Nicholson could reach the shipyard workers; Bash penetrated the public schools, heart of the English social establishment; Douglas Johnson of the IVF was the most strategic, taking on the intellectual establishment, and Tom Rees reached out to the growing number of office workers. Between them they greatly stimulated and broadened my own faith, although the greatest influence was yet to come.

All good things come to an end and so did my days as a student. I had found myself, enjoyed myself, proved my Christian faith as never before, made lots of great friends. and learnt some History and Law on the way. After the last term, two medical friends who had also been on the CICCU executive came to Rosapenna and we enjoyed our last days of freedom before the burdens of professional training took over all our working hours.

Chapter Three

A PROFESSION

On a fine September morning in 1946 I walked down Westbourne Terrace to take the Central Line to the City. I was bursting with health after two months at Rosapenna, but felt oddly encased in a new black pin-striped suit. Father had advanced the necessary 500 guineas to Messrs Price Waterhouse and Company, Chartered Accountants. The culture shock of the City was profound. I was articled to one of the twelve partners but during the years of my 'training' I never saw him, and the only communications I had from him were the curt covering letters replying to my requests to his signature on my examination forms. After the care of house-masters, supervisors and tutors, I was on my own. It was a month or so before I found out about the correspondence course of Messrs Foulkes, Lynch and Co. and stepped on to their inexorable weekly treadmill, not to escape for another five years.

I found accountancy a very precise discipline. Both sides of the balance sheet had to add up to the same figure, and you had to check and cross-check until they did. And the Foulkes Lynch marks on the previous week's paper told you candidly whether you had grasped the point or not. Never before, not in Law and certainly not in History, had my mind been so stretched.

That September morning I found myself sent out on my first job to an office in Aldwych, which looked out on a deep well clad in lavatory brick. Across the table was my senior, who sat for a long time gazing into vacancy. I also gazed, not knowing what I was to do. After a while it turned out that he was waiting for the books and when they came he showed me how to check cash book with ledger.

He was succeeded after a week or so by a much more entertaining character, an ex-colonel, who had been articled before the war. He had not qualified and, after leading a regiment, the thought of the Messrs Foulkes Lynch weekly grind was too much for him. He was excellent company and we lunched together every day at Grooms Coffee House by the Law Courts, full of briefless young barristers trying to borrow fivers from each other.

The work turned out to be a mixture of appalling boredom mixed with fascinating glimpses into all kinds of businesses and people. Usually we worked in clients' cramped offices which were almost always stuffy with cigarette smoke, though occasionally we managed to persuade clients to let us work in the grandeur and peace of the board room. In the bigger companies we usually found ourselves checking yards of print-out. The small companies were far more interesting. There was a sack merchant with clerks still on high stools and there was Batey's Ginger Beer and Soda Water still delivering on 1928 lorries, all written down in the books to £1 each.

My first audit on my own was a charity which used to write off all its capital expenditure to revenue. This naturally created a large deficit, on the basis of which it made an impassioned appeal, spending the proceeds on yet more buildings which created an even larger deficit and that made for an even larger appeal. I think that the partner finally told the client that this splendid scheme had now gone too far.

Gradually I began to get the feel for the job. When excess profits tax ended, a client in the rag trade decided to move his profits forward out of the reach of the old tax by lowering his closing stock figures for the taxable year. After testing my fledgeling experience against a series of plausible explanations backed up by irrelevant documents, he finally conceded that he was trying it on and I felt that I was learning.

Then I was sent on a fraud investigation. The cashier had kept two sets of books and had never taken a holiday (always, I was told, a sure sign of fraud). He had taken about £5,000 by entering bogus 'cashed cheques' for directors and had added these to the total of the company's debtors. With the money he had apparently kept a mistress in Bognor Regis. The company then appointed an internal auditor who had routinely asked its debtors to confirm the amount owed at the year end. When the cashier realised that the game was up, he cashed one last cheque, bought a travelling rug at the Army and Navy Stores on the firm's account, and then disappeared. His pretty young assistant was outraged to think of the lectures he used to give her about staying out late at dances! He was traced when he signed his own name to a mortgage guarantee for a nephew, but the judge let him off lightly on account of his age and the carelessness of the company.

This was small beer compared with the frauds which had been investigated by the managers, who taught me my trade. When, in the crash of the early 1930s, financiers shot themselves, Price Waterhouse would be called in to find out why. They were usually share-pushers, whose success in raising finance depended on paying increasing dividends, and when the crash came and share prices slumped, there was a great temptation to pay dividends out of capital to shore up the share values and cover the borrowings until times got better. Some promoters went even further and created fictitious stock.

It has been the same from the early eighteenth-century South Sea Bubble, Britain's first speculative boom, to Robert Maxwell in our own day. But no new generation seems to learn from those before, and greed is the same in every generation.

But at this time of socialist austerity there was no Stock Market boom. Dr Dalton was Chancellor of the Exchequer. At a discount company, whose books I had to check, they bought money at 1¾ per cent and sold it again at 2½ per cent. They would chase the money round the market each afternoon to find which banks were short of cash that day and which were long, and then went out in their top hats to settle the transaction. A very famous soldier, who was a director, wrote a note to the General Manager asking him to explain how the discount market worked. It did not seem to me to be too complicated.

More complicated was the business of passing examinations. In a big firm, specialists look after tax and company law, so, in the absence of partners who could take the time to explain them to us, we had to rely on dry textbooks and on answering questions in the weekly Foulkes Lynch paper. The result was that all our year of articled clerks except one failed the intermediate examination.

This did the great firm's reputation no good at all. The firm's brightest partner, W E Parker, summoned us to a meeting. He said that the firm's policy of leaving us on our own helped to sort out future partner material. I said that some of us were not bright enough to be partners, but the firm had still signed our articles and had a duty to help us through. To that there was no answer. A long time afterwards when he was Sir Edward Parker, President of the Institute of Chartered Accountants, we met and he said, 'I remember you as the shop steward of the articled clerks.' But from then on he himself took an interest in us, and the supervision was more helpful, though not nearly so systematic (or so ruthless) as the arrangements for articled clerks today.

We did, however, get a great deal of experience. Even an articled clerk in Price Waterhouse saw the City from the inside. We had to read the board minutes, look at the banks' comments on major loans and listen to all the gossip of the client. In those circles the major players trusted each other and vast transactions were done by word of mouth. That the frauds were relatively rare was due to the close-knit community of bankers and merchants in the City of London. They did business with those they knew and could trust and were extremely particular about anyone else. The big clearing banks did not push loans and the merchant banks, who issued shares, were very careful before they put their name to a prospectus.

While at Hildenborough we attended the Brethren Assembly in Vine Hall in Sevenoaks, where Kenneth Luckhurst was the leading elder. He was Secretary of the Royal Society of Arts in Adelphi Terrace and was wise, warm-hearted, gentle and with a vast range of knowledge. He asked me to all the interesting lectures especially on post-war reconstruction, took me to lunch at the Athenaeum and tried to teach me Greek. For the two years we went to Vine Hall he made the Brethren tolerable and when I complained of their ways he took me to conferences and encouraged me to make my point.

Father left the sale of Rosapenna too late to get a buyer and in any case his heart was not in it. He was 'someone' in Ireland, a 'has-been' in Northern Ireland, and no one in England. By 1947 the immediate post-war holiday boom was over, and Rosapenna had a bad year. The winter of 1947–8 brought thick snow and the daily journey up to London on top of evening study was both tiring and time-consuming. My sister Mary, who travelled up every day too to train as a physiotherapist, was also exhausted. So instead of selling Rosapenna, Father sold the house in Kent for double the purchase price, rented a flat in Knightsbridge overlooking the officers' mess of the old Horse Guards barracks, and he and Mother spent most of their springs and summers in Ireland.

There was no question about where we should go to church in London. A friend had already brought me to Westminster Chapel in Buckingham Gate where Dr Martyn Lloyd-Jones held a Friday night discussion. We could raise any question we liked and for the next few weeks he would persuade us to say what we thought, would put exactly the right questions to show the difficulty of our argument and, if we persisted, would lead us in logical steps until we saw the error of our ways.

He had been assistant to Lord Horder, the Royal Physician, until, aged twenty-seven, he decided that most of the complaints of his patients were spiritual rather than medical. He accepted a call to the Forward Mission Church in Aberavon in South Wales, and soon had a flourishing congregation in this working-class town, which suffered more than the rest of the country from the great slump. In 1938 he came to Westminster Chapel as Assistant Minister to Dr Campbell Morgan. Unlike Campbell Morgan he was a Calvinist, basing his teaching on the great doctrines of the Reformation.

Unhappy with the woolly teaching of the Brethren and the Evangelical pressure for conversions, I knew at once that I had found a solid doctrinal structure for my faith.

Dr Lloyd-Jones' teaching went back to the careful doctrines on which Evangelicals had based their position in the 350 years since the Reformation and before they fell into pietism at the end of the nineteenth century. 'The Doctor', as he was known, showed that Christian doctrines were like the mutually supporting arches of a great cathedral. Take away one, and it weakens the building. Take away two or three and the whole structure collapses in ruins.

I was not the only one to feel that he had found secure ground in an increasingly hostile world. The church filled up until there were fifteen hundred in the morning service and nearer two thousand in the evening.

We had been going to his church for no more than a year when Father asked the Lloyd-Joneses to come for a holiday at Rosapenna and to speak at the Rosapenna Sunday service. He and the Doctor liked each other, as did Mother and Mrs Lloyd-Jones. The Doctor, now in his late forties, had been over-doing it and badly needed a rest, so they came to Rosapenna and continued to holiday there regularly for several years. He was certainly one of the greatest influences in my own life. Though a towering preacher, with immense authority, when out of the pulpit he was gentle and humorous. His wise and balanced views carried great conviction.

His influence in the forties, fifties and sixties spread far and wide. During the war he was President of the Inter-Varsity Fellowship (now the UCCF) and he and the General Secretary, Dr Douglas Johnson, moved the IVF from the 'muscular Christianity' of the time back again into the mainstream of theological debate. The liberal Student Christian Movement (SCM), which had been the IVF's rival between the wars, faded from the scene. The Doctor was also a key figure in the foundation of the International Fellowship of Evangelical Students (IFES) immediately after the war, and indeed Westminster Chapel itself was full of overseas students.

His main work was to base the Evangelical position once more on the great reformers and the definitive creeds, the Thirty-nine Articles of the Church of England and the Westminster Confession of the free Churches, which in turn went back to Augustine and the Christian Fathers. The shallow pietistic teaching which had dominated Evangelicals since the death of Spurgeon was too subjective to influence the public debate, but the foundation creeds of the Protestant Churches could be defended against all comers. It was not enough for the Christian Church to rely on inner conviction – everyone else had inner convictions too. We had to show that the God revealed by Jesus Christ, the Apostles whom he appointed and the Prophets whom he endorsed, was the one true sovereign God who had created the universe, and that that message was the only valid analysis of the human condition, of good and evil, life and death. We were to need that conviction as secular humanism gripped the public agenda in the second half of the twentieth century.

As the excellent two-volume biography by Iain Murray shows, Dr Lloyd-Jones carried great weight in the Evangelical Churches, bringing them once more into the mainstream of theological thought, and at his memorial service in 1981 Westminster Chapel was packed to capacity. His message was seminal and his ministry unique.

In October 1949, Father, my sister Elizabeth and I went across the Channel for the first time. Father's new American Packard was hoisted on board the ferry at Dover, with two or three others, and off again next morning at Dunkirk. Mary had had to take an unexpected exam and Mother stayed behind with her. Elizabeth and I had never been to the Continent, and we were very excited.

We had lunch at Reims, sitting on the pavement outside a hotel on the broad avenue leading up to the cathedral. By contrast with Britain's austere rations, the food was superb. That evening we slept in a small family hotel in the main square in Chaumont, where a vendor of doubtful postcards hoisted a sample on a long pole up to the bedroom window as we waited for dinner to be ready 'tout à l'heure'. The visit was, after six years of war and four years of Socialist austerity, a liberating experience. We went through Switzerland to Venice, empty of tourists, to Ravenna, where the fifth-century church of San Vitale has a baptistry for immersion. Elizabeth was in her element in the galleries of the Uffizi in Florence, but the high point, even for a family of Ulster Protestants, was Rome. Jack Costello, who had succeeded Eamon de Valera as Taoiseach and who was a regular visitor to Rosapenna, had given us an introduction to the Irish Ambassador to the Vatican. He, in turn, introduced us to a tall bespectacled Irish priest, who offered to take us round St Peter's, suggesting that he meet us after mass. We said apologetically that we were Protestants and he said, tolerantly, 'Ah well, never mind about that, I'll show you round just the same.'

Monsignor O'Flaherty gave us a brisk tour inside St Peter's, telling us, as we passed the statues, 'This was a good Pope who did a lot for the poor, but the less said about that Pope the better!' He took us round the back of St Peter's, through two closely guarded courtyards, and showed us the Pope's front door and then, when he found that no one was around, the Pope's private chapel. We also went through the Sistine Chapel and there was hardly anyone else there.

He had been at the centre of the 'Rome escape line' for Allied prisoners freed by the Italians after their surrender and on the run from the Germans, who had promptly taken control. He was immensely proud of the decoration he had been given by Field Marshal Alexander for sheltering Allied prisoners in the Vatican. He told us, 'The German military commander sent a message, "O'Flaherty, if you're seen in the streets of Rome again, I'll have you shot on the spot." But I carried on regardless.'

He even sent a British major up to the German military hospital to have his appendix removed. 'We told them he was a German major and since they were short of space in the hospital, they could send him back to the Vatican hospital. So we gave him a shot of something to keep him quiet and they took out his appendix and sent him straight back to our nuns to nurse and no one any the wiser.'

A film was made of the Rome escape line, starring Gregory Peck as O'Flaherty; but the handsome actor was so far removed from the dry, humorous and rugged character whom we had met that I couldn't go on watching.

O'Flaherty suggested that we might like an audience with the Pope. Cautiously Father asked what that would involve. 'Oh sure, nothing at all, you just kiss his ring.' Father said that was extremely good of him but he feared it would be much misunderstood at home. 'Have you any Catholics working for you then?' Father admitted to that and a few weeks later two rosaries arrived, 'Certified blessed by His Holiness the Pope, O'Flaherty, Monsignor'. Father passed them on and they were much appreciated.

The breadth of business insight given by Price Waterhouse audits was immense. I remember the audits of Fisons Fertilisers, Marley Tiles, Beecham's, Mobil Oil, Kemsley Newspapers, Associated Press, Truman's Brewery in Brick Lane, the National Provincial

Bank and St Clement's Press (my first encounter with a 'Father of the Chapel'), as well as smaller companies. We not only studied the company books but listened to all the company gossip and learnt how British industry and commerce worked. It was invaluable experience but it contributed only incidentally to the very precise demands of the Institute of Chartered Accountants for accurate knowledge of company and tax law and how to apply them.

But at last, after three spring study leaves at Rosapenna to a background of larks and daffodils, I finally qualified. For years afterwards I had the recurring nightmare that I still had the finals ahead and couldn't remember a thing! But I am grateful to the very exacting discipline of the profession. It taught me how to analyse complex situations, to differentiate the key factors from the unimportant and to think logically.

One of my last audits was of a new nylon-stocking factory in Enniskillen. I spent about six weeks there in deepest winter driving home to Rosapenna over roads rutted with ice either in our big Ford station-waggon which had bald tyres and was hard to hold on the ice or a tiny two-seater Fiat which rode the ruts like a speedboat on a choppy sea. I stayed at the Imperial Hotel on the main street, populated almost entirely by commercial travellers (sales reps today) who retired to the Commercial Room after dinner, leaving the hall fire to the few professionals. On the night after the death of King George VI, there were three of us: an architect, a man from the Ministry of Agriculture and myself. The man from the Ministry had told a farmer that the King had died.

'Deed, isn't that tarrible. Was he a married man?'

'Yes, he was.'

'Did he have any children?'

'Yes, two girls.'

'Ah well, no doubt the wife'll fall intil the job!'

We both told the man from the Ministry he was having his leg pulled, but he said that the only paper the farmer read was the *Impartial Recorder* and that only for the fat stock prices. That was the world before TV and also before the last twenty-five years of grumbling civil strife during which, one Armistice Day, a massacre at Enniskillen hit the world's headlines.

Back in London, courtesy of the Cambridge University Appointments Board, I had an interview with Grigor McClelland, Managing Director of Law Stores, Gateshead, a Quaker grocery chain of sixty shops on Tyneside, which Grigor was taking over from his father. He had been to Henley Staff College, the nearest Britain had to a business school, and was fired with all the idealism of professional management. The interview went well and I was soon up in Gateshead to meet Arthur McClelland, the Chairman. That interview, too, went well and a telegram with an offer of a job was waiting when I got home.

I owe a great deal to Grigor but I owe to him especially the vision of professional management. During the six years of war and six post-war years of Socialist government, import controls, allocations of raw materials and rationing of food, there was little competition and little incentive to more effective management and better service. Companies seemed to be privileged bureaucracies, with entitlements to petrol coupons and tax-free expense allowances.

While Arthur McClelland could taste for every kind of flavour in butter and persuade a customer who had said a shilling a pound was too dear to buy a quarter pound for 3d, Grigor was going to run it all by statistics. He had bought a punch-card machine – the mechanical forerunner of the electronic computer – and he wanted a professional accountant to take charge.

The machine and I arrived at about the same time and I learnt early on the computer expert's maxim: 'rubbish in, rubbish out'. It became evident that the internal documentation for movement of goods in and out of the warehouse had no cross-check and that my predecessor had simply 'adjusted' the figures to what he thought they should be.

I was sent on a punch-card course in London. In a stocking warehouse, I discovered a system which gave cross-checks and, back in Tyneside, a simple pin-board for shops' orders on which a comptometer operator could cross-add totals for every commodity ordered.

When I'd installed the system we counted the warehouse stock and it showed a huge deficit. Grigor couldn't believe it, so we did it again with the same result. Then a tea salesman came in and said that he'd found brands on sale in a small grocery shop up a back-street which he only sold to us. It turned out that the shop belonged to the mother-in-law of one of the lorry drivers. After that there were bin cards in the warehouse, which only issued stock to the total of the weekly orders, and we had no more trouble.

After the poor digs I had found myself in Whitley Bay and Corbridge, the McClellands sent me to a friend in Gosforth, Gwen Holmes, a sterling character, whose husband's business had failed and who now took four lodgers in their big stone house, 2 Park Villas.

She picked her lodgers and we, too, were all characters after a fashion. One, Dick Joicey, was an engineer at Swan Hunter's who later won a George Cross; another, ex-RAF, with a matching RAF moustache, was an accountant at Proctor and Gamble, the big American detergent company; and the third, Whitnall Allen, with whom I got on especially well, was in adult education.

Whitnall Allen and I both had small cars. Mine was a 10 hp Sunbeam Talbot which could travel at 60 mph on a down slope with the wind behind it. But the other two had fast pre-war sports cars: a Lancia saloon and an open, long-bonnet SS Jaguar. Then they swapped cars for a consideration and the dinner talk was confined for some time to the newly discovered faults of the recently exchanged cars.

Petrol rationing had just ended, but car production had not caught up. So there were miles of open roads, especially in the lovely border country across Carter Bar up the Tweed valley and on the road home which now lay along the Roman wall and through Galloway to Stranraer and the ferry to Larne.

At Whitley Bay I joined the small Brethren Assembly led by a fine and open-minded Christian who worked for British Ropes, and he and his wife made me very welcome. In the brief time I spent at Corbridge, I went to the Wylam Assembly and began to have invitations to preach. I remember especially preaching at Seaham Harbour and having tea in a miner's home. When I settled at Gosforth, I went to the Gosforth Assembly which met above the Co-op in North Gosforth and was immediately face-to-face with the fundamental flaw of Brethren church government, the self-perpetuating body of elders.

There were three splendid families at Gosforth – Grenfell and

Margaret Arnott, Bill and Doris Cuthbertson, and John and Muriel Dawson. Grenfell was a solicitor and Bill and John were teachers. But they were not only able and intelligent; they were wise and good Christians and warm in their hospitality. By contrast, the elders were small men whose only capacity was to cling on to their position and authority. And nothing could be done about it.

I had already blotted my copybook by preaching at the main city-centre Assembly on Christian tolerance. Word went out that I was not sound and after that the invitations ceased. The crunch came at Gosforth when I gave a short word on the Christian duty of hospitality and suggested that this might be extended to some of the overseas students at Newcastle University. The leading elder rose to rebuke me. I was not the only one entitled to claim the right to expound God's word and the Lord revealed his wisdom to them too. I walked straight out at the end of the service and never went back. Eventually the Cuthbertsons, Arnotts and Dawsons left too. Bill remained a teacher at Newcastle Grammar School, and Grenfell and John both went into the Anglican ministry.

I found a temporary resting place in an Assembly at Longbenton mainly composed of those who had felt forced to come out of either Open or 'Glanton' Assemblies where they found the eldership narrow and unchristian. The leading elder, Stan Davidson, a jeweller in Gray Street, was warm and welcoming, and I stayed there happily while I was in Newcastle.

I also joined the local Gideons, the group who place bibles in hotel bedrooms and give away New Testaments. I remember especially the interest there was in New Testaments at two borstals. On one other visit I arrived in the middle of a dance in a youth club in Scotswood. The leader rather nervously made an announcement that I had New Testaments to give away and I invited anyone interested to come to another room. To my amazement, every single one followed me next door.

In the summer of 1952, my sister Elizabeth married John Marsh my closest friend at Cambridge. After the wedding I had supper with a few of our friends in the garden of the Blue Cockatoo by Battersea Bridge and afterwards we walked over the bridge to the Festival of Britain exhibition in Battersea Gardens. Dr Lloyd-Jones's elder daughter, Elizabeth, was with us. I had, until then, thought her a rather douce daughter of the manse, but, as she compared some of the more bizarre designs at the exhibition with the recent décor of the Catherwoods' small flat, I suddenly saw that I had made a profound mistake and that she was a girl of great character. She, in turn, had taken against Bash-Campers while at Oxford and had sworn never to marry one. But, next time I was in London, she did agree to come to dinner and a concert and was eventually persuaded that behind the Cambridge accent was an independently minded Ulster Scot. It is not easy to court the minister's daughter in a huge church which takes an active interest in his family. We met well away from Westminster and though Douglas Johnson saw us hand in hand from the top of a No 73 bus, no one knew until I had the ring on her finger. We were married on 27 February 1954. Elizabeth's Uncle Vincent gave her away and the Doctor married us in a Chapel packed with friends and congregation, Elizabeth's pupils hanging over the balcony. I went through the day in a happy daze. As my father used to say of his marriage to my mother, it was the best thing I've ever done. I could not have had a better companion in the ups and downs of life, a better mother for our children, anyone more interesting to talk to or more fun to be with.

After three weeks we came back to a little council flat in Gosforth and a great welcome from the Arnotts, Cuthbertsons and Dawsons, and from Grigor and Diana McClelland. The warmth of northern hospitality was overwhelming.

We were only in Newcastle for four months. I didn't set out to look for another job, but an advertisement for a chief accountant for the *Manchester Guardian* caught my eye. I had a great admiration for the paper and put in an application. The Scott brothers asked to see me and I got on very well with them. Then they wrote to say that they couldn't offer me the job simply because I was only twenty-nine and their accounts office was full of elderly clerks.

Enormously encouraged by this near-miss, I applied for the job of Secretary/Controller of a large construction company. I was summoned for interview by Peter Prior of Urwick Orr and Partners, who said I was far too young but the application was very good so he felt he had to see me. He gave me a brisk and penetrating cross-examination and passed me on to Sir Richard Costain.

The company, though public, was family-run by two brothers and two brothers-in-law. It was overtrading and at the point where it needed professional management. In this delicate transition, the thought of someone younger who would not be inclined to throw his weight around too much, evidently appealed to Dick Costain and he offered me the job at twice my current salary.

By the end of the brief months we spent in the little flat in Newcastle, our friends were as much Elizabeth's as mine and we have kept in touch with them over a lifetime. The years ahead were to be a lot tougher.

Chapter Four

CHIEF EXECUTIVE

Costain's was the toughest job I ever had and it was as well that I possessed the energy of youth.

At first it was simple enough. As Secretary and Controller, I had to point out to the board where they were losing money and it was up to them to do something about it. But as the months went on the situation worsened. Rationing of building by licences had just been abolished and there was a rush of new work and a rush of contractors to get as much as they could. But there was no increase of skilled workers to carry it out, so the costs of the new work far exceeded the estimates and Costain's, who had tried hard to get a bigger share of the market, soon found their new UK contracts deep in the red.

There were also heavy losses on a housebuilding venture in Canada, where we had an incompetent manager, and on the biggest opencast coal contract ever let. There we were paid per ton of coal plus an advance calculated on the cost of removal of overburden where the sloping seam was nearest the surface. But the engineers had decided to start at the deep end, where it cost three times as much to uncover the coal, about £3m beyond the contract finance.

It was clear that the unstructured division of the management between two brothers and their two brothers-in-law was no longer adequate. Urwick Orr, the consultants who had recruited me, proposed a professional chief executive. Dick Costain was reluctant to bring in another outsider, one who would set tough terms and who could not be dismissed without embarrassement.

His solution, against Urwick Orr's advice and against some opposition from the family, was to tell me that, since I had been telling them for a year what to do, I should now go ahead and do it. I was only thirty, so I had nothing to lose and I accepted. The view in the company was that I was another of the Chairman's blue-eyed boys and wouldn't last.

My first crisis arrived at once. Dick Costain was Chairman of the Overseas Group for Construction Industries and was arguing on their behalf that since the aid for the huge Kariba Dam across the Zambezi, the largest dam in Africa, came from Britain, it should be tied to British contractors. So he dearly wanted to put in his own bid for the dam. But we were heavily over-extended and there were not the staff to do the tender, let alone supervise the actual construction. In addition, because it was so spectacular, every civil engineer wanted to build it and the tender prices would be as keen as their interest. I suggested that, instead, we bid for the initial housing on the site which, being unglamorous, would have a much better price and profit. In the end he agreed and I used up some goodwill. But had he not agreed, the stretch on our resources would have made my new job impossible. Their unsuccessful main bid cost John Laing so much that they decided never to make such a bid again and the contract went to Italian contractors, who are reputed to have had difficulty in covering their costs.

At home, we stopped all competitive tendering at once and took only those contracts where we could negotiate our own price. Our competitors were badly overstretched, so very soon we had some much better contracts and gradually brought our turnover in line with what we could handle. Lloyds Bank gave us an overdraft to finance the opencast contract – agreed in five minutes when Dick Costain and I went to see the Chief General Manager. We had some very tough negotiations with the Chairman of the Coal Board's Opencast executive and I paid constant visits to the site until we had costs in line with these new prices (the giant drag-lines had to work 150 hours a week; otherwise we lost money). We replaced the Canadian housing manager with a young professional, Keith Morley, who spent the rest of his life in building up a fine housing company. Finally, we closed a loss-making small works department and a loss-making concrete plant.

I set up operating divisions, each responsible for their own budget capital and profit budget, and each with an executive board, which I chaired. I also chaired an executive board for the company and, after false starts with outsiders, we promoted two professional insiders to the key posts of Controller and Personnel Manager.

By the summer of 1956 the worst was over and, as we went off for a holiday to St Ives with our one-year-old son Christopher and Elizabeth's sister Ann, I had never in my life felt so totally exhausted.

The problems were not over. Costain-John Brown (CJB), a company in which John Brown, the engineers and shipbuilders and Costain's each had a half share, had, in turn, a half-and-half joint venture with Iraqi partners for their country's new road-building programme. After the joint venture had asked the British parent companies for the fourth successive bank guarantee, I went out to Baghdad with Sir Stanley Rawson of John Brown to find out what was going on.

The only pleasure on the trip was the cuisine on the Air France Super-Constellation from Orly, which carried its own chef! It quickly became clear that the rate at which the inexperienced Iraqi Transport Ministry was letting the contracts far exceeded the capacity of the local sub-contractors to service them. As each new stretch of road was let, the existing sub-contractors disappeared for the new job and higher prices and, their contracts being worthless, they had to be bought back again at the higher going rate. There was no apparent end to the process and no way of recovering our losses.

Before finally deciding to put our staff on the plane for home, we checked with the British Ambassador, who assured us that no one would prevent their leaving. Then we spent a long evening explaining the situation to our Iraqi partners. We should not have been so gentlemanly. That night one of their relations in the government signed an authority for payment for all the work up to date and wrote out a cheque. On the dot of the opening of the bank controlled by another relative, the cheque was presented and all our partners' bank guarantees extinguished, leaving us to meet the total liabilities. They did not enjoy their success for long. Soon afterwards there was a revolution, in which the former Regent and the young King were killed, and our erstwhile partners had to flee for their lives to Beirut.

We decided that we would not have got into this difficulty had CJB been run by one or other of the partners. I talked to Charles Aberconway, Chairman of John Brown, and we agreed that it fitted better with them, so we sold our share and they kept the initials, renaming it Constructors John Brown. It has since earned a long and distinguished record, mainly in chemical engineering.

As the company's profits improved, I noticed substantial buying of our shares on the open market. Though Charles Clore had done some property takeovers, this was well before the days of hostile takeover bids. But the Costain family held only 10 per cent of the voting shares and the city institutions about another 10 per cent, so, when the unknown holding got near 18 per cent, I warned the Chairman that the family were not far short of losing control and we agreed together a package to stave off a hostile bid. The dividend policy had been obsessively cautious and in any case the profits were now much better, so we announced a much higher dividend, together with a higher profits forecast. The company's star property, Dolphin Square, was heavily undervalued in the balance sheet, so we revalued it. This greatly helped the share price; but to make assurance doubly sure, we issued new shares for our partner's stake in Costain West Africa and placed all the new shares with the City institutions, which increased the proportion in friendly hands and reduced the proportion with the unknown holders.

Shortly afterwards we had a visit from two well-known City financiers, Walter Salomon of Salomon Brothers and Harley Drayton of BET, who revealed themselves as the new shareholders, rebuked us for not making a rights issue to all shareholders for the acquisition of the CWA shares, and asked for seats on the board. When this was refused, they sold their shares and took their profit. I suppose that it was at this point that I began to have some doubt as to whether the free market in capital was all it was supposed to be. Had I seen what was to follow in successive speculative booms, I don't think I would have had any doubt at all.

Up to this point, I had done everything on first principles. There were no textbooks that I knew of on professional management and a whole generation of company directors had grown up in an economy where resources were scarce and allocated by government, and where industry had been protected against foreign competition. Then, in 1957, I bought Peter Drucker's *The Practice of Management* in Heffers in Cambridge and it gave me the rationale for all that I had been doing. The splitting up of companies into operating divisions, the setting of divisional budgets, the decision to concentrate on what the business does best, were all there, together with a lot of other professional wisdom which was a tremendous help then and for years to come. It gave me courage to battle against management by hunch, to insist on rational reasons for decisions and the isolation of the key factors and numbers.

I wrote to Peter Drucker to say what a help I had found his book. Shortly afterwards I was in New York and, as a long shot, asked him out to dinner. To my great surprise he came, saying that he could not refuse an invitation from someone who wrote such a glowing letter. Since then we have kept in touch and his books and advice have been more helpful over the years than any others. In particular he taught me to look at the key questions, such as 'What is our business and what ought it to be and who are our customers?'

From then on I have always been clear that the job of a manager was just as professional as the job of a lawyer or accountant. There might be more variables, but they could be reduced to principles on which we could base our diagnosis, policy and action.

One dedicated professional at Costain's was a tremendous help. Sandy Galloway had arrived just ahead of me as Director of Public Relations. He had been Chief of Staff of the Eighth Army just before it went to Africa and after the war he was the first military governor of the British sector of Vienna. He inspired me with the professionalism of the army, which faces as many new and unexpected situations as any business. It has its bottom line too and its losses are measured in a different kind of red.

One phrase he used I've always found helpful. 'What, Catherwood,' he used to say, 'is the object of the exercise?' He would never let me start out on anything without being quite clear what it was I was trying to achieve. Only then could we begin to put together a plan as to how to carry it through. This clarity of purpose I found sadly lacking in business. But in the army it was a matter of life and death.

He also inspired me with the officer's deeply ingrained duty to look after the troops, and believed that British management would have a lot less trouble if they did the same. For that reason he was a great admirer of Field Marshal Montgomery and took me to have lunch with him at Alton Mill, so that I could be imbued with some of the same spirit.

Monty said that he didn't see why we in management could not sit on an oil-drum on the shop floor and gather the men round, just as he had done with his troops. I thought that this was a bit naïve, because the army did not have to negotiate the wages of the soldier and, especially in war, it had some pretty drastic sanctions. All the same he was far nearer to his men than any leader in World War I; he was far more careful of their lives, so they trusted and followed him. Professionalism taught us a duty of care not just to the client, but to all who worked with us and for us – and also some imagination about the little things which mattered so much.

He said that when serving in Southern Command just after Dunkirk, he had received an order that every soldier must keep his rifle with him wherever he was.

'All right on the North West Frontier! But a soldier in the back of the cinema can't hold a girl with one hand and a loaded rifle with the other. We'd have had at least an hour or so's notice of an attack. Just the kind of unimaginative order which gets the troops down.'

Monty was not popular with the British establishment, but as one German general said, 'He won every battle he fought and that, after all, is what matters.' My own impression, just on a couple of hours' visit, was that he had never got over the surprise of having made it to the top – Commander-in-Chief for the Normandy invasion and later Chief of the Imperial General Staff – over the heads of the establishment. 'Do you know I had two million men serving under me – *me*!'

Sandy Galloway was as a professional should be in his new job, very successful. I thought that, since Costain's contracts were large and spectacular, we could get quite a lot of free publicity by promoting press interest in them. Early TV seemed to have very little place for the interest and romance of industry and we wondered whether we could not inspire the BBC to do a programme. Sandy Galloway said, 'I'll get on to Ian Jacob, know him well.' So the Director General got a letter and we ended up with a programme based on a bid for a harbour in Malta, with Aidan Crawley as the front man and Jack Ashley as the producer – my own first brief appearance on TV as we were filmed discussing our bid.

Then, with the experience of the great turnround we had done ourselves with professional management in the key jobs, I did a proposal for a series, the theme being that, with good management and sympathetic government, we could get an enormous increase in productivity, but without it, we would soon be overtaken not only by the Germans, but by everyone else.

The formidable Grace Wyndham-Goldie was then in effective charge of BBC talks and she came to lunch at the Stafford Hotel with Jack Ashley to discuss the idea. Jack was later commissioned to do four programmes, with Chris Chattaway as the anchor man. They were, I think, one of the first of the series of programmes and books of the sixties on the theme of Britain's slow growth and relative decline. The commentary team on each programme was Andrew Shonfield, Jack Darling, a Labour MP, and myself.

Sandy Galloway and I were asked to Lime Grove to watch the legendary Richard Dimbleby putting out *Panorama*, which at that time had an audience rating of over eight million and we also visited the daily current events programme fronted by Cliff Michelmore. Jack Ashley taught me to not to shout at the camera, but to chat quietly and, whatever else I learnt about being in front of the cameras, it came from him. He and his wife Pauline have remained good friends ever since, a friendship which has been carried on by the next generation of both families.

Two thirds of Costain's work was overseas and that was what kept the company going. Most of it was for British consultants and they, in turn, were working for the colonial administrations, the whole process uncomplicated by corruption. We did, of course, have approaches from other quarters. There was an agent who said he was from President Batista of Cuba and that the

President wanted to spend $10m on a new palace and 10 per cent would get us the contract. I said we should ignore it. The man might not be from the President; if he were, the President might not have $10m and would want us to find it; even if he did have it, the idea of a grand new palace might simply be megalomania, signalling an imminent *coup d'état*. Shortly afterwards Batista was thrown out by Castro. There was another huge harbour about to be built in that part of the world on the same kind of basis, which we also ignored. It was never built, each Minister of Marine being baulked by his colleagues, who wanted his job – and the rakeoff – when the harbour was built.

We were awarded the early contract for the houses at Kariba and it seemed that we had to rent every old bush aircraft and every bush pilot in Africa to fly staff in and out of the mud airstrip. My first flight in 1956 was in a pre-war de Havilland biplane and the pilot insisted on skimming round the bends of the Zambezi to make sure that I saw a hippo. As the wing went down at each bend to meet its shadow on the water, I certainly saw the hippo, until finally someone at the back told the pilot to stop it. On the next visit we had a modern Cessna and when we arrived the site was alive with workers. I climbed the side of the coffer-dam in the gorge in intense heat and admired the muddy rocks below (the bottom of the Zambezi) shortly to be covered for ever. The housing contract, fortunately, was very profitable.

The Cessna took us to the Victoria Falls, which I seemed to see from an angle of 90 degrees as the plane banked for a better view. We stayed in the great colonial hotel on the south side, with its wide verandah, black waiters in white uniform and the Union Jack flying over the veldt. I was glad to have seen it, but also glad that the drain of the colonial empire was coming to an end, when, I hoped, we in Britain could concentrate our talents and resources on keeping our place in the industrial world.

In the two Rhodesias and in Nigeria, we were building those countries' modern infrastructure, hospitals, schools, universities, houses, power stations, roads and docks. As I went through the first fully equipped children's ward of the hospital in Ibadan, I thought that to be in construction was well worth while. The colonial administration in Nigeria was beginning to hand over to Nigerian ministers. In Kaduna a minister had inspected our housing and ordered us to block up the door between the front room and the back, since the man of the house might not like his wife to come in when he had visitors!

After driving north past compounds of houses, each with a guarded stockade, I boarded a BOAC Stratocruiser at Kano. The Governor General of Nigeria, who was travelling with us, was piped aboard. Then, somewhere over the Sahara as we were dining in style, the Captain told us that one engine had stopped and we were heading back for Kano – 'but dinner will continue to be served'. At 1 a.m. the Governor General was piped off again and on again at 5 a.m. Next morning, because of low cloud over Rome, we diverted to Marseilles, and when we trooped into the airport restaurant, the Governor General was directed where to sit by a head waiter who, naturally, had never heard of him. A year or so later the office was extinct.

By 1959 we had professional managers in all the key positions: Peter Lederer in the Building Division; Brendan Clancy in charge of Civil Engineering at home and overseas – the guts of the business; Jimmy Beattie in charge of the Concrete Company, and Barrie Stilwell in charge of Personnel, the heart of the business. We were beginning to work on the next layer down – but Dick Costain didn't like it. Brendan Clancy and I urged a particular appointment on him and suddenly he saw that the loyalty of the next rank would be to the professionals and not to him. Before it was too late he wanted his company back.

He had put three outside directors on the board, all since the turnround in the company and all beholden to him. One brother-in-law had retired and his brother Albert, though still on the board, was preoccupied as the MP for Folkestone. But the three other executive directors were also his appointments. He did not want to reverse what we had done; but he wanted to be in charge again.

It was a very rough situation. I had a wife and two children, Christopher born in 1955 and Bethan in 1958, but I was quite clear that Dick Costain's aims and mine were not, in the long run, compatible. I was, by now, a firm believer in professional principles of management, with objective criteria and properly argued decisions. He wanted an unquestioning personal loyalty which I could not give to any man. I started, very quietly, to look around for another job. I had three offers, but one was too staid and administrative, one was to hold the ring between two quarrelling partners and the third was 8,000 miles away and, with the children so young, that was too far. It was a tense time.

Finally I asked my accountant to enquire about an advertisement for a job as Managing Director of an engineering company which offered much more than I was currently earning. It turned out to be the British Aluminium Company, taken over the year before in a fiercely contested takeover bid, which had divided the City, and now chaired by Edwin Plowden, who had been chairing the Atomic Energy Authority. The new owners were Tube Investments, with 51 per cent, and one of the four American aluminium giants, Reynolds Metals, with 49 per cent.

I had six successive interviews, did a two-hour intelligence test and gave a sample of my handwriting (to be sent to a Dutch expert for character analysis). Only when I got back to Edwin Plowden for a second interview did I realise that I must be the front-runner; but there was one more hurdle. He said, 'I don't really know you, Catherwood, and I'd be grateful if you could find two referees whom we both know well and who will not tell me lies about you.'

It was a tall order, but Charles Aberconway of John Brown had worked for Edwin Plowden in the City and Donald Fergusson, now a director of Costain's, had been a Permanent Secretary when Plowden was at the Treasury. Both supported me and, with great relief, I went to tell Dick Costain that I had been offered a job which I would like to take. He ordered a stiff whisky but seemed comforted that he could tell the board that they were losing me because they couldn't possibly match the salary. He asked me to lunch the next day and we parted the best of friends.

Sadly he died only a few years later – and I think all the rest of the board, with the exception of Albert Costain, also died within a few years. Brendan Clancy went to John Laing, but all the other key professionals stayed in post.

Costain's did not allow much time for outside activities. I was a member of the Ealing Conservative Association and spoke in Ealing Town Hall in defence of Angus Maude's right to be a Tory rebel in opposing Macmillan's retreat from Suez, even though I supported Macmillan. I asked him to explain the Anglo-French 'impartial' ultimatum requiring the Israelis to advance to the Suez Canal and the Egyptians to retreat behind it, but got no reply. Suez was a shock of political disillusion from which I never totally recovered.

A year later, as it became clear that the European Economic Community was going to go ahead, I thought our counter-proposal of a European Free Trade Area was quite inadequate. I therefore persuaded Dick Costain to take it up on the President of the Board of Trade's Advisory Committee, of which he was a member, and to argue that it would be much better to join the EEC. He came back and said that he had tried but had got nowhere.

My one firm commitment outside work was a Sunday after-noon discussion group at Westminster Chapel, which I took over in 1955 and kept up for the next twenty-five years. This was the kind of steady church responsibility which I had always wanted. The class, aged mainly between seventeen and twenty-two, quickly built up to about thirty. It had a very persistent balance of two to one in favour of the men and the mix of backgrounds was as wide as those in the Chapel itself.

I ran it as I had seen Dr Lloyd-Jones run the Friday night discussions, on the Socratic method, asking questions rather than giving answers and leaving it, so far as possible, to members of the class to correct each other – which they normally did with great vigour. This method makes people think for themselves, since the points which we make ourselves also imprint themselves on our memories far more firmly than points made to us by other people. I never allowed anyone to quote authorities, or the whole debate would have resolved into arguments on which authority was right. If people were convinced by some argument which they had heard or read, then they had to argue it and defend it as their own.

Once a month the class decided by vote on a particular problem that they would like to discuss; otherwise we worked slowly through a book of the New Testament. To handle a discussion which can go off in any direction needs far more preparation than the set path of a talk. I read different commentaries to be clear on the several possible interpretations of the passage and then looked up books of systematic theology for the key doctrines. Then, as the discussion moved on, I raised questions to nudge it to the central issues and, once there, I tried to make sure that the class came to a balanced conclusion. If they came to a conclusion too easily, I acted as devil's advocate. I kept notes and used them to summarise the previous week's discussion and start off the next one.

From 1955 to 1980 it was, apart from holidays, a fixed point in our lives. From 1968, when Dr Lloyd-Jones retired, Elizabeth took over her mother's women's class and we both used to sit surrounded by commentaries from lunch until a quarter to three.

It needed rigid discipline in a busy life, but it was worth it. In each 'generation' of about five years, there were those who stood out, and some of the students went on to become leaders in their professions. Derek Henderson, a consultant at St Thomas's Hospital; Quin Terry, now a leading architect; Robin Wells, who became General Secretary of the IVF (by then the UCCF); Paul Leinster, an environmental engineer; and, in the same generation, with a lot of other people from the arts, Norman Stone, a TV producer, and Steve Turner, a poet.

Norman and Steve lived at 1a Shepherd Market and offered liberal hospitality for Sunday lunch, which Christopher and Bethan and, later, Jonathan, born in 1961, greatly enjoyed. It was about that time that we debated the morality of nudity and at the end, a young actress said that she had always resisted parts in which she would have to strip off and now she understood why.

In the summer they all used to come down to Cambridge in old cars and after lunch we went out on the river in seven or eight punts poled unsteadily along by macho men. Those who were found to be still dry at the tea stop were not dry for much longer. Then back home for a long supper; we never saw the last car lights disappear until eleven. It was hard work, but we made lots of friends for life and would not have missed it.

Although Westminster Chapel was a big city-centre church, with lots of students and visitors, there was at its core a strong church 'family' who stayed for most of the day on Sunday, having lunch and tea together as well as the afternoon classes and prayer meetings. It was a warm and vigorous fellowship in which all our children were accommodated too.

But most important of all was the teaching of the Doctor, which, with a two-year gap in Newcastle, I enjoyed from 1948 until he retired. He was a brilliant preacher, gripping and persuasive, compelling by the force of his informed logic, balancing Old Testament with New, the Gospels with the Epistles, and the doctrine of our individual responsibility with the doctrine of God's sovereignty.

Yet, and especially as those he influenced took up the forgotten teaching of the giants of the seventeenth and eighteenth centuries, he warned against an attitude which was correct but cold, reminding us of the width and warmth of God's love and the power of the Holy Spirit. The pillars of Christian doctrine were not like cold stone; but its object was to inspire us and to make us worship God with all our heart and soul.

He saw the enemy as theological liberalism, which had conceded one pillar of faith after another to secular humanism. He feared for the effectiveness of Evangelical ministers, increasingly squeezed by their Church hierarchies and, at a great meeting of the Evangelical Alliance in 1966, chaired by John Stott, he made a passionate plea for Evangelical unity.

But his plea was seen as a threat to the integrity of denominations and so, at a time when the Church and country were about to be overrun by secular humanism, Evangelicals divided instead of uniting. In retrospect it is easy to say that he should have left it there. But the vocal minority, who wanted to translate his plea into a united Evangelical Church, also wanted him as their leader, and he was identified with them and lost to the Evangelical majority.

He leaves many monuments: the national student movement – the IVF/UCCF was built on the foundations he laid with Douglas Johnson. He was, with Stacey Woods, a founding father of the worldwide International Fellowship of Evangelical Students (IFES), which has gone from strength to strength. The Evangelical Library owes everything to his leadership and he inspired the Puritan Conference and the re-publication of so many of the great Puritan works.

But his greatest monument is his teaching and that lives on in his books of sermons. He started to edit them in retirement and the work was taken on by Elizabeth and her mother. Now it is mainly done by Elizabeth with help from his eldest grandson, Christopher. The Martyn Lloyd-Jones Recording Trust has tapes of most of his sermons and through these and the more than forty books which have been published to date, he is reaching many times more people across the world – and in their own language – than he ever taught in Westminster Chapel.

Chapter Five

A CHRISTIAN IN INDUSTRIAL SOCIETY

Edwin Plowden was a professional to his fingertips and I learnt more from him than from any other single person about decision-taking in a big organisation. He had started his career with Tennants in the City, had gone to the Ministry of Aircraft Production during the war and, after a brief time back in the City, to the Treasury as Chairman of the Economic Planning Board under Cripps, Gaitskell and Butler, then back to industry as Chairman of the Atomic Energy Authority for five years. In 1959 Ivan Stedeford, who had built up Tube Investments (TI) by a series of takeovers, asked him to come back to the private sector and chair his biggest, latest and most controversial acquisition, British Aluminium.

He told me that he had spent his time pre-war at Tennants in undercutting Continental chemical cartels, so he certainly knew the rough side of business. To have served during the war under the maverick Beaverbrook must also have been an experience in itself, and in the Treasury he was at the heart of the economic arguments about how to run a bankrupt Britain – especially the argument when the Conservatives came back in 1951 on whether to make the pound convertible. And at the Atomic Energy Authority, committed to civil expansion, he had to hold a balance between brilliant physicists and practical managers.

His natural authority, which came from a very sharp mind and his exceptionally wide experience, was balanced by a disarmingly gentle and courteous manner. In welcome contrast to the rough-house of the construction industry, he took a great deal of care

67

with personal relationships at every level, and expected all of us who worked for him to do the same – and not only with employees. He expected us, for instance, to tell unsuccessful applicants for jobs at once and not to keep them hanging on, when they ought to be looking elsewhere. He was to need all this authority to weld together the disparate teams: the resentful top managers of the British Aluminium Company (BA), the confident Americans from Reynolds and the management of the original Reynolds TI Aluminium (RTIA), now merged with the much bigger acquisition. Those who talk glibly of the supposed synergy of mergers have little experience in trying to realise it. At an early board meeting after I joined, Edwin Plowden said that if, in future, he heard anyone arguing for a TI, Reynolds, BA or RTIA way of doing things, he would be dismissed at once. He clearly meant it and there was no more trouble.

That did not, of course, produce a professional management team. The RTIA sales director had taken over, merged and reorganised the two sales teams, so that, just when it was necessary to hold every customer's loyalty, they were all faced with a new and strange salesman. By the time I got there, our share of the market had dropped by a fifth and we had a huge stockpile of unsold ingot from the new Baie Comeau smelter on the St Lawrence (whose financing had made BA vulnerable to the takeover). We eventually got a very professional sales director, E J Timlin, from a smaller competitor.

The new Production Director, a tough cigar-chewing American looking remarkably like Groucho Marx, had been in his element as the big boss of Reynolds' great McCook rolling mill in Chicago. He had managed the two RTIA plants without too much difficulty; but he now had six fabricating plants, some of which had started losing money as our market share dropped and as the buoyant market, on which TI and Reynolds had bought in, began to ease. We promoted younger engineers in both rolling mills and I made a fortnightly visit to the biggest at Falkirk until we had reduced our manning and covered our costs. Eventually Reynolds recalled their man and we appointed BA's previous Production Director, Jack Salter, for the fabricating plants and another old BA hand, Godfrey Anderson, for the smelters. The former BA Finance Director left for another job and I asked Peter

Prior, who had recruited me for Costain's, to join us. But, brilliant and professional though he was, his humour and individualistic style rubbed against the rather more establishment attitude of his colleagues and he went off to be Chairman of Bulmer's Cider, which he ran in his own style and with great success until he retired. When he headed a government enquiry into motorway service stations, he rode up and down the motorways on his motor bike and as the slim figure with piercing blue eyes, Roman nose and full black riding kit pushed his tray along the self-service counters, no one could possibly guess who it was.

The most brilliant member of the new team was Ronny Utiger, who joined us from Courtaulds. At first he worked on commercial strategy, then he replaced Peter as Finance Director. When, sadly, my successor died in office, he became Managing Director of BA and eventually and until he retired, Chairman of TI.

We had two Highland smelters, the smaller and older at Kinlochleven and the larger and newer at Lochaber under Ben Nevis. The old smelter made money, the smelting boxes lasting their full life. But the smelting boxes in the bigger Lochaber plant could achieve only half the life and it ran at a loss. When it was clear that our management did not know how to solve the problem, I persuaded Reynolds to lend us one of their most professional managers, who not only put that right but also put right the far bigger smelter at Baie Comeau.

We were not only one of the biggest landowners in the Highlands; we were, second only to McBrayne's Boats, the biggest employer in a large area with little other employment. Great was our shock when the President of the Board of Trade signed a trade deal with the Soviet Union, which gave unlimited access for exports of Soviet aluminium to the British market. I led an angry delegation from the industry to the Board of Trade, where we pointed out that, with massive capital investment in hydro-electric power, the sunk costs of aluminium production were very high, the marginal costs very low and the temptation to dump by a country with a protected market was overwhelming.

We argued that we protected ourselves by buying up dumped imports and selling them straight back again to the dumper's best customers. We had had deep apologies from the Japanese producers when we sold their dumped metal back again in the Tokyo market and similar action had stopped one minor American producer after a second attempt. But in the closed market of the Soviet Union there were no customers and no counter-actions we could take against dumping. They had an enormous smelting industry, they needed hard currency and they would put us straight out of business.

It was clear that the Board of Trade knew nothing of this. The Ministry of Aviation was supposed to be our 'sponsor department', but they had not consulted us and had clearly not been consulted themselves. It was borne in on me forcibly how totally ignorant the British government was of the economics of the country's industries, although they were absolutely vital to Britain's economic survival. The Board of Trade said that they had just clinked glasses with the Soviet Minister and could not possibly go back on the deal.

The deal not only affected us but, directly or indirectly, the viability of the whole European industry. So I suggested to the other producers that we should offer to buy, exclusively, slightly more than the current volume of Soviet exports at a slightly higher price, sharing the purchase among ourselves in proportion to our share of the market. After considerable discussion, they agreed.

Then we had to sell the deal to the Russians and two of our number were despatched to Moscow. After endless meetings, the deal was done. I had gone with Edwin Plowden to see Richard Powell, Permanent Secretary of the Board of Trade, who was very conscious of the damage to the industry and to employment of allowing free Soviet imports without consulting us. He knew what an almighty public fuss we could make. Edwin Plowden put it to him, as one mandarin to another, that in all the circumstances, this deal seemed the most sensible action to take and he agreed.

It was as well that we went to see him. The deal lasted a long time and ten years later when we had become members of the EEC, its directorate for competition began to ask questions, and it was that meeting, where our own government had agreed to this restrictive contract, which covered us.

But we did not know at the time that the deal would stick for so long. A year later, when the deal was due to be renewed, the Soviets started to dump rolled aluminium, which affected the more open British market more than the Continental markets. I then had the even more awkward two-headed task of persuading the European industry that we should not renew the ingot agreement unless fabricated products were included, but that if they were included, we should renew it. That was difficult, but they agreed.

We had asked Warburg's to advise us, so they passed on the message. The Soviets replied that these were two different industries and that the smelters had no control over the fabricators. We said that that was just too bad, no deal. Then they asked me to go to Moscow to negotiate. Warburg's said I should refuse, saying that there was nothing to negotiate. It seemed a high risk, but I took it. After three weeks we had a message from the Soviet Embassy in London that the departments in Moscow had come to an agreement and that fabricated aluminium would be included.

But BA's big market share continued to be vulnerable and we still had the high ingot stocks which we could not sell on the American market without provoking retaliation against Reynolds. So in deciding what to charge to preserve market share, we took the cost of holding the ingot stocks into account and made a sharp reduction in the basic price for standard fabricated aluminium. That stabilised our market share.

We were also forced to rationalise production. In the middle of the summer holidays I went in the small TI company plane from a Suffolk airfield not far from our holiday house in Frinton to Staffordshire to tell the assembled workforce at our old plant at Milton that we had to close it and that there would be jobs for most of them at our plant in South Wales. We offered the best redundancy package we could and the GMWU who represented the workforce said that it was a model deal. But there is nothing more miserable than to bring to an end a whole community with its own skills, pride and traditions. Fewer than one in ten went to South Wales. We took on redundant miners at our plant near Neath and until they learnt that they should handle aluminium's immaculate surfaces more gently than coal, our rejection rate rose dramatically!

Harold Macmillan's attempt to get us into the EEC had run into the de Gaulle veto and that posed enormous problems for British companies. We were being cut out of our traditional sterling markets as one country after another raised barriers to protect infant industries. Australia, for instance, barred imports of ingot to protect its own smelters, but we went on selling rolled products; then they built their own rolling mills and we could only sell foil. Finally, as I remember, they put down a foil mill and cut off their market completely. All round the globe, these traditional markets dried up.

Our proper alternative was the booming EEC. But we had tariffs of at least 10 per cent against us, which skimmed off the profit margin from which our EEC partners were funding their new plant and machinery. This new plant produced not only higher volume, but higher specifications which we could not match and altogether new products which we could not even make.

The only answer seemed to be a rate of growth in the home market which equalled that in the EEC, giving British industry the cashflow to match the new EEC investment. Harold Macmillan set up the new National Economic Development Council (NEDC) to bring management and unions together with government to see how Britain could achieve a better economic performance. But our recent experience told me that the NEDC would need some better link to industry itself, or the six industrialists who sat round the table would be dominated by civil servants and economists. That summer I sat in the loggia outside our rented holiday house in Frinton and began to sketch the kind of link I thought might work.

Earlier in that summer of 1962 part of my past went up in smoke. On a dry and windy day, the wooden structure of Rosapenna Hotel caught fire. By the time the fire engines had arrived from Letterkenny thirty miles away, the blaze was beyond control. The only person in the dining room for lunch was the aged Duke of St Albans. The head waiter said, apologetically, 'Your Grace, I fear that the hotel is on fire.'

'Then Casey, I suppose that there will be no more lunch.'

'I fear not, Your Grace.'

'In that case, bring me another plate of soup.'

The manager and his wife tried to persuade the Duke to leave at once, but he protested that all his new spring suits were in his bedroom; nor, when they had rushed upstairs, would he let them throw the suits out of the window on to the roses.

So, as the beams crashed down behind him, the last person out of this resort of the Anglo-Irish was the twelfth Duke of St Albans, descendent of Charles II and Nell Gwynne, flanked by the manager and his wife with suitcases full of his new spring suits. It was an appropriate finale. It is as well that it went out in a blaze before the new jets took everyone off to the sun and before the civil strife started six years later, only fifty miles away in Derry.

We had paid our last visit six months before, just before Christmas, when the only guests were Ian Fleming, creator of James Bond, and his wife Anne (formerly Lady O'Neill). Father's broker, Jim McGugan, had insured the hotel well and when Father sold the land, he and Mother came to live in England, settling in the pretty Cotswold village of Wootton near Woodstock, a long way from the Atlantic storms.

Although we had not gone to Rosapenna regularly, the place in the country had always been there and now, with the increasing pressures of life and a small family, our country roots began to call. So we looked at a list of old rectories, which the Church Commissioners were now beginning to sell. The first we viewed was surrounded by a heavily overgrown two-acre garden with ivy, briars and bushes thickly intertwined. It had not been decorated since before the war and the top panes of the windows were still painted for the wartime blackout. But structurally it was sound, it had plenty of room and was close to Cambridge. For the next two years we negotiated with the Church Commissioners at the Soke of Peterborough. We offered the asking price of £5,000 but then they put it on the market. However, after a few prospective buyers had called, the Rector wrote to the Church Commission to say that he did not think that the last two people who came to see it were married to each other, while the Catherwoods were suitable and had offered a reasonable price; so if they went on sending people, he would tell them about the wet rot, the dry rot and the tiles off the roof.

So, in 1964, they finally settled for £5,500, and we paid another £4,000 for repairs and decoration, all of which we borrowed. Over thirty years the lawns have been reclaimed from bramble and bush, the suckers have been cut down to reveal all the old yews, and to those and the other fine old trees we have added a cedar, four golden Irish yews, a red flowering chestnut, a tulip tree, a weeping copper-beech, a willow and a maple, an oak, four apple trees, two more yew hedges, two beech hedges and lots of shrubs.

During the next thirty years I spent in public service, it has been an all too brief haven of timeless peace. The bookshelves have spread steadily, the big family pieces of furniture, redundant elsewhere, have gradually filled out the rooms. To turn into the drive is to enter another world, and a day or two later we feel ready to drive out to face all our problems once again. We try not to keep it to ourselves and it has plenty of room to cater for church outings; the old like the peace of the garden, the young like exploring the back stairs, the endless attics and the cellar, with its own well, and the huge wardrobes like the one in *The Lion, the Witch and the Wardrobe*. It is a Dickensian house, at its best for family parties at Christmas, with frost outside, shutters closed, Christmas cards and candles, and log fires burning.

Dr and Mrs Lloyd-Jones, who thought originally that we were mad to buy it, spent all their holidays with us, and the Doctor edited most of his books there. In 1964 Christopher was nine, Bethan five and Jonathan two, and for the next sixteen years of holidays, we were three generation all together. After the Doctor's death in 1981, Mrs Lloyd-Jones began to spend half her time with us there and the other half with her younger daughter, Ann, and her three other grandchildren, Elizabeth, Rhianon and Adam. Although the Doctor was formidable and authoritative in the pulpit, he was a gentle, interested and interesting grandfather. He played pocket billiards with Jonathan, and he and their grandmother played Christopher and Bethan at croquet. But their main memory is sitting round the table in the big kitchen talking and, as they got older, arguing, young cubs with the old lion, venturing where no one else would dare. In 1968 we went to Wales together visiting the family farm near Newcastle Emlyn and Llangeitho, where the Doctor was brought up. And in 1970 and 1972 we went to Aviemore together, exchanging houses with the minister of Rothiemurchus, where the Doctor took the Sunday services; three generations living together, and influencing and entertaining each other as an extended family should.

As Managing Director of BA, I began to live in a wider world. I was elected to the Council of the British Institute of Management, then directed by the dynamic John Marsh (not my brother-in-law). Andrew Shonfield, who was with us on Jack Ashley's TV series, proposed me for the Council of the Royal Institute of International Affairs (Chatham House) and, having served on the Finance Committee of the IVF, I now joined the Council, chaired by Norman Anderson. In 1963 I also joined the Northern Ireland Development Council, chaired by Lord Chandos, a great raconteur who brightened the Council meetings with his stories.

The outside activity most permanently recorded was my first book, *The Christian in Industrial Society*. Oliver Barclay, General Secretary of the IVF following Douglas Johnson, organised a series of meetings of Christians in business. We would look at all the hard ethical problems which we faced and try to put together some guidelines. Each of us would put in a paper for general discussion.

Richard Barclay was a banker and Murray Pickering a tax expert; the rest of us were in industry, Robin Caldecote and Kirby Laing being the best known. Since we had not included a trades unionist in the group, we asked George Woodcock, the General Secretary of the TUC, to dinner. I was rapporteur and, rather than all of us try to agree everything, I was given the job of writing it up in book form.

We were, under Oliver's inspiration, trying to counter the long influence of pietism among Evangelicals, which had taken us out of the mainstream of public argument after the great days of Victorian reformers like Wilberforce and Shaftesbury. We argued the need for deeds as well as words, for collective as well as individual protest against the injustices of society. We pointed out that the bible teaches God's care about the social order, justice for all, and love for the poor and weak.

We argued that, though there was no 'social gospel', since the good news of redemption through Christ is addressed to each individual, there was, both in the Prophets and Christ's own teaching, a social law. It might not by itself produce new Christians, but, through the work of God's common grace, shared by the whole world, it would produce a better society. To reformers like Wilberforce and Shaftesbury there was no problem of morals or behaviour which was beyond the competence of God's word.

We dealt with the Christian's proper attitude to work, wealth and economic systems. We argued for the social responsibility of big business and the trades unions, the authority of government, the duty to pay lawful taxes, and a code of fair trading (no discriminatory pricing and no bribery). We discussed the rights and wrongs of making money on the Stock Exchange, our duties as employer and as employee, to colleagues as well as to the boss. Having written it up, I ended the book with a summary of the Weber/Tawney thesis on the powerful impact on Western society of the Protestant work ethic.

The book clearly filled a need; it was translated into German and published in America under the title, *On the Job, the Christian Nine to Five*. It went through several editions, the last being in 1982, and it sold over thirty thousand copies. I never matched that again!

I not only hustled around Europe, meeting agents and customers and attending the meetings, mainly in Zurich, of the European aluminium producers, but I also went each October to New York and Richmond, Virginia, to keep in touch with Reynolds and to compare their methods with ours. I called too on Peter Drucker and he also came over to London to advise.

One year I went south to Mussel Shoals in Alabama, where I visited one of the big Reynolds rolling mills – all white – and the smelter next door – all black. It seemed to me that there was no magic in the American industry, nothing we could not match if we set our minds to it and believed that the business of Britain was business – not running the remains of an empire.

Reynolds had fewer people than BA on the shop floor, but it did have a thicker band of very well-qualified front-line management. It was that band that British industry lacked. We did not have the same weight of technical education and we had no management education to speak of. There were the Henley Staff College and

Ashridge, but they only catered for a very few and were not in the same class as the big American business schools. My first letter to *The Times* was to support the case for British business schools on the same scale as the American.

I was in an empty Manhattan during the 1962 Cuban missile crisis. At a huge cinema in Times Square there was only one other patron. I didn't feel too nervous, because Peter Drucker had said that it would be settled, and sure enough, the Soviet ships turned round without a shot fired. But it was the nearest the world came to nuclear war.

I had been over in America during the Nixon/Kennedy election. All the businessmen in New York wore Nixon buttons and all those in Richmond wore Kennedy buttons – still the solid South. I saw the famous Nixon/Kennedy debate (the first TV encounter between Presidential candidates), in which Kennedy forced Nixon, Eisenhower's Vice President, on to the defensive. I am sure that it was that and not the famous shadow on Nixon's chin which won Kennedy the few vital extra votes which put him just ahead. Kennedy's call to get America moving was one which certainly appealed to me. I wanted it to happen in Britain too.

The thinking I had done in the loggia of our holiday house at Frinton had turned into a document calling for industry-by-industry committees reporting to the the National Economic Development Council (NEDC), which would have also tripartite membership from management unions and government. Their first remit would be to do all they could to encourage a rapid increase of productivity in their industry, giving it the cashflow to invest; their second to underpin the NEDC with practical industrial advice, so that it was not wholly reliant on economists and government departments.

In 1962 I gave the paper to Robert Shone, who was to be the first Director General of the NEDC and whose office, at the Iron and Steel Federation, was only a few floors below mine in Norfolk House. To cover the possibility that Labour under Harold Wilson might win the next General Election, I got an introduction to Jim Callaghan, the opposition Treasury spokesman. He asked me to put the paper to a Fabian Society working party to be chaired by the Cambridge economist Robert Neild and which he himself would attend. I thought I should mention that I was not a member of the Labour Party, but he said that since it was a Fabian group, that didn't matter.

I was quite clear what I wanted out of the working party and, as is often the case, those who know exactly what they want prevail over the more uncertain ideas of those who do not. The working party included my proposal in its submission in early 1963 to the Home Affairs Committee of the Labour Party, where it was introduced by John Grieve-Smith, a Labour Councillor from Croydon. I went along to the meeting at the Bonnington Hotel where I met Harold Wilson for the first time, and others, like Roy Jenkins, on the front bench team. The paper went through on the nod. I could hardly believe it.

That summer we went for a week to the Isle of Wight, where Jim Callaghan was staying in a cottage with his family. They came over for coffee and I spent the evening arguing fiercely with his son-in-law Peter Jay under Jim's benevolent gaze.

I was increasingly doubtful if any good would come of the Conservative government. I was a member of a small dining club, all of whose members had been made chief executives before they were forty. Peter Walker, then a Tory backbencher, was our Chairman and he asked the Chief Secretary to the Treasury, John Boyd-Carpenter, to speak to us. The talk was almost wholly negative – this was so difficult and so was that. There seemed to be no urgency to make changes to get Britain out of its economic doldrums. Then Harold Macmillan resigned and, hoping that Rab Butler would bring the party to life, we were given instead the thirteenth Earl of Home.

On the other side it was all go. Harold Wilson had decided on a Department of Economic Affairs alongside the Treasury and the dynamic George Brown was its spokesman. George Brown at once organised a conference of academic economists and his fellow front-bench economic spokesmen. I had not met him and was asked, I suppose, as an industrialist prepared to advise the Labour Party.

The academics argued that British industry was too labour intensive and needed more investment, with which I agreed. But their proposal was that wages should be taxed to make labour more expensive, forcing industrialists to spend more on plant and less on labour. Although there were one or two union representatives there, they said nothing, so I intervened to say that were I a trades unionist and the government had announced that it needed higher labour costs, I would oblige at once and they needn't bother with any fancy new taxes. The proposal died, to the evident pleasure of George Brown and his front-bench colleagues who talked to me afterwards. Though I thought nothing of it at the time, this was probably a decisive moment in my life.

I had been pressing for some time for a high-level executive from Reynolds to get a freer and more systematic transmission of Reynolds know-how to BA. In the summer of 1964 Bill Strath, who had taken over as Chairman when Edwin Plowden became Chairman of TI, told me that at last Reynolds had responded, and proposed to send us their corporate lawyer, Gus Margraf. I thought that was just what we wanted. Then Bill Strath said anxiously that there was one condition. Though Gus would only take on the BA jobs that he, Bill Strath, did now, they wanted him designated as Joint Managing Director. To his obvious relief I said that I didn't mind a bit. I would be doing exactly the same job and it was I who had pressed for the appointment, so we should not let the title stand in the way.

So when Labour won the election and on the day that I was unexpectedly sent for by George Brown and asked to be the government's Chief Industrial Adviser, Gus Margraf arrived and there was someone readymade to take my place.

Although Robert Shone did get the Conservatives to accept the idea which I had put to him of the Economic Development Committees (quickly dubbed 'little Neddies'), they did not seem to take much notice of industry. Jim Callaghan and George Brown were, in sharp contrast, full of enthusiasm and, though they accepted my ideas and knew that I was not a member of the Labour Party, it occurred to me that they might be embarrassed if it were known that they were accepting policies put forward by a paid up member of the opposite party, even if not a very active one. So I told my local party that for various reasons I thought it best to put my membership in suspense.

Yet it was a big jump to serve, even as a civil servant, under a Labour government. Edwin Plowden asked me whether I wanted to do it. I said that it seemed an exceptional opportunity and too rare a chance to miss. He was sympathetic, having done the same himself at about the same age. He warned me that some people in the City would never trust anyone who had served, even as a civil servant, under a Labour government, but 'Even if you make a mess of it, you're young enough to come back and start again'. So I was seconded to the government on full pay for two years. However, I was to stay a lot longer than that.

Chapter Six

GOING FOR GROWTH

The Labour government did not start well. True, it inherited a fragile economy. The outgoing Conservatives had run a full five-year term, leaving themselves no time to curb the Maudling boom and passing to Labour a trade deficit of £400m a year plus an overall deficit of double that amount, a record £800m payments deficit. Knowing that they would have to fight another election soon, ministerial speeches made the most of the deficit, but that undermined confidence in sterling. To make matters worse, they had, against advice from their civil servants, imposed an import surcharge of 15 per cent. Besides being against all our trade obligations, this was thought by the currency markets to be an action taken only *in extremis*. As a result there was a huge loss of currency reserves, the first of many runs on the pound. Roly Cromer, the Bank Governor, had put together a rescue package, but the outlook remained dark.

Against this rather gloomy background, we started to put together the Department of Economic Affairs (DEA), which was supposed to pull Britain out of its growing economic problems. Arthur Peterson from the Home Office was in charge of regional policy; Donald Macdougall had come from Neddy (the common abbreviation of the National Economic Development Council) as Chief Economic Adviser to put together the National Plan; I was Chief Industrial Adviser, and Douglas Allen from the Treasury made the fourth of the Deputy Secretaries. He was in charge of administration and, shortly afterwards, of incomes policy.

Without the experience of four years with Edwin Plowden, I

doubt whether I could have switched from industry to the Civil Service. He taught me always to consult before making decisions and to listen carefully to what people were actually saying. He had a sharp eye for the weak point in a case, so that you had to have it all buttoned up before you saw him. After four years of putting proposals to him and arguing them through, I had no difficulty in doing the same at the top level in Whitehall.

I persuaded George Brown that the economic plan he proposed should be based on consultation with industry, so Neddy (which brought together monthly the six economic ministers, plus six members from management and six from the TUC) should be kept on and the six little Neddies already set up by Robert Shone should be expanded to cover the rest of the private sector.

It was quite another matter to persuade Whitehall. I was summoned to a meeting in a large panelled chamber, decorated with portraits of the kings and queens of England. Most of the Permanent Secretaries seemed to be there and, at their first meeting after the election, there was a lot of gossip, taking the measure of their new masters. I felt that I had gate-crashed the country's most exclusive club.

Eric Roll, our Permanent Secretary, freshly back from Washington, said that our new Department of Economic Affairs (DEA) proposed to keep the six little Neddies and, since he knew little about it, I would answer any questions.

I had a very rough time from the assembled company in a first-class turf-fight. They believed that the little Neddies infringed the excellent relations which each of the industries had with their sponsoring department, and they wanted the new government to wind them up at once. Lucidly, eloquently and with great depth of Whitehall experience and equal depth of feeling, my proposal was torn limb from limb. Some inner instinct told me that I could not meet this onslaught head on and I found myself saying:

'There may be a lot in what you say; but the government has only a tiny majority; it needs to create confidence, not just in the currency markets, but also in industry. If it wants to offend the maximum number of influential people in the shortest time, it will tell all those on these six little Neddies that it no longer needs their advice. So I suggest that, for the moment, we play safe and do nothing.'

To my amazement there was a murmur of assent round the table. I had, instinctively, met the Whitehall argument on Whitehall terms.

My first job was to recruit a team of industrial advisers, asking industry to second them to the government free of charge. It was not always easy to persuade industry to part with top executives, especially when the grapevine had given us the names of the best. But John Berkin of Shell and Ernest Woodroffe of Unilever led the way and, despite an attempt by Paul Chambers of ICI to oppose the effort, others followed.

Arnold Weinstock of GEC parted with Jack Scamp and almost instantly regretted it. But Jack was a superb industrial relations negotiator and government did not want to let him go again. Hill Samuel gave us Derek Palmar (later Chairman of Bass); the *Financial Times* gave us Michael Shanks (the only member of the Labour Party); the British Motor Corporation gave us Richard O'Brien, whom I had met through Sandy Galloway, and Noel Bond-Williams came from Delta Metal. It was an excellent team, each responsible for advising on particular industrial sectors and, collectively, for giving advice on industrial policy. Our individual advice might have been ignored, but it was not so easy to ignore all of us together. Peter Thornton, later Permanent Secretary of the Department of Trade, was our Under Secretary, gearing us into the Whitehall machine and the vast flow of paper which passed through the Department.

Though we were not, like Nicky Kaldor, Tommy Balogh and Robert Neild, political appointees, we still worried the Civil Service. Familiar faces at the Oxford and Cambridge Club turned out to be top mandarins, including the Head of the Civil Service, Sir Lawrence Helsby, who asked me to crack a bottle of port with him. They didn't need to worry. Edwin Plowden had played it by the rules in his time and, like him, I decided that we would get further faster if we worked with Whitehall and not against it.

Of course we had fights. The government introduced a capital gains tax and the City complained bitterly that it was a breach of contract to charge it on the redemption of securities issued under par. The silky minds at the Treasury denied this absolutely and the argument reached very high levels of abstraction before they made some concessions.

Then we advised George Brown to hold down the cost of postage to concentrate the minds of the Post Office on improving efficiency. That brought a summons to lunch at the Reform from Otto Clarke, formidable Second Permanent Secretary at the Treasury, and a worried explanation of the need for long-term expenditure plans, for which he had fought such a strenuous battle. It also brought a visit to George from the Postmaster General, Anthony Wedgwood Benn (as he was then known). In the end we compromised with a little Neddy for the Post Office, the only one in a nationalised industry.

We had difficulties with both the Ministry of Transport and the Ministry of Labour when we wanted to set up a little Neddy for the movement of exports. There were long delays in the docks, especially in London, where queues of ships waited in the Thames, and this played havoc with delivery dates for British exports, which damaged our exports and undermined confidence in the pound.

The Ministry of Labour were convinced that it was a labour problem. I argued, from my Northern Ireland Development Council experience, that we needed a massive change in the use of containers and, for the short Continental passage, roll-on roll-off ferries. We should not keep ships waiting in port while we stuffed their holds just as we had stuffed the holds of sailing ships. The way to free the ports was to fill containers at the factories or inland depots and turn the ships round in a day. If Northern Ireland could deliver to Britain overnight, then we could deliver to the Continent overnight. But we needed to get together representatives of all those involved: exporters, shippers, shipowners, dock owners, customs and trades unions. This was not 'government intervention'; it was commonsense partnership of the interests which needed to be organised nationally.

The Ministry of Transport had commissioned and had just received a massive study on the modernisation of the ports, which said nothing of all this. I suggested to the Permanent Secretary that the Minister come to discuss it with George Brown. He blanched and said, 'No, let's keep it at our level.' George, whose father had been a docker, talked to Ray Gunter, Minister of Labour, and settled it. Robin Caldecote was appointed Chairman. He did a superb job and Britain's ports were transformed.

Tony Crosland was DEA's Minister of State, and Bill Rodgers and Maurice Foley the Under Secretaries. George and Tony made an excellent team, Tony from the intellectual, Fabian side of the party and George from the populist, trades union side; each respecting the other for their complementary qualities.

Harold Wilson had ruled out devaluation of the pound, which was Tony's preference. So, instead, he wanted a package of economic measures which, put out together instead of being dribbled out separately, would carry credibility in the currency markets and help the economy to expand without another currency crisis. We went to Chequers to discuss it.

I was surprised to discover that Chequers, though a large house, was warm and friendly, with rooms on a human scale and a central hall in which everyone gathered to chat. The package was agreed, but a mobile BBC transmitter on the hill above reminded us that Winston Churchill was dying and, when the time came, the Prime Minister would be expected to address the nation. The announcement of the package was postponed for the broadcast. The grand old man clung to life longer than anyone expected, the moment passed and the announcement was never made. The policies came out in dribs and drabs and did nothing for confidence.

Confidence was certainly needed. Only the few people who needed to know were told when there was a run on the pound; but those of us who had to talk to those few knew at once. Their time horizon was a matter of hours and any talk of policy beyond that was met with glazed eyes. The big hope was that an incomes policy would restore confidence in the currency markets, and George spent most of his time and emotional energy in negotiating with George Woodcock, General Secretary of the TUC, and Maurice Laing, President of the British Employers' Federation, and his General Secretary, George Pollock.

On paper the argument was persuasive. If wages costs could be stabilised, export prices could remain competitive, companies would have the extra funds to match the industrial investment being made by our competitors, and the better trade balance would give government the reserves needed to back the currency without recurrent and debilitating crises. That, in turn, would allow a higher growth rate, which would help profits and give workers more to spend.

George Woodcock, under his shaggy eyebrows, could see all this. But, though he wanted to help a Labour government to get a working majority, he did not know whether he could carry his General Council with him. He pressed very hard for price restraint as a quid pro quo; but how was that to be enforced without a statutory policy?

I was content to agree with the theoretical case, but I was deeply sceptical of the ability of either management or unions to deliver the needed restraint. It seemed to me that the best way to get the reserves needed to back growth was to reduce our defence commitments and to use fiscal incentives to reverse the British bias in favour of overseas investment. Then economic growth would keep unit wage costs down and give industry the cashflow needed for the investment that would sustain it.

That alternative was politically difficult for a government with a wafer-thin majority, but there was another possibility. The little Neddy for the machine tool industry had suggested that investment grants for new plant would be far more effective in persuading companies to buy new equipment than tax allowances against eventual profits, if and when they were earned. The grant had exactly the same effect as a subsidised rate of interest; it was certain and bankable, and it offset the commercial risk. By contrast the allowance depended on the early success of the investment, did not offset the risk and did not impress the bank manager.

This seemed to me to be politically practicable and I took it up. When we met with the Treasury advisers, Nicky Kaldor said that it was against Leontief's theory, which demonstrated that there was no correlation between the rate of industrial investment and the rate of export growth. Leontief's theory, of which I had never heard, was against all my experience, so I made immediate enquiries. I was told that it had been based on research in California no later than the 1930s (when California was not even an industrial state). So I formed Catherwood's theory, which was that economic research took ten years to produce, another ten to get into the textbooks and another ten to become established economic wisdom, by which time it was out of date. In addition, business had to reckon pay-back from sales over five to fifteen years ahead, so the total time gap between economic theory and business practice was nearer forty years.

We also had trouble with the Inland Revenue, which did not want to give up the investment allowances, and with the Board of Trade, which did not want to administer the grants. We could not consult industry on a specific tax change. When we had won the Whitehall argument and the grant was announced, we found the CBI was against it because they regarded the grant as a government hand-out, to which they were opposed, while the same benefit as and allowance against tax was a tax-reduction and politically acceptable. But whatever the CBI politics, there was a remarkable increase in the figures for investment in plant and machinery, which rose by 25 per cent between 1966 and 1970 (see following chapter and Appendix). When the Conservatives, at the request of the CBI, abolished the grants in 1970, investment dropped promptly, sharply, and against the other factors which should have supported it: the arrival of a Conservative government, the improvement in the trade balance, and the prospect of a successful outcome of the negotiations for our entry into the European Community. It did not recover the 1970 level until 1978 (see Appendix).

George Brown finally persuaded George Woodcock and Maurice Laing to sign a 'Declaration of Intent' for a voluntary prices and incomes policy at a ceremony in Lancaster House in front of TV cameras. I talked to Maurice Laing on the way in and he doubted its effectiveness, but felt that, in all the circumstances, it was right to sign. My own feelings were much the same.

The National Board for Prices and Incomes was set up to run the policy, and public attention was diverted from the DEA's effort to achieve an economic breakthrough to the more newsworthy question of whether the price of baked beans was to be referred to the Board.

After this we lost Tony Crosland to the Ministry of Education and although Austen Albu, who replaced him, had sterling qualities, he was not the political counterweight to George Brown which Tony had been. The DEA retained its powerful engine, but had lost its navigational system.

Now that the prices and incomes policy was up and running,

I persuaded George to get out into the country. I went with him to Teesside and Tyneside in a tiny Heron of the Queen's flight. At Middleton St George we changed to a large red helicopter, also of the Queen's flight. We were saluted aboard and strapped ourselves in. The rotors started up – and then died. They started again and died again. After several more attempts a red-faced officer opened the door and announced that they couldn't get the engine started. We transferred to a large black Austin limousine and drove off briskly, leading the convoy, for a mining village.

After about five minutes, George tapped on the glass partition and asked the driver whether she was quite sure that she knew where she was going. She said that she hadn't had time to check the map. So George told her to draw up at the next bus-stop, wound down the window and the lady waiting there was suddenly confronted by his famous face, asking the way. She obliged without a flicker of expression and the convoy moved on.

The village's mine had closed and George was there to publicise the new industry, which had been started up to provide jobs for redundant miners. In this strong Labour area he was received like a hero, men and women crowding round him wherever he went. He might be seen as a maverick in the chilly upper echelons of Whitehall, but there was no doubt about his popular support or the strength of feeling for the man who was fighting their cause.

The red helicopter caught us up and we flew straight over ICI's Middlesbrough chemical plants. George looked down worriedly at the mass of pipes and tubes and wafts of steam. 'If the engine failed on the ground, it could fail here too.' We decided that it would be all the same wherever we hit the ground.

We were met by the local top management of ICI and bussed up to their big headquarters house. George chose this moment to announce, 'You ought to know that this department is run by Christians. I'm high church and Fred is low church, but before I've finished with him, I'm going to raise him up!'

At Newcastle he spoke to a large gathering of businessmen. Afterwards he asked one of them what he could do for him. 'Nothing,' said the businessman.

'Surely there must be something?' said George; but the

businessman persisted. It was the same clash of cultures which made the seventeenth-century Huguenots reply to a similar question from Colbert, the great French Minister of Commerce, *'Laissez faire et laissez passer.'*

We also went to South Wales, starting with a large factory near Monmouth. George was in his most cheerful mood. It was, unfortunately, one of those companies where the management did not know the workers, so George took over, chatting up everyone on the shop floor, while the manager, great beads of sweat breaking out on his forehead, did not know where to put himself. I was not surprised that, a few months later, the company had a prolonged strike.

The next visit, to a smaller company, was a complete contrast. The Chairman knew all his workers. As we went round, he introduced everyone we met, told us how each apprentice was getting on, how long each worker had been there and a bit about them. From boss to apprentice, it was a team.

We drove through central Cardiff with a police escort and on the wrong side of the road to the Temple of Peace, where George addressed a full house of businessmen; but what pleased him most about the whole visit was was a shabby old man at the entrance to the station, who said, 'Keep it up!'

Harold Wilson, in contrast to the grouse moor image of his predecessors, had campaigned for the white heat of the technological revolution. The result was a new ministry, presided over by Frank Cousins, the union leader, on secondment from the TGWU; the donnish novelist Charles Snow, and Pat Blackett, the President of the Royal Society. Both the latter were peers without political experience, and Frank Cousins was uneasy in his new role in the House of Commons. So some of their more politically sensitive decisions were referred to the DEA.

The first was whether to support the remaining British computer company in order to protect us from total American dominance. I remembered the response of BA's American shareholders when I asked for their technology on aluminium engines. They said that the American market was ten times our market, so their American customers were ten times more important than our customers, and they were not going to pass on their technological advantage to our customers until their own customers had established a decisive lead in the market. So my advice was in favour of keeping an independent British company.

The second and much bigger proposal was that government should set up an Industrial Reorganisation Corporation to achieve economies of scale in research and development. Britain, in the mid-sixties, was facing Continental competitors with a tariff-free market four times our size, giving a far bigger payoff for each generation of new products, where research and development could be even more expensive than new capital equipment.

I asked Kenneth Keith, merchant banker and member of the NEDC, whether merchant bankers achieved all the mergers for which there was a strong economic case. He said that boards could take a long time to see the need and banks were there to help those who actively wanted to merge, not to chase around trying to persuade those who did not see the need, however strong it seemed to be. Given the much bigger payoff for European companies and the civil market spin-off from the research for the US defence and space programmes, I advised in favour of setting up the Industrial Reorganisation Corporation.

George was attacked in the Commons for 'back-door nationalisation'. He said that when the government wanted to nationalise, it would do it by the front door. The IRC had nothing to do with nationalisation and would be run by an independent board of industrialists with Frank Kearton, Chairman of Courtaulds, as Chairman.

The DEA also accepted responsibility, this time against my advice, for the 'Fairfield experiment'. I was not against the experiment, an attempt to keep a yard open by new methods of working which would be an example to Clydeside shipbuilding. I was simply against George hazarding his political credibility on an experiment which might easily fail. There was certainly a need for improvement. Les Cannon, President of the Electricians' Union (and NEDC member), and Frank Chapple, his deputy, had complained to me of the archaic methods of the shipbuilders, which prevented their members earning the kind of wages they could get elsewhere. I had taken this up and was told that we knew how to build ships and our foreign competitors didn't! What saved the experiment was the energy and enthusiasm of

Iain Stewart, a Scottish industrialist, and, until we were undercut by Far Eastern builders selling to flags-of-convenience owners, the company kept going.

There was one assignment which I could not escape. Short and Harland, the Belfast aircraft company, were coming to the end of the orders for their huge underpowered transport plane, the 'Belfast', which the air marshals did not want to see or hear of again. As a Socialist, George was not specially keen on bailing out the Ulster Unionists, but, as a trades unionist, he felt he had to help a plant employing several thousand workers. So he told me that, as an Ulsterman, I'd better go and look after my own, adding that if he had known I was an Ulsterman he was not sure that he'd have taken me on.

Short's had diversified into machine tools, small missiles and vacuum cleaners, and had also developed the prototype of a squat little plane which they called 'Skyvan'. I decided that they could never maintain their level of employment on vacuum cleaners, and as Phil Foreman of Short's watched one of the Belfasts soaring into the sky, he said to me, 'The trouble with machine tools is that they don't take off.' The company's heart was in aircraft.

So I asked Arthur D Little, the Boston-based consultants, to look at the Skyvan. Their report was surprisingly favourable. It had, they said, a unique niche in the international aircraft market, in between the scaled up Pipers and Cessnas and the scaled down airliners. I said that it was so squat. They said, 'It's the same shape as a bee, and just as suitable for what it does.'

The government put up the development money for the Skyvan which was, for years, a great success on the feeder routes from small up-country airfields in America and also in the outback and bush throughout the world. Every time I see a Skyvan or its successor, the Shorts 300, I think that, if only for that, my time at the DEA was worth while.

The crowning glory of the DEA, however, was to be the National Plan. Donald Macdougall and his deputy, John Jukes, were working on the macro-economic figures, and the little Neddies, where they had already been set up, or the trade associations where they had not, were asked about the prospects for their industries.

91

It is a long time since anyone has had the audacity to ask a government to make public, industry-based, firm-figure forecasts on the effects of its policies and to propose alternatives where the figures were shown to be inadequate. This is not because the need today is any less – our rate of unemployment is much worse – but because the most ambitious attempt ended so quickly in failure.

George Brown's was not the first attempt. The NEDC was set up by the Macmillan government in 1962 and Robert Shone, the first Director General of the NEDC, had been asked to produce a document to show how we might achieve a growth rate which would match that of the European Community and give our industry the resources to remain competitive. 'Conditions Favourable to Faster Growth' aimed at a rate of 4 per cent. The key was a shift of resources to manufacturing industry. It left open the exact policies needed to achieve this; but Robert Shone and many other economists thought it could be done by a devaluation of the pound.

Instead, in 1963–4, the Conservative government had simply relaxed credit and allowed the economy to expand in what became known, after the Chancellor of the time, as the 'Maudling boom'. With extensive overseas holdings of sterling and the drain of defence commitments, Britain's reserves were not strong enough to sustain the Maudling boom, and the Conservatives left behind inadequate currency reserves to support the exchange rate of the pound and an economy heavily dependent on the confidence of foreign holders of sterling.

The Labour government argued that the problem with the NEDC's 'Conditions Favourable to Faster Growth' was that it did not carry the commitment of the Conservative government. What was needed was a plan produced by government and to which its reputation was committed.

It would have been a mammoth task at the best of times; but in addition to the fragility of sterling, the government only had a Commons majority of five, shortly to be reduced to three. So the National Plan was produced against an urgent electoral timetable. Government departments put in figures for the nationalised industries and, naturally, these assumed funding for public investment to achieve output to meet growth of demand at the target figure, now 3.8 per cent. For the much more critical figure of the growth of productivity and investment in the private sector needed to sustain the growth rate, the plan was supposed to take the view of industry. But the timetable just did not leave enough time for the consultation and dialogue necessary to make the figures secure. So it was not industry's plan; it was government's.

The biggest omission of all was the action which government would have to take to translate aims into achievement. Those who wanted devaluation assumed that there would be an export-led boom which would sustain the balance of payments and get Britain on to the virtuous spiral which had so helped the Germans. I believed, with most of industry, that government should make some hard choices about the allocation of resources, cutting back on all commitments which drained our currency reserves, and, in my own view, through policies like the investment grants, it should use its fiscal powers to shift resources into export industry. So everything depended on whether one believed that the government would, if re-elected, devalue or make some other hard choices.

When the CBI team on the NEDC discussed the document the evening before the Council meeting, they found themselves, initially, four to two against. George Brown, suspecting problems, wanted to talk to them before they came to a conclusion; but when he started to phone round, none of them were in their offices and their staff would not say where they were. That made him quite sure that they were plotting and he became desperate to find them. His civil servants told him that there was nothing more to be done, but his political assistant Pat Kelly went on faithfully ringing round and finally found a colleague of John Davies at Shell who had not been warned that the meeting was secret and who told her that they were at the Courtauld Staff College.

George rang at once to say that he was on his way and they were not to leave until he got there. By two in the morning he had swung the vote to four to two in favour. He stepped thankfully into his Austin limousine, which then broke down on the A4 at Heathrow. Wanting his night's sleep before the crucial meeting, he thumbed a lift for the rest of the way in a passing Mini and later in the morning the NEDC gave its blessing to the one and only National Plan.

The election came early in 1966 and, with ministers away, there was a steady but unrecorded debate in the highest reaches of Whitehall on devaluation. The case for devaluation was that it would produce the needed shift of resources to manufacturing industry and give us export-led and self-sustaining growth. The argument against was that devaluation put up import costs immediately and, since export volume took time to grow, our short-term balance of payments would worsen; the higher cost imports would raise the cost of living and inflate wage claims, and the price advantage would only be temporary. We would in any case have to restrain domestic growth to make room for exports, and by fiscal and other policies we could still achieve a transfer of resources to export industry without risk of devaluation.

At that time the British economy was not so far out of line with the Continent and the shift of resources without devaluation was not outside the bounds of possibility. We had very heavy currency payments for our forces overseas in the Middle East and in Germany while, on their defence account, the Germans were receiving hard currency from both British and American forces stationed in Germany. At that time I estimated that the difference between the substantial German and totally inadequate British currency reserves was exactly accounted for by the accumulated difference between German currency receipts and British currency payments on defence account. Yet when there was a scrap on the Tibet/India border, Harold Wilson had said that Britain's frontier was on the Himalayas. But though he was committed to a British presence east of Suez, he did not want to devalue. I thought that he should make up his mind.

George Brown had his rough side. He did not have a drink problem so much as a low tolerance for alcohol and some of the dinners he had for industrialists one would sooner forget. Nor did he suffer fools gladly. But he respected those who stood up to him. He had a very clear and usually correct view of what mattered and what did not. He had the quality of which every mandarin dreams: the ability to carry his colleagues in cabinet and, outside cabinet, he also had very sensitive political antennae.

And he could be most charming and very persuasive to those he wanted to influence.

One of my jobs before the election had been to look for a successor to Robert Shone as Director General of the NEDC. I put up lists of names, but got no response from George Brown. There was a press report that I was to have the job, which I at once denied, explaining that in four months I was due back in industry.

Then George saw me and told me that he had put my name to all three parties at the NEDC. He said, 'The CBI are of course happy with your name, because you are one of them. The TUC seem, for some reason, to trust you and I've managed to persuade my colleagues in the government that you are all right. You are the only name on which I can get the agreement of all three parties. I think you would do it well and I would like you to do it. And if you won't do it, never come to me for anything ever again!'

I made a few conditions, the most important being that I should continue to be seconded from industry. I did not want to be a civil servant and felt that the job needed the independence which secondment gave. Edwin Plowden had been very firm that a two-year secondment was the limit, but after a session with George, he rather ruefully agreed to another three years.

I thought that I was going from the centre to the periphery, leaving an effective and influential job at the heart of government's economic policy, for an institution which the DEA had sidelined. I could not have been more wrong.

Chapter Seven

NEDDY:
PARTNERSHIP FOR FULL EMPLOYMENT

Ministers came back from the election with a strong overall majority and in a euphoric mood. They felt that they now had a full five years to get everything right and instead of the hectic 'hundred days' of 1964 when they wanted to do everything at once, there was a long pause, while they caught their breaths.

It didn't last. Very soon there was a strike of British seamen and overseas trade came to a standstill. The loss of trade put pressure on the pound and there was a severe currency crisis. Had Roy Jenkins or Tony Crosland been at the Treasury, they might have overcome the Prime Minister's reluctance to devalue the pound, but Jim Callaghan supported Harold Wilson. In the absence of alternatives to devaluation, government was forced once again to restrict imports by cutting back domestic demand. It was, after all the talk of new policies, the same old vicious spiral.

These measures were imposed in July against furious opposition from George Brown, who resigned. But Bill Rodgers persuaded him to stay and Harold Wilson bought him off with a promise of the Foreign Office. Diplomacy did not suit George, who liked ruffling feathers for the sheer fun of it. But it did give him the chance to launch Britain's second application to join the EEC.

When the moment came for the change, John Burgh, George's Principal Private Secretary, went over to tell Murray Maclehose, PPS to the Foreign Secretary, Michael Stewart (who was going to the DEA), that George was to be his new master. John came back to say that in the true diplomatic tradition, Murray's only sign of emotion was the slight flicker of one eyebrow. But very shortly afterwards he accepted a posting as our man in war-torn Saigon.

George Brown's departure marked the end of the DEA as a power in government. Michael Stewart was no slouch. He was an orderly schoolmaster, who knew his brief and could hold his own in debate. I remembered seeing him from the Commons gallery in the late 1940s running rings round Oliver Lyttleton, who was reduced to speechless rage. But he had none of George's vision, nor the determination and drive which made strong men step smartly out of the way.

Michael Stewart left it to me to tell the post-Council press conference that the National Plan was dead. It must have been obvious, but no one had so far said it. Having taken that press conference, I took all the high-profile monthly post-Council press conferences for the next five years, and that alone was of enormous assistance in filling the vacuum left by the DEA and in making Neddy the focus in those still-hopeful days for the great debate on Britain's economic development.

I was also helped by an instinctive decision to play straight with the press. Government, unions and management put their own spin on their statements, which the press had to allow for and discount. So, when experience gradually convinced them that we really were an unbiased source for discussions by key figures on critical national economic issues, it was a help both to them and to us.

There was nothing especially brave about this frankness. If I were to say anything in public, then the truth was the only defensible position. If one of the three partners complained, then the other two were there to defend me. In fact I had only two complaints in five years. One arose because the CBI had been taken in by Harold Wilson's manner and had not listened to his words. I suggested that they call Downing Street and check. The other arose because *The Times* had sent their economic correspondent, who did not understand that the TUC's lack of public opposition to a Labour government policy in the run up to an election did not mean that they actually supported it. When the

TUC complained about *The Times* piece, I referred them to the reports of the labour correspondents in all the other papers. The distinguished labour correspondent of *The Times* did a corrective piece a few days later.

I was also helped by Harold Wilson's decision to fill the economic policy vacuum by calling a National Productivity Conference for mid-September, which he asked us to organise. The CBI were sceptical, but reluctant to offend a newly elected government. So, after a lot of phone calls and heavy use of the Prime Minister's authority, the key people agreed to attend. As with the National Plan, it seemed to me best to use the occasion to get government's public commitment to a few important policies which would be helpful to British industry, so we prepared papers along these lines. Hywel Evans, the Secretary of the Council, was a tower of strength. Because we had given it a practical and limited theme, the Lancaster House conference was considered, much to everyone's surprise, to have been a success.

But in the longer run the reason why Neddy now took centre-stage was that, unlike the one-man band of the DEA, it was solidly based on the work of the industry committees. While I was still in the DEA, I had, with Tom Fraser, Neddy's experienced Industrial Director, gradually extended the little Neddies until they covered most of British industry and commerce. By including the trades unions, representing millions of voters, each little Neddy had far more political clout than its trade association alone. By joining senior government officials in the dialogue, industry was no longer an outside supplicant in Whitehall, but an equal partner with government in the discussion and conclusions.

And whereas macro-economics was an esoteric subject under-stood by very few, the wool industry mattered to Yorkshire, the hosiery industry to Leicester, chemicals to Teesside, metal-bashing to Birmingham and cars to Coventry. Even an industry as widespread as hotels and catering made national news when the little Neddy recommended self-service in place of the maid with the early morning tea. So the little Neddy reports had wide press coverage and we never had any need to promote Neddy as an institution. The monthly post-Council press conference and the Neddy by-line on the reports from the twenty or more little Neddies were enough to show what we did and why we were there.

Industry was as much as ever against government interference in the millions of daily transactions between buyer and seller. The open market had to be the basic mechanism to match what a customer wanted and needed with what the producer could provide. But government was a powerful giant in the economy and could, by acting in ignorance, enormously increase the uncertainty and risks of conducting business. That was a compelling reason why industry wanted to engage government in the detailed examination of the factors which made for the success and failure of each industry, and to persuade them to base national economic policy on a closer and more up-to-date knowlege of British industry as a whole.

It also helped government to have reports which were agreed by the unions and by their own departments, and which were visibly free from bias. And it was, of course, an enormous boost to the trades unions to be part of this constructive process which not only helped their members, but gave them a much more positive public image. Above all Neddy and the little Neddies were trusted where government alone was not.

There were those outside industry who still had the vision of a perfect market mechanism which could settle everything without cumbersome committees. I had a half-hour radio debate with Enoch Powell (all alone by ourselves in a studio). He was without any practical experience; his views were based entirely on theory. He thought that government should not bring businessmen together in little Neddies, since it would encourage them to conspire against the public interest. I said that if they wanted to do that, they would hardly do so in the the presence of the unions and government officials; it would be much easier and more agreeable over lunch at the Savoy.

A market is only as good as the information on which its decisions are based. Our job was not to override the market, but, by making sure that it was informed, to reduce the risks, especially the risks of investment. I remember a Council exchange at which Les Cannon of the ETU argued that business should invest during a recession for the next upturn, to which Kenneth Keith, our City member, replied that capital would never take that kind of risk during a recession; it wanted to see the upturn first. Les Cannon said, 'I always thought that capitalism was a lousy system; now I know why.'

So we worked hard to increase the transparency of the market and to minimise risk, especially the risks of industrial investment on which so much else depended. As industry became more capital-intensive and equipment more complex, the lead times grew longer; so the risks of misjudging the timing of upturns and the underlying level of demand became greater. This was especially true of the big new chemical and petro-chemical plants, and if giant companies like ICI and Shell had a forecasting problem, their suppliers and sub-suppliers were even more at sea. So when the upturn came and all the big projects were commissioned at once, there was not sufficient national capacity to meet it. The rush of imports to fill the gap was enough to tilt the trade balance and bring the whole upturn to a halt.

By agreement between the chemical little Neddy and its suppliers in the engineering and construction little Neddies, we set up a process plant working party so that they could not only co-operate on demand forecasts, but look at the bottlenecks in supply. We also set up a working party on the organisation of the new and complex large sites in all industries, which had more than their fair share of labour troubles.

No one doubted that market pressures should, in the end, concentrate resources in the effective companies and drive the ineffective out of business. But it was not so simple. In an imperfect capital market, it could result in the survival of the fattest who had the size to resist takeover bids, rather than the fittest who might not. Without much closer shareholder control than the savings institutions would give, there was no self-correcting mechanism to protect the workforce from poor management. But, most important of all, our exclusion from the EEC weakened even the most effective British companies and made their market share vulnerable to imports, threatening our whole economy.

So the broad remit to the little Neddies was to co-operate on market forecasts and on the major structural issues, problems which would not be solved constructively by the simple process of market pressures.

As I arrived at Neddy, the wool textile little Neddy had just concluded that if the industry were to survive, it would need major restructuring, the scrapping of old plant and substantial investment in new capacity. But the industry itself had doubts and the little Neddy thought that it would help if I were to tour the Yorkshire mills to support their case. So I spent several days going in and out of topping, spinning and weaving mills, and talking to everyone in sight. My sister Mary had married Alan Clough, whose family had been in the industry for generations and who was shortly to become the Chairman of the Wool Textile Delegation, and that was a great help. Tom Fraser, the wise and widely respected Industrial Director of Neddy, had been Director of the Delegation and he carried great weight. So the industry agreed, and another wool man, Bill Bulmer, put together firm proposals with which government agreed. The wool industry lived to fight another day.

The leaders of British industry responded enthusiastically to the idea that we could do something to get out of the economic trap in which we all found ourselves. With this enthusiasm I had no difficulty in finding some excellent industrialists as chairmen of the little Neddies. They believed that there was good management in most industry; it was a matter of getting best practice more widely adopted. The backing of the trades unions was a great help in getting broader support in companies and wider interest outside, and in arousing a national sense of purpose.

There were only two industries where the problems seemed to be incorrigible.

The newspaper and printing industry was dominated by the trades unions, whose financial stake in the industry seemed a great deal larger than that of the owners. The union leaders, Briginshaw and Bonfield, told me that the reason was that none of the newspaper owners trusted each other. If one of them had a strike, the first thought of the others was how they could pick up and keep the stricken paper's circulation. But, they said, 'If they all stood together, we'd never get away with it.' As it was, jobs in the print shop were so valuable that they were handed down in the family from father to son.

But it was not just distrust between the owners. The economics of newspapers made them especially vulnerable to wildcat strikes.

Garrett Drogheda, Managing Director of the *Financial Times*, told me that 90 per cent of the cost of a newspaper had been spent before the presses began to roll and, since there was no sale for yesterday's paper, none of that cost could be recovered if a wildcat strike in the press room made the papers miss the overnight trains. But the damage, though great, was mainly domestic. The newspaper industry was not vulnerable to imports and we did not depend on it for exports; nor did it have a vast substructure of dependent suppliers.

Our other problem, the motor industry, was much more critical to the economy. It was one of the last to be persuaded to have a little Neddy. Pat Hennessy, the red-headed Irishman who ran Ford's, said that there was no need; he could see the Chancellor any time he liked. I asked him when a Chancellor had last done anything he had advised and there was a long silence. At last they all agreed and I asked Hugh Tett, the Chairman of Esso, to chair it, which he did with great competence and authority.

But when Hugh Tett's term had finished, I couldn't find anyone else to take it on and had to chair it for a time myself. At my first meeting, with thin attendance from the unions, the new American Chairman of Vauxhall, fresh from Australia, said that the key problem was labour relations. All the management side agreed. I suggested that we should discuss it next time with a fuller union attendance. Next time the unions, including Reg Birch, the TUC's only Maoist, also agreed. At the third meeting both sides were there in full force. I said that we now had to decide on our programme, only to find that the management were not so sure after all. I pointed out that it was their proposal, that these things were not done in a corner and if they backed out as soon as the unions agreed, it would look extremely bad in public. But they would not agree.

Instead they asked me to dinner at the Dorchester and told me that when the unions accepted so promptly, their people had become suspicious. I said that they were in no position to have such bad labour relations. They had 90 per cent of the home market, but this would not last. Germany, France and Italy, the big Continental producers, had only 70 per cent of their home market and they had to make up with exports. As soon as we were members of the EEC, if not before, they would have to be competitive to defend their home markets and to make up what they lost by selling in the very competitive Continental markets. That needed reliable delivery dates and no wildcat strikes. They thought they knew better.

Bill Lyons, founder of Jaguar, was sitting next to me and told me that he liked long order books (and long delivery dates) because that gave steady production without ups and downs. That policy explained precisely why Jaguar was fast losing its place in the market to Mercedes. The motor industry was still a business of tycoons, in the tradition of Nuffield and Lord of Austin's, still guarded by tariffs and restrictive dealer networks at home and still clinging to the protected markets of the colonies where standards were not too high. It took two decades of fierce external competition and tough professional management to turn the industry round, but not before they had lost a huge share of their market to foreign producers.

The motor components makers saved themselves by switching their sales towards the Continental car producers, and when membership of the EEC finally removed the tariffs against them, they were both competitive and successful.

The motor industry did not have quite the vulnerability of the print industry to wildcat strikes, because cars were not as perishable as newspapers and the amount already spent before the assembly line was lower, maybe about 70 per cent. But huge assembly plants, operated by relatively few people, enabled those few to hold the company to ransom. I remember Frank Chapple's comment that, in the half-way stage between heavy dependence on manual labour and complete automation, small groups could pull the plug and stop the whole works.

These were the newly discovered dis-economies of scale. When we talked to directors and managers privately, they all admitted this vulnerability, of which they never spoke in public. But in private their accountants quietly pointed out that it cost twenty, thirty or forty times as much to suffer a strike as it did to concede the wildcat demands. I remember the Chairman of one of our biggest companies telling me that the cost of winning back lost market share in consumer goods was so many times greater than the cost of meeting a wage demand that it was not even worth calculating.

The growth of shop-floor power was one reason for the CBI's scepticism about the effectiveness of devaluation in shifting resources from consumption to export industry. So, when it came in November 1967, they did not have the same optimism as the Treasury. They were right. It took a long time for the volume of exports to catch up with the higher prices of imports, but, most important, the higher cost of imports put pressure on the policy of wage restraint and the TUC found it harder and harder to hold the line.

Not long afterwards George Brown resigned as Foreign Secretary. Britain's second application to join the EEC had failed and he had lost political credibility. Michael Stewart went back to the Foreign Office, the Prime Minister took the chair at Neddy and the Chancellor returned to the Council as his deputy. The DEA was split between Barbara Castle at a strengthened Department of Employment and Peter Shore. NEDC agendas were decided in consultation with the Permanent Secretary of the Treasury. Neddy was back at the centre again.

The Treasury's models still knew nothing of the deadly virus of shop-floor power. They worked to the theory of the 'Philips curve', which showed that when demand and employment go down, so does the rate of wage awards, and when they go up, earnings go up too. So the Treasury justification for every credit squeeze was that the current level of demand would put up wage rates and make our exports uncompetitive. But the squeeze also reduced company cashflow and cut the funds companies needed for the new products needed to keep their market share.

If the Treasury was still in ignorance, the union leaders were beginning to discover, especially after devaluation, how the power of the wildcats undermined their own authority. They could no longer fulfil the central purpose of the trades union: to use the bargaining power of the strong to help the weak. Jack Jones, leader of the TGWU, and Hugh Scanlon of the Engineers, both members of the Council, went to Dagenham to deal with a wildcat strike in Ford's. They exerted all their joint authority and got a settlement. For this Hugh Scanlon was rebuked, in his absence, by his executive. They felt that he should have been on the side of the strikers. Jack Jones, determined that the same thing should not happen to him, saw his executive, explained that the authority of the Union was at stake, and his action was endorsed.

Wildcat strikes were not only a symptom of shop-floor power; they were also a way, after three years of incomes restraint and the increase of import prices, for the skilled workers to recover their wage differential over the unskilled – maybe one reason why the engineering union, whose members' differentials had been squeezed, were not so happy about the Dagenham settlement as the TGWU. An incomes policy could not start without some protection to lower-paid workers. This was tolerable to begin with, but as time went on, the narrowing of differentials put increasing strain on the unions who were trying to keep within the agreed guidelines.

We had an all-day meeting of the Council at Chequers on a weekend in December 1968. The TUC pointed out that George Brown's 'Declaration of Intent' in late 1964 had been followed by the voluntary restraints of 1965, the July measures of 1966 and the further restraint after the devaluation of 1967. On all of these occasions they had undertaken to continue wage restraint against the promise of higher economic growth to come. After four years that promise was beginning to wear thin and unless there was a change fairly soon, they could no longer hold the line.

The government was unbending. Roy Jenkins, who had now succeeded Jim Callaghan as Chancellor, argued that we could not afford expansion until our balance of payments was in surplus. Against that Anthony Wedgwood Benn had argued on Council that the Board of Trade figures for exports, which relied on exporters' voluntary co-operation in providing the data, were lower than the industry figures. So, he maintained, the balance of trade was much better than appeared – and later upward revisions of the trade figures were to support his view.

Barbara Castle, now Secretary of State for Employment, had published 'In Place of Strife', her response to shop-floor power being a proposal to tighten trades union law, which, since the problem was a shop-floor rebellion against the power of the unions, seemed to the unions (and on my own analysis) to be especially perverse. She had told the TUC that as a socialist she believed in planning, and planning had to cover everything, including their wages. Jim Callaghan took the unions' side, but, as Home Secretary, he was no longer on the Council. We were at stalemate and I went back to London to explain this to the press in terms which were as constructive as possible. Len Murray's last words were, 'Go easy, Fred.' By this I took him to mean that I should not put the TUC in open opposition to a Labour government, but also that I should not say that they supported the present policy (see pp 97–8 above).

In the following year not only was the incomes policy broken, as the shop floor took the law into their own hands, but the Philips curve was broken too, as employment fell but earnings rose. When I produced these figures at Council, there was a murmur of disbelief from some on the TUC who knew that they had not authorised the increases and could not understand how it had happened. Although the government dropped 'In Place of Strife', Labour lost the election and, with the arrival of the Conservatives, wage restraint disappeared completely.

The disastrous swing of the Labour Party to the left from 1973 to 1983 must owe something to the feeling of being let down after all the long years of restraint during the sixties. And, as the Conservatives also moved towards extremes in the same period, much rhetorical scorn was poured on 'tripartism', the united efforts of government, management and unions. But the trade, employment, inflation and growth figures as well as the investment figures (see Appendix) show that, on the contrary, it was a success story.

Britain's balance of payments moved into surplus in the first quarter of 1969, just after the Council's Chequers weekend. The rate of growth was much higher than it would be in the next two decades; the rate of unemployment only a fraction of what it is now. All that was achieved while traditional Commonwealth markets closed against us, while we were still excluded from the EEC and without the huge one-off bonus of North Sea oil which insulated us from currency crises for a decade and paid for the high consumption of the eighties.

The one great advantage of the sixties over the seventies was the currency stability, still maintained by the post-war Bretton Woods agreement and anchored in the American dollar. Given currency stability it was possible to construct some kind of economic model to show where government policies might take

us, and to look at options which might take the country out
of its economic constraints. This had enabled my predecessor
and Neddy's first Director General, Robert Shone, to produce a
credible document in 1963. The CBI had opened their industries
for inspection through the little Neddies and saw no reason why
the government should not now do the same.

So, after the devaluation of 1967, the CBI felt that we should
have another attempt to put figures to the likely outworking of
current government policies. John Davies, Director General of the
CBI, asked for a 'first rough cut' of the figures, which industry
felt would be helpful to them in making their own corporate
forecasts.

The Treasury were not too keen on this exercise. Treasury
forecasts are highly sensitive, since they can show disaster ahead
and that might put pressure on sterling or lead to panic among
those who could be affected by counter-measures. But Labour
was politically committed to 'planning' and, since this was the
nearest they were likely to get to it, the Treasury agreed and
gave us one of the best people they had, Tom Kennedy. He
was a superb Economic Director, wise, numerate and courteous
in argument but very firm. The DEA, now under Peter Shore,
did the work, but the document was for consultation with the
Council and the little Neddies had a substantial input. 'The Task
Ahead' was published in February 1969 and it is interesting after
all these years to look through it again.

The preface, which stated the object of the exercise, read:

'For the past ten years Britain's economic performance has
been poorer than that of other industrial countries. More important, it has lagged behind what people believed to be both possible
and desirable.'

So the paper would look at 'The possible courses of the
economy up to 1972' and 'The consequences of better or worse
performance'.

The document itself made it clear that this was only a basis
for consultation with both sides of industry, to help them and
the government make key decisions. Although new factors could
throw the whole calculation, it argued that it was better to have
a basic framework into which those new factors could be fitted,
rather than none at all.

All the major companies were represented on the Council. The little Neddies had to do their own forecasts and the joint effort was very helpful. But industry also wanted to argue with the government about the figures which only government could influence. So the government gave the figures on public expenditure and overseas defence expenditure, which industry saw as constraints on the economy. Government, in turn, was also interested in the constraints imposed by British investment abroad. The CBI had argued that overseas investment was helpful to exports, but Professor Reddaway of Cambridge, whom they asked to look at the case, decided, to their consternation, that the outflow of capital really was a constraint on domestic growth.

Within its higher and lower figures, 'The Task Ahead' had more modest central figures for growth than the National Plan; though it argued that with lower unemployment, its 3 per cent figure of growth of productive potential could be higher. The aim was to get domestic production (GDP) up to 3.2 per cent and to keep consumption at 2.4 per cent in order to build up our exports and give us the reserves we needed to avoid the recurrent currency crises. Then Labour lost the election and no more was heard of 'The Task Ahead'.

When, despite George Brown's best efforts, we had been turned down for the EEC a second time, I had begun to look at the possibility of a North Atlantic Free Trade Area (NAFTA), to give us a tariff-free export market comparable to that of our main competitors. At best this would include, on this side of the Atlantic, our own EFTA partners, including the Scandinavian countries and the two Alpine republics, Switzerland and Austria; on the other side not only Canada and America but beyond that, if possible, Australia and New Zealand.

The intellectual driving force behind this idea was Professor Harry Johnson, who taught at both the LSE and the University of Chicago. Its forum was the British North-American Committee chaired by the head of the Baring family, Lord Howick, and bringing together businessmen and politicians for meetings about once or twice a year alternating on each side of the Atlantic.

I talked to the Danes first. They were open to the idea, but they were equally dependent on British and German trade and did not want to lose either. But if we went into a NAFTA, they would probably have come with us. The Australian High Commissioner was extremely interested, but when his Foreign Minister came over, the High Commissioner could not persuade him to discuss it. I saw the Canadian Foreign Minister when we were in Canada for Expo 67 and he was very friendly but non-committal.

American opinion was, of course, critical. They were quite clear. They wanted us in the EEC for exactly the same reasons as de Gaulle wanted to keep us out. We were their traditional friends and they wanted us in this new big block, so powerful economically and politically, putting an Anglo-Saxon point of view. So, they said, did all our friends on the outside, including the Canadians and Australians. The American policy from the beginning was a united Europe. It was safer for the West; it forced America's European friends to settle their own differences, rather than coming running to them; so it was easier for America to deal with. I was to get it into my head that that was and would ever remain the policy of the United States of America.

I had said nothing in public, but George Brown, then Foreign Secretary, sent for me. He gave me a lunch in the Commons and was at his most charming, friendly and persuasive. He used his full range of political skills. It was really a joy to behold. His punch line was:

'Europe is about politics, not about economics. If we went in with the Americans, they would outnumber us five to one and they would run us. If we go in with Europe, then, dear boy, we are all the same size and we will run them!'

Then George resigned and Michael Stewart once more became Foreign Secretary. He also sent for me and the treatment was quite different, but just as impressive. He saw me in the Foreign Secretary's great room in the north-west corner of the Foreign Office, sitting at his desk surrounded by advisers. I felt rather like a naughty schoolboy in front of the Headmaster. The message was the same. This was not just an economic arrangement; this was a political issue and, his eyes gleamed, 'Think of the prizes!'

As if that were not enough, Michael Halls, the Prime Minister's PPS, rang me and told me that if I advocated NAFTA in public, then he thought I ought to know that the Prime Minister would attack me in public.

More compelling, friends and colleagues whose opinions I valued were against it. Tom Kennedy was steadfastly against and I ran into Ronnie Macintosh, an old colleague from the DEA, who said, 'You chicken out quickly, Fred.'

Not long after the 1968 student riots in France, President de Gaulle resigned and Pompidou was elected in his place. After a decent interval, the British government put in its third application and after the 1970 election, the incoming Conservative government brought the process to a successful conclusion.

However, in view of the recurring opposition in Britain to our membership of the European Union, first on the Labour side and now on the Conservative, I am glad I studied the alternatives. Almost all of the opposition to the EC assumes that there must somehow be an Anglo-Saxon alternative – compare Mrs Thatcher's eulogies on America with her criticisms of Europe – and it is absolutely clear to me, if it is not clear to all those who still want it, that an Anglo-Saxon alternative is not and never will be on offer.

When, towards the end of my three-year term, I was asked whether I would serve another two years, I thought I had better make sure that I was acceptable to an incoming Conservative government; so, in 1969, I went to see Ted Heath. After he had consulted his colleagues, he said that they would abide by any decision made by the Council. When Roy Jenkins, then responsible as Chancellor for Neddy, consulted the rest of the Council, they wanted me to stay on.

On the morning of the next Council meeting, our elder son Christopher was in hospital with an injured eye and just before I went down to meet the Chancellor at the door, Elizabeth rang to say that they wanted to operate and she would not allow it without my agreement. I said that I would ring straight back. Coming up in the lift, I explained to Roy Jenkins what had happened and asked that they should start without me, rang Elizabeth and supported her in the decision to let the operation go ahead. I then went in to find that Roy Jenkins had held up the meeting so that they could begin with the announcement of my reappointment. I was very touched.

The Conservative leadership, at a weekend meeting at the Selsden Park Hotel in Croydon, had decided on a policy of disengagement, which seemed to lead, if elected, to the abolition not only of the Prices and Incomes Board and the Industrial Reorganisation Corporation set up by George Brown, but of most of the other institutions of co-operation between government and the two sides of industry. So I felt that, though Neddy was a Conservative creation, I should leave no stone unturned to preserve it.

I talked to Selwyn Lloyd, its first Chairman, and to Reggie Maudling, its second, and of course to Ted Heath. But I thought it was necessary to do something wider, so I asked the management side of the little Neddies that, if they felt that the NEDC and the little Neddies were doing a worthwhile job, they lobby whoever they knew best in the Conservative leadership.

I couldn't keep in touch with them all, but George Howard and Nigel Strutt of the Country Landowners asked me to lunch at Boodle's. The shadow spokesman for Agriculture was Joe Godber. Over lunch they said, 'We have sent for Godber and we have told him that he is not to wind up the little Neddy.' I thought, thus did the great Whig landowners send from Boodle's for their placemen in the Commons to tell them where the Whig interest lay.

Another landowner may have had an even greater influence. The Chairman of their little Neddy was Mindy Bacon, premier baronet of England, KBE, Lord Lieutenant of Norfolk, Pro-Chancellor of the University of East Anglia, a staunch Conservative, and no doubt important to the party in East Anglia. Because he was such an establishment figure, I had my doubts about his suitability as Chairman, but I was told to wait until I met him. When I did, it was clear that he was a formidably able figure and just right for the farmers.

Right up to the day of the election it was thought that Labour would be re-elected, but there was a late swing and the Conservatives came back with a small but workable majority. After the 1970 election, the Conservatives abolished, among others, the Prices and Incomes Board, the Industrial Reorganisation Corporation, the British Productivity Council and the British National Export Council; which, in view of the success of

British exports and the huge voluntary effort which had gone into export promotion, caused a tremendous outcry. But Neddy survived. We were asked to cut the number of little Neddies and we had no difficulty in picking out four of the least effective.

Where Harold Wilson had sat puffing his pipe, listening to all that was said, but seldom joining in or committing himself to an opinion, Ted Heath, by contrast, was part of all the genial give and take round the Council table. He was, naturally, least at ease with the unions and hankered somewhat after simpler times when people were content with a fair day's pay for a fair day's work.

Although the Conservative government kept Neddy, and the Prime Minister thought it worth taking the chair from time to time, their slogan was 'disengagement'. They ridiculed Harold Wilson's 'instant government' and his government's growth targets, and believed that industry could get on far better without too much interest from government. Of course they had a point, but I was anxious that government and industry should continue to have a well-briefed and constructive dialogue.

I have always believed as a Christian that unemployment is against the dignity and worth of the individual, and against all the instincts God has given us. So I believe that full employment should be central to government policies. It cannot be a prime objective of business, so it must be the responsibility of government and that responsibility puts a practical limit on disengagement.

I also argued in the 1971 annual lecture to the Manchester Statistical Society (not as esoteric a body as it sounds) that only political decisions could reverse the misallocation of national resources; but these political decisions had to be based on constantly updated industrial economics, not on the Treasury macro-economic model, which had given wildly optimistic forecasts after the devaluation just over three years before, and then, when they turned out to be quite wrong, equally wild pessimistic forecasts.

The plea fell on deaf ears. Instead, when disengagement produced rising unemployment, there was a crude U-turn; Neddy was swamped by the effort to introduce a new incomes policy and my successor, Frank Figgures, was taken off to set up the new Board to run it. The Barber boom echoed the Maudling boom of the decade before, and instead of national resources going wholeheartedly to export industry to exploit our new membership of the EEC, far too much was diverted into an unsustainable domestic property boom which crashed at the same time as the government (see Appendix).

Yet I have a very soft spot for Ted Heath. He did understand that we simply had to have the greater market of the EEC, and he not only got us in, but he has, as the anti-European mood gripped the Labour Party and then his own party, stuck, as no one else has, to his advocacy of our European partnership. He has had the courage to say so loud and clear when few others dared. He sees, as all leaders in Europe see, that we need each other and that to go back to the narrow nationalisms which triggered the Second World War would be disastrous.

I held the rank of Permanent Secretary, and was knighted in January 1971 at the tender age of forty-five. I was especially glad that this happened while my father was still alive. He died three years later just before Christmas 1973, followed not long after by his elder brother, Ernest, the last of the Catherwoods of the Creagh. He and Mother greatly enjoyed the ten years at Wootton. The Catherwoods, Cloughs and Marshes, six parents and eight grandchildren, used to get together with them after Christmas; the last occasion was in the George at Stamford, and I can still picture Father, white-haired against oak panelling, smiling at the head of the table.

I owe my father a great deal. His determination made sure that I stuck at my profession until I qualified and he was right that this was, in its day, the entry card to management. His close interest and encouragement also made sure that I pressed on to tougher and more interesting jobs. He was a pioneer, a visionary, a great traveller and, in his latter years, a most warm-hearted father-in-law and grandfather. Whatever faults he had were offset by an outsize sense of humour, so that in the middle of being difficult about something, he could suddenly laugh at the absurdity of what he was saying. When he went, life was duller without him.

I carried away a lot of happy memories of my five years at

Neddy, especially of people. George Woodcock, the intellectual General Secretary with the bushy eyebrows, who could see the case for incomes policies, but was never quite sure whether he could carry his Council. Vic Feather, a complete contrast; a practical Yorkshireman with an enormous sense of humour and the capacity to give sound advice in earthy language which everyone could understand. Alf Robens, who knew how to close mines while making the miners feel that he was on their side. He was the first to question the cost and the wisdom of nuclear power and was quite clear that had he not gone to the Coal Board, he would have been Prime Minister. An emaciated Les Cannon, near to death from lung cancer, coming to his last Council to make an appeal to the Conservatives to keep the IRC. Frank Cousins, sitting uncomfortably on the government side as Minister of Technology and a lot more easily among the TUC, when he finally gave it up to go back to his union. Peter Runge, the first CBI leader, looking just like Robert Morley, reasonable and accommodating. John Davies, the first CBI Director General, a charming and intense Welshman who lost his way when he went into politics. And one of the biggest personalities of them all, Frank Kearton, boss of Courtaulds, a tough tycoon who found it hard to keep to the CBI line, but whose shrewd common sense rode above sectional interests and party politics.

My only disappointment was that I was unable to tie the City into Neddy. The merchant banker Kenneth Keith was on the Council, but the City regarded him as something of an outsider and he did not represent them in any formal sense. I was very conscious of the continuing commitment, by Continental banks and investment institutions, to those companies in which they had made a long-term investment, as compared with the arm's-length attitude and short-term policies of Anglo-Saxon investors. I thought that, at least, the City should be engaged in the Council's dialogue, but at best there should be a little Neddy for financial institutions.

I talked to Leslie O'Brien, who had become Governor of the Bank of England when I had gone to Neddy. He directed me to the Chairman of the clearing banks, John Thompson, Chairman of Barclays, and we had a long talk in his office. He not only saw me out of his office, but came down in the lift and saw me out of the door to Lombard Street, the greatest courtesy a visitor can receive in the City.

They were not all against it. But they did not see their way round the protocol. The Governor might be appointed by the government to head a nationalised institution, but he was also their representative to the government and they did not see how they could have any other. After my time the problem was solved by bringing the Governor on to the Council. But it made no difference to the City's habit of spreading its investment small and wide, and selling out at the first sign of trouble or at the first ridiculous offer. Things were to get worse, not better.

Chapter Eight

BRITISH MANAGEMENT

I had a longstanding agreement with Maurice Laing that, when I left Neddy at the end of April 1971, I would join them to replace their retiring and much-respected Chief Executive, Ernest Uren.

There had been other offers, but I knew the Laing brothers, Kirby and Maurice, well. I also knew the construction industry and another quite compelling reason was John Laing's excellent reputation in labour relations. Having been so close to the trades union movement, I did not want to find myself fighting them the next moment, especially for some doubtful cause.

But shortly after I arrived, the building industry had its first national strike for decades and, since Laing's were a big company which preferred to deal with recognised unions, our sites were the easiest to bring out on strike. The union leadership was very apologetic, but said we would realise how difficult it was to make the strike effective on the smaller sites.

That was not good enough for the militants. They organised 'flying pickets', coachloads of militants who would descend suddenly on a small site and, using strong-arm tactics, so terrify the few workers that they dare not return. It was very clear from accounts from our managers on smaller sites that this was very far from the peaceful picketing allowed by the law.

Kirby Laing was the current Chairman of the National Joint Council for the Building Industry and, after the strike had gone on for some time, I suggested to him that I should use my trades union contacts to see what kind of settlement might be reached. Vic Feather put me in a room beside his office with the General

Secretary of the building workers' union. Long strikes did not help them either and we worked out a deal which we thought might be saleable on both sides.

But the construction industry was still run by tycoons and Godfrey Mitchell of Wimpey told me to keep out of it. 'My people tell me that the unions are on their last legs and will soon crack.' He was wrong. The strike went on for as long again and the settlement in the end was roughly the same as the one we had worked out in Vic Feather's back room.

Not long afterwards we also had to face a 'rent-a-mob' at the new St Thomas's Hospital site opposite Parliament. An electrical sub-contractor had a wildcat strike not recognised by the Electrical Union and the strikers tried to bring the whole site out in sympathy. Failing to do this, they raised pickets wherever they could find them. We kept the site open in agreement with the Electrical Union, the London police and Home Office with all of whom Maurice Laing kept in close touch. Very soon we had to start bussing the workers in from collection points away from the site, but we had harrassment at the gates until someone found stock-car racing drivers to drive the buses. Then there was no more trouble.

Apart from excitements like this, it was not easy to gear down from work at the centre of the national economy to the problems of one company. It might have been easier had there been more problems. But my predecessor, Ernest Uren, had done an excellent job. He had organised the company, much as I had done at Costain's, into operating divisions with decentralised managements, and all were profitable.

But to begin with I had to tour the company's operations and that was always interesting. We had three sites in the no-go areas of Belfast. One was a huge impersonal block of flats with concrete walkways in the Nationalist area of the city centre. The IRA had just paid a visit and removed the payroll at gunpoint. As they went off with the cash, their small Ford had found an army Saracen blocking the exit, so the gang sounded their horn and the Saracen obligingly backed off to let them out.

At the other site in the Nationalist area, I asked the agent whether he was not worried about the loss of stores. He said

117

that there was no problem because the chief storekeeper was also said to be a big boss in the IRA.

In the Unionist area we were building houses on the south side of Carlisle Circus. The agent there had just had a visit from a local armed 'loyalist' who told him that he had Catholic tilers working on the site and they had to come off. The agent told me that when you looked down the barrel of a revolver, you knew that if you made the wrong decision, it would be your last.

On the later site visits that year, I was instantly recognised because during the summer the Catherwood family had appeared three times on a popular TV show, *Ask the Family*, which had an audience rating of over twelve million. Trying to be quick-witted in answering difficult questions in front of an audience of that size, who are also listening as you whisper to each other, is not an experience I would recommend. But Bethan, whose head teacher gave our names to the BBC, had been adamant. By the quarter final I had decided that it was time we lost by a narrow margin, otherwise we would be slaughtered by some bright teacher's family who knew all the answers, and that is all that viewers would remember. It so happened that we were ahead all the way through the quarter final, but level at the last question, which we then lost. As we found afterwards, that left viewers' memories with the impression that we had done well and happily confused as to whether we had lost or won.

Even though critical problems at John Laing did not arrive daily as they did in the public service, it was as well to keep in close touch with all that was going on. Construction being a dangerous industry, I asked for all reports on fatal accidents and I remember these vividly.

Big sites are covered with electric cable and the movement of mobile lifting equipment was strictly confined to daylight and to marked roadways, and always with the jib down. One driver was killed because he drove the crane at night across the roadways and with the jib up. Another, building a temporary railing around a stairwell, fell down the well himself. A group working on a motorway decided to drive back from a pub one evening on the blocked off roadway. They removed the barriers, and drove along the road until the car turned over when it hit a pile of gravel.

But soon there were decisions to be taken. We had started to face very low bids from competitors on motorways. Laing's had built the first major motorway in Britain, the M1, and had more experience than anyone else. We also had very skilled estimators. If our bids were accurate, the company taking work on low bids would become bankrupt. I supported the civil engineers in the view that they should rely on the accuracy of their own bids and not try to follow the market down. It was a wise decision. The successful bidder did become bankrupt.

I also agreed with the civil engineers' suggestion that, in place of the motorway work, they should bid for the first of the North Sea oil production platforms. These had to be 400 feet high in order to sit on the sea bed; so they had to be built on their sides and tilted over into an upright position as they sank. They were of an altogether different magnitude in concept and construction from the small exploration rigs built so far.

We joint-ventured with a French pipeline company; we were awarded one contract and Wimpey the other. We decided to go for skilled and unionised workers living at home and bought a small harbour at Graythorp near Hartlepool. Wimpey decided to go where there were no unions and to bring labour from wherever they could find it. They took a site on the Moray Firth in north Scotland.

We took on the Boilermakers' Union and had a tough negotiation far into the night once a year – with a token day's strike from the Engineers' Union, just to remind us that they were there too. But all our workers were skilled and experienced and went home in the evenings. It was said that Wimpeys ended up with a dozen competing unions and their workers lived on a boat with nothing to do at night. It was a race to see who could float their rig out first to Britain's first big North Sea oilfield.

We won the race and no company could have wished for a greater public relations splash than our float-out. Maurice Laing invited everyone he knew for three open days beforehand. I went up for one of the days and toured the site with Len Murray and Danny Macgarvey of the Boilermakers, whose members were as proud as anyone. Len Murray made me come along to his meeting with the shop-floor committee.

George Edwards of British Aerospace was also there. I explained that people were crawling all over the rig to see that all the stop-cocks opened and shut properly, 'Otherwise the tilt will go wrong and we'll end up with the most expensive lot of scrap metal ever to hit the bottom of the North Sea.' He said that it was the same with aircraft, but, 'There comes a time when you have to tell them to put someone in the cockpit, point it down the runway, rev up the engines and see what happens.'

We built two more steel rigs and then there was talk of building a concrete rig. The engineers found that the deepest sea nearest to skilled workers was off the Kilcreggan peninsula in Dunbartonshire at the great bend of the Firth of Clyde. I went up to see the committee of the Dunbartonshire County Council to get planning permission. The Labour majority were strongly in favour and the small Conservative minority, sitting together right at the far end of the table, were against. At a public meeting in the Kilcreggan village hall I found out why. The engineers' survey had done a good job on the depth of water and the location of labour, but it had not done a social survey of Kilcreggan. I had a rough time.

'What will a thing that height do to our TV reception?'

'It will put up all the wages and how will we afford gardeners?'

And finally: 'We have nothing personal against you, but would you please just go away.'

In the end the bottom fell out of the oil market and the rig was never built.

Arriving on top of the deregulation of the financial markets the Barber boom produced an explosion in property development. The big clearing banks were pushing money out to secondary banks, which were pushing it on to developers. Laing's had large property holdings and also a major property development division. Property prices soared to absurd heights. In the end customers had to be found who would be prepared to pay rents which justified the new price level; but neither the developers nor those financing them seemed to have done any market surveys. The big clearing banks should have insisted on surveys, since there was an assumption that if the big clearing banks were prepared to lend on those property values, they must be all right. But it was the blind leading the blind.

I remembered the lessons learnt from the managers of Price

With my father in 1931

Wedding day at Westminster Chapel, London
on 27 February 1954

The family at Rosapenna in 1954 with John, baby Alison
and Elizabeth Marsh and my sister Mary (front, 2nd left)
with my parents

Dr and Mrs Lloyd-Jones in 1968

Harold Wilson takes the Chair at Neddy in 1968

With the Duke of Edinburgh at the launch of Export Year 1976

g chopsticks at a church lunch in Tokyo in 1976

With Aike Morita, Chairman and founder of Sony, in 1976

th Jimmy Saville at the opening of Laing's Saville Building in Leeds, July 1973

Giving degrees at University of Westminster, 1974

On the shop floor as Chairman of BOTB in 1978

Support from Ted Heath in the first Euro Election in 1979

The family at home with Dr and Mrs Lloyd-Jones in 1980

With Christopher, Bethan and students at Schloss Mittersill in 1982

Meeting Tip O'Neill, speaker US Congress, in 1993

Support from John Major in the 1989 Euro Election

Four generations: Bethan Lloyd-Jones , Elizabeth, Bethan and Myfanwy Marshall in 1991

With our first grandchild

Meeting Perez de Cuellar, Secretary General of the UN, in 1992

Meeting Nelson Mandella in 19

As Vice President of the European Parliament with staff:
Debbie Moss, Jane Kelsey and Lillian Philips

My last day in the constituency at the
Holme School, Peterborough in 19

Waterhouse who had cleared up the mess after the 1931 financial crash and, two centuries before that, the instructions of Sarah, the great Duchess of Marlborough, to her financial advisers, who had invested heavily in the South Sea Company: 'The thing is ridiculous, sell all our share!' Laing's did not run with the pack.

At the climax of the boom we were offered a loan at 6 per cent to build the second block of an office development in Manchester, where we had already laid the foundations for both blocks. I found that the current office space then under construction in Manchester was eight times the annual take-up of new office space in that city; so it didn't matter how cheap the money was; it wasn't on.

Laing's had a lot of property development and when the crash came, the market went down so far that we had to make some reduction in valuations, but it was well within our ability to absorb. But elsewhere secondary banks and developers were completely wiped out. It was the end of Slater Walker, that financial star of the late sixties. The old Jewish merchant banks like Warburg's and Kleinwort's kept out of it. Cyril Kleinwort said that he had been in New York during the crash of the thirties and he would never forget. But it did great damage to the reputation of the big clearing banks. Without their funding it would not have happened and they should have known better.

Ted Heath's greatest achievement was to negotiate Britain's entry into the EEC. Without his persistence and energy it might not have happened. It is not easy to go back for a third try, but he did. He said that President Pompidou had written to him apologising for the two de Gaulle vetoes. On 1 January 1973, the United Kingdom became a member, along with Denmark and Ireland, and the Six became the Nine.

There was a transition period, but business could now invest for a Continental market of 250 million people. We had a level playing field and nothing to prevent our making the best of it. But, at that precise moment, the Barber boom diverted attention and energy to the home market. A year later I looked at the list of Laing's major UK building contracts and, out of about thirty, only one, a chemical plant in Welwyn, was for a manufacturing company. The rest were hospitals, schools, office blocks, shopping centres and, creeping on to the list, major offices for the new upper tier county councils which had emerged from the reorganisation of local government.

It was not easy to stay right out of the public arena.

My successor at Neddy, Frank Figgures, had been a senior Treasury official, a great character, extremely able and very good company, but not at all accustomed to saying anything in public. And, after five years at Neddy, I had a lot of good friends in the media, who kept in touch. As the disengagement policy was clearly not working, and unemployment and wage rates kept on rising, I was asked to comment. One day, on the BBC's *The World at One*, I said that I thought that the government would shortly try to introduce an incomes policy.

A few days later Ted Heath gave a reception to celebrate the tenth anniversary of Neddy. At the top of the stairs he shook Elizabeth's hand, at the same time berating me for forecasting a change of policy.

'You had no right to say that on *The World at One*; it will ruin my reputation with the party.'

By the time he had finished, Elizabeth's hand was quite crushed. At the reception, George Brown was exuberant. 'They'll have to have an incomes policy!' Michael Stewart said that he wanted to support the Prime Minister on Europe, 'but with what he is doing to my constituents he makes it very difficult'. Within a fortnight the U-turn was announced.

I returned formally to public affairs through the British Institute of Management, where I was again on the Council. I was elected a Vice Chairman in 1972 and chaired an enquiry on the effect of the new business schools. These had been funded mainly by the big manufacturing companies in the hope that they would give them a steady stream of young professional managers. But instead, the graduates of the schools were going into the City and very few were going to the companies on whose efforts in Europe our future now depended. With the cash squeeze on industry one could hardly blame them.

I was also on the Advisory Board of the Davos Management Symposium, which met at the end of January in the Swiss ski resort of Davos. Klaus Schwab, who founded it, seemed to have found a winning formula. The meetings were in the morning and evening, leaving the afternoon for skiing, an ideal formula for combining business with pleasure. And, given the kind of audience of top European businessmen to which this appealed, he was also successful in persuading the most distinguished speakers that it was worth their while to come to the Swiss Alps to address them. I co-chaired the plenary sessions in 1973 and 1974 with Olivier Giscard d'Estaing, the brother of the French Finance Minister, and in 1973 was able to bring the family too. One evening, sitting in the Hotel Belvedere with Olivier, I asked after the health of President Pompidou. Olivier said it was bad. I asked who would succeed him. He said, 'Maybe my brother.'

I chaired a small panel which included J K Galbraith and Raymond Barre (later French Prime Minister) who was a monetarist. In straight debate with the monetarists, Galbraith won hands down. But in the questions, a practical German businessmen said that, though he had been very impressed, 'I still do not know what to do with my money.'

The European Commission was heavily represented by Commissioners and Directors General and, in the sessions and seminars, I began to get a feel for the Community we had just joined.

Next year, 1974, we had just had the first oil shock and one of the plenary speakers was Gyllenhammer, the young Chairman of the Swedish car company, Volvo. Instead of putting forward policies which might see Europe and its industry through the oil crisis, he made an impassioned political appeal for strength through European unity in order to face down the OPEC cartel. I thought a rising European business leader should have been less rhetorical and more practical – and Sweden was a neutral country and not even a member of the EEC. So I used the chair to cross-question him, which provoked even more impassioned appeals. But there was no doubt which of us carried the audience with us. They did not want to think it through as a problem; they wanted to demonstrate.

When it came later to discussion of the 1975 symposium, Klaus asked me to find another Chairman from Britain and I suggested Ted Heath, by then out of office. He did it for another two years, until he also took too much on himself as Chairman!

From 1971 to 1977 I was Chairman of Council of the Inter-Varsity Fellowship (IVF). It was a time of great expansion of higher education and we tried to increase the staff in line with the need. We also began to feel that, with the increase in polytechnics and technical colleges, the division of the work into universities and colleges was wrong, and that we should merge the work, changing the name and constitution.

No one should ever to try to chair a voluntary organisation when it is changing its constitution or its name; but we succeeded. There were lots of suggestions for the new name and I had a twelve-page letter from the first General Secretary, the redoubtable Douglas Johnson, giving the likely student adaptions of the resulting acronyms. At the end he suggested 'Universities and Colleges Christian Fellowship' and I put it to the Council that unless we wanted more letters like the one I had in my hand, we had better settle for Douglas Johnson's proposal. They all agreed. So the IVF became today's UCCF.

Most of us had become accustomed to agreeing with DJ. He was the founder of the movement and had very clear ideas of where it should go. He wanted to put the Evangelical wing of the Churches back in the mainstream of public debate. To do that, he had to found a movement in the universities which was prepared to go back to the doctrines of the Reformation, to rescue biblical scholarship from the domination of liberals, and to bring Evangelicals back from decades of pietism and to have a firm position from which to challenge the rise of secularism. Yet, although he was a leader, DJ's approach was oblique. He maintained that the IVF (now UCCF) was a student-led movement, not a mission to the universities run from outside. So the students must make the decisions. Yet he was also concerned that they take the right decisions and this involved a web of consultative committees with DJ, active but invisible, at the centre. But, like his letter to the Council on the name, it worked, because he could always persuade good men and women to help. Theologically he was greatly helped by Dr Lloyd-Jones, who was President throughout the war. Financially he was helped by Sir John Laing.

DJ was responsible for the setting up of Tyndale House,

124

the centre for biblical studies at Cambridge, and the London Bible College, which was to offset the domination of the liberal theological schools at the universities. He was, with Dr Lloyd-Jones and Stacey Woods of the IVCF (USA), responsible for the founding of the International Fellowship of Evangelical Students in 1947 and he has been responsible for the rise of the Evangelical sector of the Church, when all other sectors are in decline.

I believe that the IVF/UCCF has had great influence in Britain. In many universities, the affiliated Christian Union is the largest voluntary student organisation. It puts the Christian faith to many students who know nothing about it and at a time when they are most open to new ideas. Constitutionally it is, as DJ intended, run by students themselves, so all depends on the student leaders, and that responsibility breeds leaders for the Church. Yet the staff workers of the UCCF are there to help, advise and give continuity. At graduate level, its specialist groups do great work in applying the Christian faith to the ethical problems of medicine, the law, teaching and other professions. I am very happy to have had a part in it.

One of my predecessors as Chairman of the IVF, Professor Norman Anderson, had been asked by Frank Longford to serve on an investigation into the effects of the new and much more liberal laws on pornography. After talking together and to Lord Justice Edmund Davies, we all three agreed to serve. I was asked to be Treasurer. We had no idea what we were letting ourselves in for.

It was not so much that Frank Longford liked talking to the press; it was that the whole thing was such a superb story. The Chief Rabbi, the Archbishop of York, Peregrine Worsthorne, Lord Justice Davies and other similar pundits, all sitting round trying to decide whether pornography corrupted. Had they looked at the latest pornography; if not, how could they know whether it was likely to corrupt? If they had looked at it, had it corrupted them and if it had not corrupted them, then what was the problem?

The problem with Frank Longford was not that he had views, but that he broadcast them freely. I had a letter from the Charity

Commissioners to say that the Inland Revenue had, for the first time, questioned the Commissioners' judgement on charitable status. Lord Longford seemed to them to have made up his mind on the issue of pornography and was running a pressure group, which was not entitled to tax exemption, rather than an enquiry, which was. I managed to persuade them that what Lord Longford said was on his own account and not on behalf of the group of distinguished judges, archbishops, bishops, rabbis and experts on the enquiry, who had yet to come to a conclusion.

We finally agreed a document and held a packed press conference in the Waldorf Hotel. Someone asked whether we had taken evidence from any pornographers, and Malcolm Muggeridge replied that that would be as useful as asking a madam to give her views on prostitution. At once a woman in the audience rose to say that she was a madam and was outraged to find that no one would publish her memoirs. This brought the entire army of photographers to their feet to get a shot of the madam and Mary Whitehouse in the same frame and that, as I recollect, was the end of the press conference.

But Frank Longford's flamboyance did get the issue on the national agenda. The breaches of the current law could no longer be ignored and a number of police officers, including some of fairly senior rank, were prosecuted for receiving bribes. And, to protect children, newsagents agreed to put pornography on the top shelf. It was a gesture – and maybe no more – against the tidal wave of the permissive society.

In 1973 John Arkell, Chairman of the BIM, asked me whether I would let my name go forward as his successor in the following year. It was a post very much in line with my enthusiasm for professional management and, with the agreement of Kirby and Maurice Laing, I accepted.

The end of 1973 saw not only the impending collapse of the Barber boom, but also the first huge price rise in oil. The Americans, having financed the Vietnam war on borrowed money, had just been forced to float the dollar. This ended the post-war era of currency stability and with it, the longest period of high economic growth in the history of the world. The industrial countries were now especially vulnerable.

The government hoped that an incomes policy would offset the effects of the Barber boom on wage rates. At Neddy, Frank Figgures had been sucked into the effort to hold down wages, as had the very distinguished head of the Civil Service, William Armstrong, whose health was broken by the strain.

Since the Conservatives had put something like Barbara Castle's trades union proposals into effect, there was limited trades union goodwill for the Conservative incomes policy, which was doubly difficult because it was not underpinned by a curb on demand, but was imposed to offset a boom, which put it under strain from the start.

The crisis came when the National Union of Mineworkers tried to use the oil crisis to recover the differential which they had lost to the private sector industries where shop-floor power had set the pace. They had a genuine case. Even with the special award they had had in 1972, they were losing 600 miners a week and at a time when oil was suddenly more expensive than coal. But the inflexibilities of the new prices and incomes legislation did not allow for their claim. So they banned overtime and coal production dropped by 40 per cent. In addition to the oil price rise, the nation now faced an acute shortage of coal in the middle of the winter.

The government decided to declare a three-day working week to conserve coal stocks and took charge of the negotiations. Early in the new year I had a phone call from John Marsh of the BIM and also a part-time director of the National Coal Board which was now on the sidelines as government negotiated directly with the miners. John asked whether I could use my contacts with the TUC to find a way through. I asked my colleagues in the construction division how long they could go on with the three-day week and they were very gloomy, so I rang Len Murray, who had just taken over from Vic Feather as General Secretary of the TUC.

I said that I thought the only way to get the government off the hook was for the TUC Council to declare that the miners should be allowed to recover their differential and that the other unions would undertake not to base their claims on the miners' award. Len said that he agreed with me, but it would be difficult to carry the Council and anything I could do in public would be a great help.

I rang ITN and the BBC, and did peak-hour interviews on both channels. I also did a piece for one of the national dailies and was discussing a possible piece for the *Observer*, when the news came through that Sid Greene of the National Union of Railwaymen had just made the offer at Neddy which I had discussed with Len Murray.

Sadly, Tony Barber, who was in the chair, turned it down out of hand. It is said in defence of his action that government could not trust the TUC. But if not, then why had they made such efforts over the previous two years to bring them back into partnership? The TUC's view was that the government could not lose. Had the offer been accepted and failed to work, they would have had complete justification for their Industrial Relations Act and incomes policy. And had it worked, it would have given the government a political triumph. Instead the government raised the political stakes and called an election on the issue of 'Who rules the country?'

It became clear to me that, whoever won, British management was living in turbulent times and that, however well-organised the management of John Laing, being Chairman of the BIM was not compatible with a full-time executive job. In addition, John Marsh was no longer Director and there was as yet no successor. The board of Mallinson Denny, the large timber company, asked me to take over when their present Chairman retired. Kirby and Maurice asked me to stay on the Laing board and soon afterwards I accepted two similar offers.

Labour won the election, but were without an overall majority until a second election in the autumn. However it was clear that there had been a large swing to the left inside the party. Michael Foot was at the Department of Employment and asked the TUC to write his policies. Len Murray told me that they were being given far more than they had ever asked for. Tony Benn (as he now liked to be called) was at the Department of Industry and where George Brown had been careful to assure business that his Industrial Reorganisation Corporation (IRC) was not a back door to nationalisation, Tony Benn made his National Enterprise Board (NEB) sound like the firm first step to socialism. As a result he could find no industrialist to chair it until Harold Wilson persuaded a confident Don Ryder, Chairman of Reed

Paper and The Mirror Group, but outside the mainstream of politically experienced industry leaders, to accept a peerage and to rely on him for support.

The new government decided that all negotiation with employees had to be through TUC-affiliated unions, thus firmly excluding managers, who were not normally unionised. In negotiation about the nationalisation of the shipbuilding company at Barrow-in-Furness, Tony Benn refused to talk to the local managers and the Council of the BIM decided that we had to make our 70,000 members into a representative body. Since we were an educational charity, this was a long and complex process; but we were determined. We were greatly helped by our new Director, Roy Close, who had done an excellent job in succession to Tom Fraser as Industrial Director at Neddy. I had encouraged him to apply and the selection committee found him by far the best candidate.

We kept the educational charity as a Foundation and proposed that the BIM Council be elected by the members. It was not easy to persuade eminent industrialists to stand for election; some of them were involved through the Foundation and others as Fellows. To make sure that we had total support, we held a meeting for all members at the Festival Hall, which filled the main floor. I explained the proposals; Terry Beckett, Chairman of Ford's (later Director General of the CBI) made an impassioned speech; there were wide-ranging contributions from the floor and when I took the vote, it was overwhelmingly in favour.

My predecessor had asked the new Conservative leader, Margaret Thatcher, to speak at our annual dinner at the Hilton and I went to the House of Commons to brief her. The previous year, Ted Heath had made a speech more suitable for a group of fervent political supporters. It was suggested that I mention this to the new leader and point out that we were a professional and non-political body. She lifted an eyebrow and said, 'So you're a lot of political eunuchs!'

She was taking home three books on monetarism for weekend reading and at the time I thought this a rather specialist subject for a party leader.

When it came to the dinner, I asked Edwin Plowden to sit on her other side, but neither of us had much conversation because she wanted to get the speech live on the nine o'clock news in order to denounce government's efforts to keep open the Rootes plant at Linwood in Scotland. The man from Central Office asked me to make sure that a thousand people were through to the coffee stage by nine! He kept passing her drafts and she spent the dinner in scratching them out and writing her own. When we eventually got her to her feet – introduction to follow after the nine o'clock news – her hands trembled as she spoke, whether from nervousness or passion it was hard to say. Then she had to go off to vote, so I saw her out. I came back, introduced her and thanked her in her absence to a very understanding audience. Fortunately for Scotland's employment and the British balance of trade, Linwood remained open until, with so much of British industry, it was killed five years later by the unrestrained rise of the pound.

My term of office as Chairman of the BIM, from autumn 1974 to autumn 1976, was a traumatic time for Britain and especially for British management. In the autumn of 1974 a left-wing Labour Party was elected with a working majority. High personal taxes combined with record inflation cut into the real earnings of all the professional classes and government seemed intent on undermining the residual powers of management to look after our vital industries. Margaret Thatcher seemed, in the words of one cynical mandarin, like a 'poor man's Ted Heath', determined on the market as the answer to all economic difficulties, but without Ted's ability to see its limitations.

It was not enough to organise the BIM to represent the views of professional managers. Unlike the trades unions, managers were not trained to wait for initiatives from elsewhere. We were responsible for running the nation's commerce and industry and, drawing on all the expertise available, we had to put our own proposals. We had more flexibility than the company chairmen of the CBI, who were legally responsible only to their shareholders; as managers we had to reconcile all the interests including employees and customers as well as those who found the capital.

We had responded to the issue of employee directors, proposed by the European Commission's Fifth Company Directive, by setting up a small working party on Company Affairs, which

I had chaired. This reported in the spring of 1974. We argued for more accountability by management and more participation by employees, but in favour of keeping the British system of a unitary board (as against the German model of two-tier boards). We proposed a formal split between Chairman and Chief Executive, and more outside directors with a stronger role.

We were in favour of works councils, freely elected by all employees, from which two members could be selected as board members by mutual agreement between board and council, and we wanted the legal obligations of boards to be extended beyond the shareholders alone to include other interests. This report reflected not only the consensus of the committee but very much my own views too.

The government then set up a committee under Alan Bullock, the Oxford historian, to look at the issue of worker representation on company boards.

But the Bullock Committee, dominated by Clive Jenkins whose trades union represented office staff, insisted that the only way to have representation of workers was through the trades unions who had fought for and obtained recognition by the company. The BIM's view was that works councils should be elected by all workers whether unionised or not. If the trades unions wanted to put up their representatives as candidates, like an organised political party, they would no doubt be elected. Len Murray told me that I was not a democrat. I said that we, who insisted on one worker one vote, were the democrats and the TUC were the oligarchs. Our main anxiety, and that of the CBI, was that many companies had up to a dozen recognised unions, competing with each other for members, and most were trying to maintain their pay differentials against other unions. The thought of introducing this cacophony of conflicting interests into the board room filled us with horror.

At the 1976 annual dinner ending my two-year period of office, our guest of honour was Jim Callaghan, who had taken over earlier in the year from Harold Wilson. In his speech he challenged us to overcome our nervousness and accept the Bullock Committee report. I had to reply unscripted. I said that we were not nervous. Along the tables in front of him were many directors with companies in Germany, all of whom happily

131

accepted worker directors and who had far more experience about the way they worked than the Bullock Committee. But in Germany there was only one union to each industry and the Bullock Report was asking us to paralyse the direction of companies by bringing on to our boards the rivalry between up to a dozen unions.

The applause this received made it clear that the members were with me and we heard no more about Bullock. But it was a pity, for the financial stake of the employees in a company is usually about ten times that of the shareholders and I believe that our idea would have worked. We had set up a further committee under a Council member, Bernard Cotton, exclusively on worker participation. But, given the backlash against Bullock, especially by the CBI, the baby was thrown out with the bathwater.

It seemed to me that professional managers were not the only professionals who would not be represented under this Labour government and, with the help of Kirby Laing, who was President of the Institution of Civil Engineers, I got in touch with the presidents of the eighteen senior professional institutions who all met together regularly. I suggested that we should found a professional forum (for which I thought PROF was a suitable acronym), where we could debate the issues which were critical to both the country and the professions, and support each other in promoting them.

St John Elstub, the President of the Mechanical Engineers, was enormously enthusiastic and made the running within the professions; almost all were supportive. The President of the Royal College of Surgeons was very shrewd – and a superb bridge player. He saw me alone and supported the idea. His opposite number at the College of Physicians was an expert on rhesus negative babies and for this discussion he was surrounded by experts. The President of the Obstetricians on the other side of Regent's Park said that he would follow the two larger colleges and told me not to forget the Scottish colleges. The Chemists and Physicists were also in favour. The only two firmly against were the Chartered Accountants, who were anxious that they might lost their privileged access to the Chancellor, and the Barristers who clearly thought it much beneath them. Had we been able to swing the Law Society we might have done it, but they changed presidents every year and so we had to start all over again. We had a dinner in the Institution of Mechanical Engineers chaired by St John Elstub and we were nearly agreed, but both of us were now running out of time and there was no one left to clinch it. It seems to me that over the twenty years since then, when standards of all kinds have slipped, it would have been a great help to have had a powerful voice to point the way to professional standards of service, as an alternative to collectivism of the far left and unrestrained individualism of the far right.

Another growing concern was the blind pursuit of so-called economies of scale, which led to giant impersonal plants that could easily be held to ransom. It was aggravated by huge unmanageable conglomerate companies, which had grown as a result of the takeover booms, and of tax rates which tempted entrepreneurs to sell for capital gain as the only way of getting their profits out. The more shop floors I visited and the more confidential talks I had with company Chairmen, the more I became convinced that unnecessary size was the source not only of chronic inflation, but of poor labour relations and ineffective management.

I set my conclusions out in measured terms in the 1975 Graham Clark lecture organised by the Council of Engineering Industries and, in more popular form, in the summing up of a series of four seminars for BBC TV. I said that small was not only beautiful (the Schumacher thesis), it was also practical, bringing management nearer to both customers and workers. We needed to alter the bias against the small company in both taxation and monopoly legislation, and meantime management could do a lot on its own. From both the Engineers and the studio audience of managers, I had warm support.

Meantime we had only a few years until both the EC tariffs and our own would be removed, and British industry, much knocked about by the oil shock and the resultant inflation, had to survive. In an article in the *Contemporary Review* I pointed out that industry's net liquidity had deteriorated by £3.5bn in 1974 and that *Business Week* had estimated that Britain had to invest £21bn in new plant and equipment to become competitive with the EC. I suggested that government divert £3bn a year from public expenditure to industrial investment and that the investment institutions make a similar commitment. It was not just a question of making better use of existing investment; we had to compete with the latest products and these could not be turned out on plant installed twenty to thirty years ago – one might as well send in the cavalry to attack tanks.

I did not limit these arguments to papers given to professional societies. I addressed meetings organised by the BIM up and down the country, I spoke at dinners of trade associations and, looking back at the diary for 1975, I seemed to have been on radio or TV at least two or three times a week, doubling up as Chairman of the British Overseas Trade Board, my next major job.

Chapter Nine

EXPORT DRIVE

The European market should have been Britain's first economic priority as soon as the ink was dry on our agreement to join the European Community. Yet not only did the Conservative government divert our investment into a home-based property boom, but when Labour took over in 1974 they demanded a renegotiation of the Treaty of Accession, followed by a referendum, before they decided whether or not to pull Britain out and no company could invest for the new markets before they knew the answer.

When the limited renegotiation was complete and the referendum was announced for the spring of 1975, all those of us who believed that Britain's political and industrial future depended on a 'Yes' vote, threw ourselves into the campaign.

One of the leaders of the 'No' campaign was the Secretary of State for Trade, Peter Shore. I had been asked by Peter Thornton, now his Permanent Secretary, whether I would be willing to replace Peter Thorneycroft, the newly designated Chairman of the Conservative Party, as Chairman of the British Overseas Trade Board (BOTB). Just as the referendum campaign was starting, he came back with a firm proposal. I thought that, if the referendum went the right way, I could help to practise what I had been preaching with such vigour about our need to go for the European markets.

I went to see Peter Shore and we agreed as old friends that, if I took the job, I would not attack him personally in the campaign and he would not attack me. At the start the opinion polls showed two to one against membership, but at the count it was two to one in favour.

Because of the strong feeling in industry against the winding up of the British National Export Council, Peter Thorneycroft had run the BOTB in a very low key, but the Board agreed that we now had to become far more active; however we were there to help and not to try to persuade companies to act against their interests. There was to be no ministerial exhortation. It should be business to business and we should keep ministers out of it.

Our formula was to hold export conferences in major cities, in which four or five local companies told how they had built up their export business. We tried to balance large companies with small, capital goods with those producing consumer goods. When we had picked the best as case studies, the Central Office of Information (COI) made an audio-visual and, on the day, two executives from each company took the stand, where Robert Mackenzie, an experienced TV interviewer, questioned them and invited the audience to join in. And he pointed out that, since they were local companies, they would still be around if anyone wanted to find out more.

For each conference I topped and tailed hundreds of letters, also inviting managers to bring a representative from the shop floor with them. This not only involved the shop floor in the export effort; it also avoided shop floor and management blaming each other at the conference. Almost every company brought a shop steward. We also asked the Export Credits Guarantee Department and local bank managers to answer questions on finance. We had an average attendance of about four hundred.

We wanted these conferences to make as big a local splash as possible, so we arranged three teams from the Board to make well-publicised visits to about a dozen successful exporters the day before. We found that the press, radio and TV were proud of their local success stories and made the most of them.

Almost every conference was also a royal visit, including visits to four of the companies. The Duke of Kent was Vice Chairman of the Board, and came to most conferences, sometimes with the Duchess too. Once, at Southampton, the Duchess took his place; in West London we had Prince Philip, and in Birmingham, Earl

Mountbatten. Between them, they gave each conference a great sense of occasion.

In the mid-seventies, just after the election of a left-wing Labour government, I had had had some doubts about involving the Royal Family. But, after our first conference at Sheffield, I knew that I need not have worried. Every businessman who had been invited came to the dinner with the Duke on the first night. On the second night there was a reception for the whole conference in the great Cutlers' Hall and after a first awed hush on their arrival, there was a crowd around the Duke and Duchess until they left. The local press and TV gave excellent coverage to this royal encouragement of each city's successes.

After so many royal visits I could see that one of the major jobs of the Royal Family is to encourage and commend those who are doing a worthwhile job. All of us need to feel that what we do has some significance to our community and country. But, to do that, those who commend our work must themselves command great respect, so those whose actions forfeit public respect cannot really fulfil their proper function.

We went south to Bristol and Southampton; across the border to Glasgow and back to Newcastle; north-west to Liverpool and Manchester, where Brian Redhead took over from Bob Mackenzie; over the Pennines to Bradford; to Birmingham and Nottingham in the Midlands; around London, to Dunstable, Slough, Croydon and Maidstone; west to Cardiff and east to Cambridge, and then over the water to our very last conference in Belfast.

Bob Mackenzie and Brian Redhead also created a sense of occasion and enjoyment, and their skilled but friendly questions pin-pointed the difficult issues. There was a lot of backchat and laughter and none of the companies tried to cover up the very real difficulties they had found on the way. The COI audio-visuals were superb, reducing to a few minutes' presentation the outline of the company, its export strategy, the failures and the successes.

Some memories stand out:

- The schoolboy who exported model railway stations, complete with (indecipherable) graffiti on lavatory walls and smoke where the trains went under the bridge. Asked about cut-price competitors he said, with innocent youthful puzzlement, that he wondered how they ever stayed in business. That brought a lot of laughter.

- The shop steward from Llanelli, replying very positively on her relations with the management, then hesitating and adding cautiously, 'so far'.
- A shop steward on Merseyside, asked whether he realised the importance of exports, replying, 'What do you think keeps us in business when everyone around is out of work?'
- Mountbatten on the receiving line, challenged to tell the tough Midland businessman from the tough Midland shop steward: 'I think the stewards are the younger men with the better dressed wives.'
- Jack Jones, asked by the press at Liverpool to talk about a wage claim, and replying, 'Wage claims are yesterday and tomorrow; today is for exports.'
- Prince Philip, asked to launch Export Year, with its aim of a 10 per cent increase in the volume of exports for the Queen's Silver Jubilee, reminding us of the country's long history of failure to achieve such targets, but recovering at last to add that he had no doubt we would succeed this time.

Export Year was the idea of a Lancashire exporter, Roy Earnshaw. The two thousand or so companies who signed up to make a special effort, all set up export committees, including the shop floor. These not only did a good job; they also had their crop of good stories. One company thought that the committee might at least solve the problem of poor performance on one key piece of plant. Those who worked on the machine sent in their considered proposal and the problem was solved at once. Management asked why they had never suggested this before. They said, 'You never asked us before.'

Export Year (third quarter 1976 to third quarter 1977) did just hit its target and I wrote hastily to the Queen before the increase levelled out. But the trend held. Exports of goods and services went up from £27,011m in 1975 to £32,896m in 1979, a real (volume) increase of 22 per cent over the four years, taking Britain's share of world trade up to 10 per cent. It was backed by an increase in investment in manufacturing plant of 23 per cent (see Appendix). We have not seen its like since. These results were achieved by a switch to the new Continental markets and they showed that, given a level playing field, we could hold our own with the best of our European competitors.

The other part of my job was to travel abroad to talk to British exporters and, especially, to their customers. We all see the foreign imports in our shops, but very few of us have the chance of seeing the British product in foreign markets and of finding, as I did, that we can do as well abroad as they do here. The big exception was the motor industry, though even there, the component manufacturers did very well.

I concentrated on Europe, with a first visit of many to Dusseldorf and also to Cologne, Stuttgart, Munich, Hamburg, Vienna, Milan, Paris, Barcelona, Madrid, Copenhagen, Brussels, Rotterdam and Amsterdam.

Richard Sykes, our Ambassador in the Hague, took me to the Amsterdam boat show, where we were doing well, and he and his wife invited me to dinner in the evening in the old Residence in the centre of the Hague. It was also a farewell dinner for their friends, a cheerful occasion of talk about what they would do in retirement. He never got the chance. Shortly afterwards he was gunned down on his doorstep by the IRA.

I visited an old Dutch merchant, agent for many British companies, who said that he had called his salesmen together to find out what advice he could give me. It was that the British were the most inventive people in the world and when we put a proposed new product to them, they were always very excited. 'But,' he said, 'you do not put your money behind your own inventions; someone else picks them up, makes and sells them and, because we like doing business with you, we are all very sad.'

British companies were not entirely blameless for this squeeze on their cashflow. In addition to the export conferences, I would take a day trip once a month with other members of the Board to go round companies and meet with local management. Taking Neddy, the BIM and the BOTB together, I suppose I must have tramped round more British shop floors and talked to more management and workers than almost anyone else.

139

It reinforced my view that the bigger the plant, the worse the labour relations. In the small plants, the boss knew everyone and introduced them as we went round. In the bigger plants, they clearly knew no one and when we stopped to talk to a worker, they became embarrassed. In the smaller plants the relationships were good; in the big ones you could cut the atmosphere with a knife.

I asked a Lancashire maker of machinery for tufted carpets about his labour relations. He said, 'My labour relations policy is never to have more than five hundred of them in any one place. We once had five hundred and ten and we had trouble.'

Five hundred seemed to me too to be the critical point and it was backed up by the statistics of time lost in strikes, which was very small up to that size, but rose sharply over a thousand workers and, above that, in steep geometric progression. So not only were big plants vulnerable to enormously expensive unofficial stoppages by a small number of workers, but their human relations made them much more likely to have disaffected workers with no feelings of personal loyalty.

Part of our job as a Board was to promote inward investment. Of course this might introduce a competitor; but since industry argued for the right to make outward investment, we needed an inflow on capital account too. The biggest office for the promotion of investment in Britain was in New York and in 1986, when the Queen was to visit Philadephia for America's bi-centenary celebrations, she had suggested that the Consul General in New York might like to have *Britannia* for a day. He, in turn, asked whether the Permanent Secretary at the Department of Industry, Peter Carey, and I would like to co-host a day aboard the Royal Yacht *Britannia* for the heads of the major American corporations. I was a bit doubtful, but was told that there had been a small trial run in Mexico which had gone well. So I agreed and on 8 July found myself leaning over the rail of *Britannia*, watching the black stretch-limousines swaying along the uneven road through the New Jersey naval base and down to the quay.

Gordon Booth, our Consul General, told me that everyone asked had come, flying in private jets from all over the States. The speakers were Paul Volker and Mike Blumenthal from the

American side, and David Orr, Chairman of Unilever, from our side. Peter Carey told me that, though he was co-host, he was an anonymous civil servant and I had to chair the formal session.

We were escorted by a British frigate and a US coastal protection vessel. After we had left the Manhattan skyline and were through the narrows and beyond the Verrazano Bridge we went downstairs. Facing the powerful and loquacious Walt Wriston, Chairman of Citibank, in the front row, I said that all of them were sufficiently distinguished to be entitled to speak for twenty minutes each and I had to rely on each of them to keep their interventions short, which happily they did. With the pound in free fall and soaring inflation it was not the best time to sell Britain and, at this distance of time, I can't remember what we said or how it was received; but none of our European rivals for American investment could have cooped up so many of America's capitalists for so long.

At lunch my immediate neighbour, a quiet New York lawyer called Vance, supported Jimmy Carter for the 1976 Presidential election, while everyone else supported the Republicans. Gordon Booth said he had invited the lawyer because they thought he would be the next Secretary of State. His diplomatic skill was spot on; Cyrus Vance did indeed become Jimmy Carter's Secretary of State.

After lunch we had a tour of *Britannia*, where the engine rooms were kept so clean that a lady could not soil her dress. There were three bridges, one for the Captain, one for the Admiral, and the third, if he wanted to look forward, for the other naval person, Prince Philip. As we got near New York we met a spectacular procession of 'tall ships', the great sailing ships which had been visiting New York for the bi-centennial. After the last guest had gone down the gangplank, David Orr and I climbed into our car, tired and happy, and headed across the Verrazano Bridge for Kennedy airport and home.

In 1977, after six years, I left the chair of the UCCF Council, having not only helped to change the constitution and name, but having also presided over the transfer of the office from London to Leicester. At a time when the permissive society was fastening an ever-increasing grip on Britain and all the social statistics were sliding fast in the wrong direction, the steady growth of the Christian Unions in universities and colleges was an enormous source of encouragement to an embattled Church. I was glad to have been a part of it.

In 1977 I was elected annual President of the Fellowship of Independent Evangelical Churches (FIEC), to which Westminster Chapel, where I was a deacon, was affiliated. As the Free Churches became more liberal in theology and declined in numbers, so the theologically conservative FIEC increased in size and, at that time, numbered about four hundred churches.

The President chaired the half-yearly Council, spoke at the opening and closing annual assemblies and, on a Saturday morning and evening, at about a dozen regional meetings during the year. The first meeting was in mid-Suffolk and the singing was led by two brass bands – shades of a Salvation Army foundation. With the deteriorating moral order, I spoke in the morning on the relevance of the ten commandments (later published as *First Things First*). Since I was a deacon and the usual ministerial Presidents did not like to talk about money, I spoke in the evenings on the Christian's duty to tithe our gross incomes and to make sure that ministers were paid the 'double honour' as instructed by the Apostle Paul. Shaking hands after the morning service, I got the usual thanks; but in the evening the congregation could not pass by fast enough. However I had the impression that cases of poorly paid ministers were a lot fewer after that.

I was also the statutory Evangelical on the Council of St George's House, Windsor, which was reported to be Prince Philip's idea of finding the Dean and many Canons of Windsor something more to do than attend to the needs of the Royal Family. It was to be a meeting place between the Church and the leaders of modern society. Under the inspiration of Robin Woods, the founding Dean who roped me in, it became just that.

The Council itself was an oddly composed body, six or so aged Knights of the Garter, Prince Philip, and an assorted body of the good and the great, from the Secretary of the cabinet, to the statutory trades unionist, a woman Methodist, Hugh Parker, the Chairman of McKinsey and one or two backbenchers. The only time I remember it expressing strong views was when a very liberal Canon suggested that we celebrate the 500th anniversary of St George's Chapel with a multi-faith service.

I was and am strongly in favour of religious toleration. In the open market of ideas, Christians have nothing to fear. If we want toleration for Christians in countries like Egypt and India, we must give Muslims, Hindus and Buddhists equal rights here. Yet pantheism was a breach of the first commandment. I hesitated to argue theology in that company. Instead, I said that the tradition of St George's was about the application of Christianity to the life of the country, and that we were inexperienced in other faiths. We should celebrate our traditional activity and not matters of which we had no experience. I held my breath and then an old KG said that was quite right, we had no business getting into things we knew nothing about. Prince Philip came in breezily to say that it was the business of the Church of England to reform itself and not to tell other people what to do and then, as the bandwaggon rolled, I was rather sorry for the Canon; but not long after, he was made a bishop.

I got out of touch with St George's House when I became an MEP, but persuaded them in the early eighties, when cruise missiles were being deployed in Britain, to have a weekend consultation on the ethics of nuclear weapons. As usual, they had an excellent mix. There was Field Marshal Lord Carver, the thinking man's soldier, recently retired as Chief of the General Staff, and two other senior soldiers, three admirals, three air marshals and the man at the 'holocaust desk' of the Ministry of Defence. The Church was represented by, among others, the Bishop of London, a Professor of Systematic Theology and a Catholic bishop; the CND by Mary Kaldor and a silent student, and politics by a couple of MPs.

Surprisingly, the Church and the armed forces agreed. The Church was against nuclear weapons beause they could not be used without mass destruction of innocent life, and Jewish and Christian teaching was specifically and repeatedly against the taking of 'innocent blood'. The armed forces agreed, because it was not war; it was mass slaughter. The navy would prefer another flotilla, the army another tank regiment, the air force another squadron. The Catholic bishop wondered whether it would be all right to threaten nuclear weapons, while not intending to use them, but the suggestion fell flat.

Business ethics, a speciality of St George's House, were very much on the agenda of exporters. The sharp rise in oil prices had resulted in a great expansion of construction and other projects by the oil producers, and also a big increase in demands on the companies of the industrial West for bribes – known in the corporate jargon as 'extra-contractual payments'.

Western governments professed to know nothing about bribery and companies would not talk about it. But, with the responsibiity for promoting exports to markets, a third of which were subject to demands for bribes, it seemed to me to be wrong to say nothing. So, as the only person prepared to talk, I became the country's acknowleged instant expert on bribery and corruption. One day, on which there was an allegation (later proved to be false) that British Leyland had paid bribes, I did four interviews on TV, four on radio and four for the national press.

My advice was that professional managers had only one reputation and they must not allow it to be destroyed. Those who pressed them to give bribes would walk away from them as soon as it was found out and they would bear the whole blame. At a dinner given by Gordon Booth in New York I had sat next to the Chairman of a famous electronic company, who told me, 'I don't care how many orders I lose, I am not going to to lose my reputation by being hauled before a Congressional Committee for bribery.'

The head of Lockheed had to resign and went to live in obscurity at the other end of the country. I once saw Reggie Maudling, who had got too near to the Poulson scandal, standing all alone at one of Edwin Plowden's big receptions, no one prepared to talk to him. Prince Bernhard of the Netherlands was in disgrace and the famous Bilderberg Conferences which he chaired had come to an end. It might be the custom of some countries to give bribes, but it was always against the law and the contract gained would only last until the next *coup d'état*. Then the incoming regime would indict not only those they had thrown out, but the companies that had bribed them.

To strengthen the hands of managers, I also argued that in

terms of world trade the countries where bribery was a problem were in a minority, and that there was enough business for any company in the much bigger markets where ethical standards still held. And, at national level, it was in Britain's interests to switch our export efforts to the European markets from those markets where technical standards as well as moral standards were low.

For the three years following the oil price rise I also spoke on the subject at the Davos Management Symposium and once, on the way back from Davos, I visited one of the big three Swiss banks and remonstrated with them on the ease with which their restrictive laws against disclosure enabled the huge bribes to be concealed.

The British Goodyear Tyre Company received an instruction from the Akron head office, issued to all their managers world-wide, that no extra-contractual payments were to be made by anyone to anyone at any time under any circumstance whatever. Laing's made a similar decision and we got no more contracts in the oil-producing states, but the company and its reputation survived without them.

Some companies who had not been so careful discovered that their own staff were being offered bribes by sub-contractors and found that there is no watertight door which prevents the process from seeping back to corrupt the company which gives the bribes. That is the ultimate danger. Industry and commerce in the industrial democracies are based on trust, and if we could no longer rely on the professional integrity of those who design and build our aircraft, on the exact specifications of our chemical and pharmaceutical plants, on the safety standards of our bridges and buildings, on those who trade billions every day in banks and merchant houses, then our heavily interdependent industrial society would collapse. We have only to look at the poverty of the countries where bribery is endemic and no one trusts anyone outside their own extended family.

Every summer from 1974 to 1986, with only two exceptions, Elizabeth and I were at Schloss Mittersill in the heart of the Austrian Alps, first as house parents to the International Fellowship of Evangelical Students' (IFES) conference and, for the last four years, as leaders of their graduates' conference.

Back in 1966 when Stacey Woods, the IFES General Secretary, proposed to accept the castle as a gift, I had, as a member of the Finance Committee, opposed it. It would cost $100,000 to put right and would need an annual subsidy; it was over two hours' drive from Munich airport and we did not have the reserves if anything went wrong. Stacey was not put off; he passed photographs round the Finance Committee and it looked most romantic and stood in a truly beautiful setting; he persuaded two colleagues to go to look at it and they came back hooked; he raised $250,000 from the German American donor, John Bolten, to convert it from a country club to a conference centre, and he persuaded the IFES fund-raising trust in the USA to accept ownership and responsibility.

The bible talks of the Church of God from 'every people, tribe, nation and language'; this was the reality. Every year 120 students came from about 25 different countries. It was an enormous inspiration to find those from such completely different racial and cultural backgrounds with so much in common.

Stacey's vision to have the conference centre in Austria made sense. Austria was a neutral country and students from the surrounding Communist countries of Central Europe, Yugoslavia, Hungary, Czechoslovakia and Poland, allowed their students to travel there for holidays so long as they had a bare minimum of Austrian Schillings and the address of an Austrian citizen who would take them. Stacey's strategic aim was to build Christian student movements in those countries and, on our first visit in 1969, there were lots of Czech students, many of whom afterwards became pastors in the churches. In 1971, the IFES held its general assembly there; John Bolten was a guest and Dr Lloyd-Jones gave the main addresses. By then Stacey's castle had hooked us too.

The Japanese movement always tried to send one student, even though it was a long way. A lot of Arab Christians came and in midsummer it was hard to persuade them to take strong shoes and heavy clothes for treks above the snowline. Two very tall boys came one year from the Dinka tribe in southern Sudan and wanted to know whether a Christian had the right to rebel. That was also the pressing topic for South Americans, where even the Catholic Church was preaching 'liberation theology'.

146

From 1975 for a few years, an extrovert staff worker for the IVCF (USA), Beckey Manley, brought a group of rumbustious American students as part of a European tour and we learned how to distinguish 'preppy' students from the rest. One year we had one from each of the four racial groups in South Africa and the coloured boy could not believe that he was allowed to bathe in the same pool as the white students. The Spaniards were far the most musical, breaking into body rhythm as soon as the music started.

In 1974, Noor van Haaften, who started the IFES work in Austria with a book table in Vienna University, came with a group of very fine Austrian students. They had all been baptised formally into the Catholic Church, but they had all only just found a personal faith and were full of questions. If you gave too easy an answer, they were soon back, wanting to probe deeper.

In the early eighties, the great argument was on the women's movement. The Scandinavians and Californians were on one side and the Asian students on the other, with those from Catholic countries somewhere in between. The African men did not know how there could be a problem about women's place. Each side pointed out that the other side's views were culturally conditioned until, at last, after enough of the cultural conditioning had been admitted and peeled off, they were all able to examine Christian teaching with a more open mind. If for nothing else, that process recognising our cultural prejudice made these conferences worth while.

There were other East/West shocks. The students with the big back-packs could not understand why those from the Communist and Afro-Asian countries could do with so little and those who had nothing much more than a t-shirt wondered why the rich students wanted so much.

I served as Treasurer of the IFES from 1979 to 1983 and was more than happy to raise funds for this unique movement. It encouraged evangelism within cultures; no government could prevent students from talking to each other, no church could have the same access to universities. Even under Communism, we were able to show students how to build up their movements in central Europe. In 1994 Elizabeth and I attended the European students' conference in Warsaw, where hundreds came from each country in central Europe and hundreds more, mainly new converts, from the countries of the former Soviet Union.

The summers at Mittersill helped to keep our growing family together. Christopher, Bethan and Jonathan came every year and made friends from all round the world. We never seemed to have a communication barrier between generations in our family. On the contrary, communication went on all the time; even when Elizabeth and I retired to bed, the family tended to follow us, the TV being over, and the talk went on and on. But we did make the effort also to be with them and not only on holiday. I made it a rule not to be away on a trip abroad over a weekend except on the rarest occasions. I also made it a rule to be home every night, even if it meant a late-night drive or a late-night plane – there used to be a quiet turbo-prop Vanguard which left Glasgow at 11 p.m., so that you could attend a dinner there and still get home that night. On Sundays at Westminster, a core of the church used to stay all day, bringing their own lunch and using the church ovens, going to the classes at three and then having tea together. There was a swarm of children and they entertained each other.

After the export conferences there was more time to travel further afield. The rapid expansion of the Japanese market from a protected home base was causing a lot of worry; so I travelled to Tokyo. But before I was able to get to grips with it all, our Ambassador, Michael Wilford, told me, with some doubt in his voice, that there was a Japanese girl who kept on ringing and who insisted on speaking to me. It was Kyoto, who had just been at Mittersill. Her mother was a Christian and her father was not. If I came to their church in Yokohama on Sunday, they might persuade her father to come to meet me.

On Sunday morning I found the embassy Rolls at the door and was told that it was most inconvenient to change it now for a less conspicuous car. So we set off in air-conditioned luxury for a rendezvous with the pastor's car, an old station-waggon filled to the brim with children, which we followed down roads that became narrower and narrower, until we had to stop and walk.

We sat in a room above a shop, shoeless and cross-legged, singing Brethren hymns in Japanese, but to the old familiar childhood tunes. Afterwards we walked to a restaurant where we again sat cross-legged and I tried to cope with chop-sticks while everyone laughed and took photos of me looking foolish. I met Kyoto's mother, but her father had not come. After lunch, the church walked back with me to the Rolls and waved goodbye.

The Honda plant which I visited had only 1,500 employees and was manned mainly by men in their twenties who ran from job to job. Most of the work was done by robots and the stock of parts was in the suppliers' trucks lined up outside the plant. At Sony I was taken round by the legendary founder, Aiko Morita, dressed, like the rest of his staff, in blue overalls. He had high standards for components and showed me British components which were not up to standard. At the end of all the high technology of the production line was a man hitting TV sets with a mallet – 'If the picture moves at the blow, the set is sent back.'

Michael Wilford gave a dinner for the chairmen of the big companies which owned the banks, the distributors and the manufacturers through a dense network of cross-holdings that made it almost impossible for any foreigner to find local finance or distribution for mass-production products. The biggest Tokyo department store sold very high-cost British consumer products right at the top of the range and the Tokyo mafia were said to be partial to second-hand Rolls-Royces. But in all mass-production products, the Japanese exporters could keep out foreign competition, and cover their development costs and overheads on a secure 100 per cent Japanese share of the home market.

I went on to Seoul where the Chairman of Hyundai gave a great lunch accompanied by a palm court orchestra, and later sent flowers round to the Residence, followed by a massive oil painting (which we decided had better be kept there – upstairs in case he saw it again). I asked why the remarkable treatment and was told that our Export Credit Guarantee had helped him finance the building of the shipyard; one of the British yards had taught him how to build ships and he was now taking away our customers; a senior manager from British Leyland was helping him into the car business, so he was very grateful to the British and wanted to show it.

At the end of 1977 I visited Houston, where the Mayor had just been to Europe, seen some wonderful old buildings and wanted some like that for Houston. In Atlanta I was told of a fighter plane which was 'British electronics wrapped round with Boeing aluminum'. In Greenville, South Carolina, time seem to have stood still, but they imported British textile machinery. Back through Washington, the Jays put me up, Peter, in the corner of the huge sitting room, tapping his own typewriter as I came in. I saw a junior official in the State Department, who talked of the 'special relationship'. I asked why they kept their market open to the Japanese without any reciprocation, and he said that the Japanese were their key allies in East Asia and they did not want to offend them.

In early 1978 Elizabeth came with me for the longest journey of all: Bangkok, Singapore, Auckland, Wellington, Sydney, Canberra, Melbourne, San Francisco, Los Angeles and the ten-hour flight back home.

In Singapore I was due to speak to the Christian graduates and to a Christian business and professional lunch, so the High Commissioner invited the Bishop to the first night's dinner. He had been a liberal, but, after a dramatic spiritual experience, had become an Evangelical Charismatic and was at the centre of a wide movement of conversion to Christianity which had swept Singapore. We went to the early service in the cathedral on Sunday and it was packed.

We flew out of the hothouse of Singapore to the very refreshing breezes of New Zealand, met old friends in the Laidlaw family and made a pilgrimage to the headquarters of the Farmers' Trading Company in Auckland. I also met the Prime Minister, Muldoon, but it was more of a courtesy call, as there was no longer much business for Britain there.

I was also billed for a brief courtesy call on the Australian Prime Minister, Malcolm Fraser, which was neither brief nor (to begin with) courteous. He was a cattle farmer and took the restrictions of Europe's CAP personally. I got the full blast of his bitterness from this powerful personality; but I decided that it was best to give as good as I got and said that if he treated all his friends as if they were his opponents, there would be no one left to put Australia's case.

While I was in full swing, I also questioned whether Australia's restrictions on inward investment were in their own interests.

150

There was tremendous rivalry between the countries which all wanted to build their own competitive industrial base and which all fought to attract the capital, skill and international market access of the multi-nationals. If Australia could live for ever on exports of commodities, that was fine, but if not, they shouldn't insist on prohibitive levels of local participation in inward investment.

Our next call was to the Minister of Trade, but we were told that he had just been summoned to a meeting with the Prime Minister, as were all the other ministers we wanted to meet. Next day I was listening to his speech to the Melbourne Institute of Directors, when Malcolm Fraser announced a committee to review the laws on inward investment. I saw him three months later in London and thanked him. He said that the committee was just about to report and I would be very pleased with the result.

In Los Angeles, we went on Sunday to a church in Orange County, built up from a work among the beach hippies and drug addicts by Chuck Smith, who said that he owed a lot of his inspiration to Dr Lloyd-Jones's books. They now had three Sunday morning services with about three thousand at each.

At the Consul General's dinner the following night we met the husband and wife who owned the splendid new shopping mall we had visited in the morning, and who were major landowners in Orange County. I told them of Chuck Smith's huge church and the Consul General's wife made a few cynical remarks about American sects. But they wouldn't have a word said against Chuck Smith. He had rescued their son from drugs; he did a great work among the young people; the new church building was on their land and, had they realised who was building it, they would have given the ground free.

We had a day in San Francisco, visited some high-tech companies, had dinner back in LA with Peter and Doris Drucker and flew back to London in a plane with the film star John Travolta, star of the newly-released *Saturday Night Fever*, in the front and a party of schoolgirls in the back, who were taking it in turns to peep at him through the curtains.

My last long trip was to Buenos Aires. The British Ambassador had been recalled and there was not even a Chargé. But it was thought that there should be some contact and since I was clearly not a political figure, too much would not be read into the visit.

I visited the Economics Minister, Martinez de Hoz, a very cultivated man from an old Argentinian family. By strict monetarist measures he had got the rate of inflation down to two figures and hoped that in another year, he would have conquered it. 'The trouble,' he said with a smile, 'is that people think it more likely that in a year I will no longer be Minister.' Nor was he.

I went to the Casa Rosada to see the military dictator, President Videla. He spent a good ten minutes in telling me that he did not want to be a dictator and I certainly had the impression that he was more of a front man for the army than the moving spirit. Then we got on to Anglo-Argentine relations and agreed that two countries with such longstanding relations should not let 'the islands' come between us. I think he really meant that; but he was shortly afterwards replaced by President Viola, who did not last long before he was replaced by President Galtieri.

I had spent the sixties in urging the cut-back of all our expensive and far-flung colonial commitments and in arguing that the cost of fulfilling our military commitments would be out of all proportion to any benefit. Once Galtieri attacked the Falklands, we were committed to defend them, but it was a great pity that the House of Commons turned down the constitutional proposals put to it shortly before the Falklands war.

Jim Callaghan was expected to hold an election in September 1978 but decided to hang on through the winter. The incomes policy unravelled in the 'winter of discontent'. The country was worried by the apparent power of the extremists in the Labour Party. The mood swung towards the Tories. The rise in exports had been backed up by a rise in investment in plant and machinery, which, given a stable currency, would have sustained a continuing rise in exports. And that same year, Roy Jenkins, now President of the European Commission, persuaded Helmut Schmidt, German Chancellor, and Valéry Giscard d'Estaing, French President, to end five years of severe currency fluctuation by introducing the European Monetary System. That would have restored a stable currency to Britain, as it did to the eight other countries in the EEC. But Denis Healey foolishly refused to link the pound.

In July 1977 Michael Alison MP had arranged for me to see Mrs Thatcher and she gave me about forty-five minutes in her room in the Commons. I said that that I had been looking at the economic results of North Sea oil and that when she found herself in government, she would, unbelievable as it was then, have to decide what to do about a hard pound.

Exports, I told her, were currently doing very well, but, to achieve our potential share of the EEC market, industry still needed a major increase in investment to bring our plant and products up to their level. If the oil revenue forced the pound up, then it would squeeze industry's cashflow and make it very hard to get on level terms with our competitors.

I said that the hard pound would, of course, reduce the costs of imports and keep down retail prices, offsetting wage increases. So it would avoid any need to be beholden to the unions for incomes restraint and so, politically, it would be easier just to let the pound rise. But that would cripple British industry just when it needed the cash to build on its gains.

She listened patiently, but was very non-committal. When the time came, she followed the easy path of allowing the pound to rise and had no problem with the unions; those in work gained for the while, but unemployment rose to over three million; we lost nearly a quarter of British manufacturing industry, and fifteen years later, after consuming all the oil revenue and after spending all the reserves, we have been left with a huge external deficit and have to borrow billions a month to keep going (see Appendix). It is almost certainly the reason why, as the money began to run out in 1988, she turned from the rhetoric of success to the rhetoric of nationalism. Fortunately we in the BOTB could not foresee this arbitrary destruction of all our efforts.

I saw the effect on one company, Goodyear Tyres. As the pound rose against the Deutschmark, we lost our Continental markets and tyre imports rose. The company's profits plunged. We closed our Craigavon and Clydeside plants. Our main British competitor, Dunlop, went out of business, the residue sold off to the Japanese. Our huge plant at Wolverhampton was in doubt, so I went over to see the main Goodyear board. The corporate jet picked us up at Kennedy and after a wash at Akron, we went into a board dinner. The Chairman, Chuck Pilliod, steered me over towards the Finance Director, saying, 'There's your problem.' I said that the hard pound was entirely due to oil and as oil production came down, so would the pound. The board next day agreed to give us $35m and Goodyear UK survived; but it was less because of my eloquence than because Chuck Pilliod and Ib Thomsen, his International Director, had both managed the Wolverhampton plant and didn't want to see it go. On such threads did the survival of British industry now hang.

It was argued that the high pound weeded out the less efficient part of British industry and left it 'leaner and fitter'. We had discussed the effect of a rising pound at the BOTB. Arthur Knight, Chairman of Courtaulds, said that they were trying to move up-market as fast as they could; but the money for the new plant to make this change needed the continuing cashflow of the old low-tech part of the business. Wipe that out with a sudden rise in the pound and the financing of the move up-market fails.

But the strongest argument against was the abandonment of a policy of full employment. A forecast of one and a half million unemployed made black headlines in the mid-seventies. The hard pound put it well over three million (see Appendix); higher than in the great slump of the early thirties. There were no beneficial side-effects. The huge cost of this unemployment benefit raised public expenditure and it had no effect at all in moderating wage awards to those in work. The gap between those out of work and those in the rest of society got wider.

Chapter Ten

REMOVING EUROPE'S FRONTIERS

Jim Callaghan's government was not so doctrinaire as Harold Wilson's, but the marginal rate of income tax was still 98 per cent and very discouraging to export industry. I visited a most successful export company in Consett, employing two hundred, and asked the owner why he did not try to double his business. He said that he would then have to take on two hundred new people whom he did not know, with all the trouble that would bring, and in any case the government was not anxious for him to expand. If the expansion failed, he would lose his money, if it were successful, he would get only 2 per cent of the profit and, if he ploughed the money back into the business, the new capital transfer tax would take it away. He had got the message: the government did not want the British businessman to take any risks.

I put the argument to Denis Healey at a small dinner at No 11 Downing Street. He was a politician of strong common sense and high intelligence, and certainly saw the damage done by high marginal taxes, not only to exporters, but also to managers and skilled workers, and the way in which it was beginning to create an unofficial 'grey economy'. But he seemed to be at the mercy of the dominant left wing of the party and his answer was, 'That's socialism.'

I think that that was the point at which I decided that I had spent too long in advising governments and that if I really wanted to get things done, there was no substitute for the democratic process.

There was another even stronger reason for moving into active politics. The Wilson government, pushed by Tony Benn and the anti-Europeans in the Labour Party, had put the issue of our membership of the European Community to a referendum in 1975 and Britain had voted two to one for staying in. Now, only three years later, the very people in the Labour Party who had argued that we needed a referendum to settle the issue were advocating that we pull out. The referendum had settled nothing.

British industry now seemed to be set, for the first time, for the steady export-led growth which had been the dream of policy-makers for so long. If Labour won the election, that growth would be strangled at birth and there would be no second chance.

I talked to two Conservative MPs: Michael Alison, who was a very old friend, and Peter Mills. I said that I had doubts about some Tory policies. Peter Mills told me not to worry; every MP had doubts about some policies. He said, 'You only need to be 70 per cent Tory; no one can ask better than that.' I was greatly reassured!

I was due to speak at the Cambridgeshire Junior Chamber of Commerce in September 1978 and I decided to announce then that, after my long years in public service, I had rejoined the Conservative Party. Our elder son Christopher, who had started off in the Labour Party at Oxford and had been a junior research assistant for Tony Crosland, had also been getting restive about the leftward drift of the party. He had been told that there was now no future in the party for someone from Westminster and Oxford. I had urged him in a fatherly way that life was long, parties changed and he should not make up his mind too quickly. But when I decided to rejoin the Tory Party, I could hardly urge caution any more.

So I made the announcement for both of us and most of the nationals carried the story. The *Telegraph* even turned up to take a photograph of both of us outside our home and put it on the front page. I took all this as a matter of course and had no idea how rare it was for the average politician to get that kind of publicity.

Elizabeth and I went to the party conference at Brighton and Francis and Valerie Pym gave us a most agreeable lunch at the Grand Hotel with Geoffrey Howe and Nicholas Edwards and his wife. Geoffrey Howe had been brought up in Port Talbot at the same time as Elizabeth, when his father was Town Clerk and Elizabeth's was a minister of the Presbyterian Church of Wales, so they picked up where they had left off. We began our political life to a rosy glow.

About that time, I realised that my second term as Chairman of the BOTB came to an end a month before the first elections for the European Parliament. These elections, unlike the General Election, would be centred on Europe, and would be the country's definitive answer to the Labour Party's policy of leaving the Community. So I asked Francis Pym and Harold Watkinson, a former Chairman of the BIM, if they would sponsor me for the Conservative list, which they kindly did.

I was called for an interview at Central Office. I assured them that I had never been a member of any other party and, when I was asked whether, with my background in industry and public service, I would know how to get on with ordinary party workers, I said that I was a deacon at Westminster Chapel, just a mile away, and that a great many of the folk who dropped in there would be a bit out of place in a respectable Conservative wine and cheese party. That answer seemed to satisfy them.

Getting a seat seemed to be more chancy. There had been some totally misleading publicity about the kind of salaries which would be paid to MEPs and, as I recollect, there were thousands of applications for 78 seats, only half of which might be winnable. Central Office winnowed them down, but I think there were still 500 on the list. I had been in public service since the early sixties and, with the pressures of business, not at all politically active before that. I would also be fifty-four at the election.

However, bold as brass, I wrote to the Chairman of Cambridge-shire's selection committee, Sir David Sells, a former Chairman of the National Union. I said that I would like to represent my own county and, though I realised I might not be offered anything, I didn't want to accept anything else if there was the slightest chance of Cambridgeshire.

He, in turn, realised that the constituency which selected first would have the pick of all the candidates and called his selection committee before Christmas – and before everyone else. I *was* summoned and found myself up against the brightest and best,

157

including Henry Plumb, who had assured me previously that he wanted a seat in the Midlands.

After two preliminary rounds, Henry, Amadee Turner QC and I were left in for the final in a packed school hall in Huntingdon. Henry had the farm vote, but there were others pointing out that only 6 per cent of the county's population were in farming and so 94 per cent were not. We could hear Amadee Turner keeping them rolling in the aisles and we thought he must get the vote. Elizabeth and I were last and, a very short time after we had left the hall, David Sells came back to say that I had an overall majority on the first ballot. Francis Pym said later that he had never in all his experience known anyone travel so fast from a state of political innocence to a safe seat. The selection committee told me how much I owed to Elizabeth.

Our first constituency engagement was in the Town Hall in Peterborough at the beginning of a great snowstorm. Afterwards we drove out on the city's ring roads in a 'whiteout' and when we got to Norman Cross the A1 was closed behind us. We took another two hours to get home. But we were lucky. All the other final selections took place in heavy snow. Who got the nomination depended on who could get through the snowdrifts.

Francis Pym gave a lunch for me in his flat in Westminster to meet the four other Conservative MPs in Cambridgeshire and to lay down some ground-rules for our relationship. I had not realised how much MPs are monarchs in their own constituencies and how alarming it could be for them to contemplate an MEP who had just the same right to go trampling about all over their patch, making speeches, sending out press releases, turning up at their AGMs. In the event MEPs had so much to do that we were only too happy to pass on all Westminster problems to our colleagues as fast as we could. In any case I found I had a most friendly and understanding group of Westminster colleagues and even at the times of high tension which were to come, nothing impaired our mutual trust and support.

Their election came first. I shared a constituency office with John Major, the candidate for Huntingdon, and his energetic and enthusiastic Scots agent, Andrew Thompson, was my first Euro-agent. He made sure that I got around to help all the six candidates, including Peter Fry in Northamptonshire.

I went to John Major's eve of poll rally. He was elected to follow David Renton. Brian Mawhinney, a fellow Ulster Scot, won Peterborough and Robert Rhodes-James, Francis Pym and, in East Northants, Peter Fry retained their seats. Clement Freud kept the Isle of Ely for the Liberals. Mrs Thatcher succeeded a dispirited Jim Callaghan.

The European election followed the General Election within a month. None of us had had time to get known in our huge Euro-constituencies and party workers found it hard to work up a new enthusiasm only a month later. Widespread Labour abstentions also depressed the turnout, but the issue of pro and anti Europe was quite clear and we won an overwhelming victory, with over 60 per cent of the vote and 60 out of the 78 seats, leaving Labour with only 17 and the Scottish National Party with 1.

This 'avalanche effect' of the British 'first past the post' electoral system produced a centre-right majority in the European Parliament. The centre-right parties had agreed that their candidate for the President of Parliament should be a Liberal and they chose Simone Veil. As French Minister of Health she had done a great deal for the women of France. But, when elected, she showed that she had little Parliamentary experience with which to face the turbulence of a new, directly elected, multi-national, multi-party Parliament.

Ian Paisley gave her her first point of order; why had the British national flag, flying outside, been hung upside down? Far more difficult was the Italian radical, Marco Pannella, who wanted to protect the rights of the smaller groups against the dominance of centre-right or centre-left coalitions. Every resolution before the Parliament was flooded with hundreds of Pannella amendments. I asked our leader, Jim Scott-Hopkins, why the European Parliament's governing council, the 'Enlarged Bureau', was being so difficult. He said that it was because otherwise some poor committee chairman would have to cope with Pannella.

In the end the Enlarged Bureau had to give in, Marco Pannella was assigned to the Foreign Trade (REX) Committee, to which Jim, because of my trade experience, had nominated me as Chairman.

At the Committee's first working meeting in the grand atmosphere of the Palais d'Egmont in Brussels, Marco Pannella

159

made an impassioned plea that we should put world hunger on the agenda. Arms flailing and eloquence apparently unstoppable, he roused an angry little old Belgian Christian Democrat to shout at him and Pannella, his righteous indignation given an immediate target, shouted back. I felt that it was now or never and banged the gavel hard. I insisted that they both addressed the chair one at a time and said that Mr Pannella had made a valid proposal. The Bureau of the Committee would look at it and give an answer next morning. Suddenly there was silence. Ian Paisley, another member of the Committee, told me later, 'You handled that well.' I thought he should know.

My first Vice President was Heide Wiezoreck Zeul, a young red-headed German socialist, former leader of their Young Socialists and known, naturally, as 'Röte Heide'. She had apparently once told the German people on TV that no one needed more than 5,000 Deutschmarks a year to live on and they had never forgiven or forgotten.

But for some reason we got on well. She was always able to balance her strongly held convictions with a clear understanding of what was needed to get agreement and action. We both realised that, with little real power, we needed to carry the majority of the Parliament with us if we were to get anything done. So we always tried to get an agreement which would carry both right and left.

One of our first problems was the destruction of one European industry after another by the 'laser-beam' penetration of the Japanese. The share of Japan's production which went to export markets was no better than that of Britain, France or Germany. But they concentrated their effort on particular industries, which could not fight back by similar tactics in the Japanese home market because of the grip of the big Japanese holding companies over mass-market outlets and local finance.

By the end of the seventies, the Japanese had taken over much of Europe's shipbuilding, almost all the motor cycle industry and large sections of the electronic industry. They had already achieved a 10 per cent share of the motor industry and, if they took any more, the home market share of the European companies would be fatally weakened.

The REX Committee, and then Parliament, decided that this

was not free trade and the Commission, which supported us, believed that there was a clause in the General Agreement on Tariffs and Trade (GATT) that allowed us to impose countervailing restrictions on Japanese exports. The Council of Ministers supported this view and Roy Denman, the very able Director General of the European Commission's Overseas Trade Directorate, DG1, went to Tokyo to negotiate an amicable settlement. The result was the voluntary agreement by the Japanese to restrict their exports of cars to about 10 per cent of our market.

One ultimate result of this was the decision of some of the Japanese companies, starting with Honda, to invest inside the European Community. Britain, whose share of the European car market had fallen drastically, benefited greatly from this decision.

The early eighties were overshadowed by the malign results of the second explosion of oil prices. Huge cash surpluses were built up, especially by the Arab oil producers, and these were destablising the world's money markets. It seemed absurd that the European Community, which had formal trading relations with countries and groups of countries all over the world, should have none with the Gulf States. They had just formed the 'Gulf Co-operation Council' and, on our own initiative, the Committee started a report on relations with the Gulf States, with Heide as rapporteur.

Our first problem was the emergence of a hostile Israeli lobby in the Parliament, with the Israeli Ambassador urging all the many members with an interest in Israel to oppose it. This was before the Israeli invasion of Lebanon lost them so much support and, though I knew that the Israeli lobby was strong in America, I was surprised at its strength in Europe.

Finally I managed to see the Israeli Ambassador and explained that we had no hostile intent to Israel; it just seemed a good idea to have the same kind of relationships with the Gulf States as we had with South America or the states of South-East Asia. I said that if he was worried in future, would he please come to see me before getting his lobby so wound up. After that we had no trouble.

There were those who argued that the banks were quite capable of recycling the huge cash surpluses of the Arab oil producers.

Heide, of course, never had any faith in the banks, but, with my recollection of the boom and bust in the early seventies, neither did I. We argued that, to avoid a slump, the funds should be attracted to industrial investment in the first world economies, which were the motor of growth for the world trade on which all the developing economies depended.

Heide wanted to help the Gulf States industrialise by easing them into the chemical industry. I said that the centre-right would never agree to this and it was not essential to the report. She made a terrible face, which was her habit when put in a corner, and the negotiation went on until the day the report came to a vote in the full, 'plenary', session of Parliament. In the course of a sleepless night I thought of a compromise amendment and got this agreed at the last moment by everyone, including Heide.

It was one thing to get a report through and supported by Commission and Council; it was quite another to engage the Gulf States. The Commission wrote to the Secretary General of the Gulf Co-operation Council (GCC), but it seemed impossible to take things any further. Then I asked Klaus Schwab, Director of the Davos Management Symposium, if he could help. He arranged a lunch by the shores of Lake Geneva with the Director General of the GCC, who was also the Saudi Finance Minister. Heide and I explained the thoughts behind the proposal. He was intelligent, agreeable and charming and from then on things started to move.

Finally Klaus Schwab arranged a private lunch at the Belvedere Hotel in Davos during the week of the Management Symposium, when everyone would be there. The Director General and Secretary General of the GCC came, together with Willy Hafferkamp, the Commission's trade Vice President, and Stevie Davignon, the formidable industry Vice President, plus Heide and I. At the Davos lunch we found that the oil boom was over and the producer surpluses had disappeared.

So though we won the argument, it was too late to stop the folly of the banks. They matched their massive dollar liabilities for the Gulf States' deposits with investments in the third world. But, in the absence of growth in the industrial democracies, on which the third world depended for their exports, they could not pay the interest on the loans. This was the origin of the third world's terrible debt crisis, not to mention the severe liquidity crisis of Western banks, when they could not get their money back.

As a postscript, the Parliament formed its own delegation to the Gulf States and the President elected to lead it was Heide. Their first visit was to the Yemen. I wish I had been there to see Heide's confrontation with a male-dominated society!

Despite our very different backgrounds, the Committee worked well together. The leader of the Socialist Group was Hans Jochen Seeler from the great trading city of Hamburg. There was little difference between his views and mine. The real negotiation was between him and Heide. There were nine Italians and the Italian Communists were in the general consensus, while the French Communists were outside. The small number of Liberals were led by an old Dutch senator, who was well to the right on most issues. The most eloquent Christian Democrat was another from Hamburg, Eric Blumenfelt, who had his own view on everything, but who was unfailingly helpful.

I discovered that committees were entitled to meet once a year outside Brussels and proposed that, in 1980, we should meet in Cambridge. The University gave us the Senate House and we decided to concentrate on the Community's trade with the Commonwealth. The Commonwealth was represented by Australia, New Zealand and Malaysia, and I had long negotiations with 'Sonny' Ramphal, its Secretary General.

I thought that our discussions would make a real impact on the local press. But the reporters in the gallery were much more interested in the wonders of simultaneous translation, switching back and forwards between melodious Italian, guttural Dutch and staccato German. They also noted the exit of members during the more boring agenda items to see the sights of Cambridge and the return of Red Heide with her purchases in a Marks and Spencer's bag.

The unreformed Common Agricultural Policy was a challenge, especially to the British members. The farm lobby in the Parliament, which was very powerful and dominated the Agricultural Committee, insisted that that committee alone was competent to deal with the subject. But the REX Committee got authority to do a report on 'World Trade in Food Products'.

The head of the FAO, the world food organisation, came to give evidence on the report, for which I was rapporteur. He told us of the damage caused to third world producers by the huge export subsidies which the Community gave to get rid of our agricultural surpluses at prices which undercut all competition. The American farm subsidies also produced surpluses and, though they were not directly related to exports, they also drove down the world price. Third world producers of temperate products like grain could not compete in world markets with the cut-price European and American products, and were forced off the land into shanty towns around the capital cities where they had to be fed on imported grain bought with scarce hard currency.

The FAO estimated that the third world could feed itself if it could earn enough from hard currency exports to invest on a large scale in irrigation, fertiliser plants and transport. Aid would never be adequate; they needed the hard currency from exports.

I was greatly helped in this report by Dr Michael Schluter, an agricultural economist who had just come back from Kenya to live in Cambridge. With financial help from an American trust he produced the specialised economic input. The report proposed a mutual reduction of subsidies on both sides of the Atlantic, which would restore world prices to a higher open-market level, and the saving on subsidies could be used to compensate the farmers for lower income from the domestic market.

We were, of course, opposed by the farm lobby in Parliament which dominated the Christian Democrats, the Liberals and the French Socialists and Communists. They were offset in that first Parliament by a combination of the sixty-three-strong European Democratic Group (EDG) of British and Danish Conservatives, all the Socialists (except the French) and the Italian Communists. But that majority was not secure and, once the report had passed the REX Committee, I had to try to persuade the newly arrived Greeks that the subsidies were a benefit to the northern farm products and that if they went on unchecked, there would never be enough money left over for the needs of the poorer Mediterranean countries. I will never forget the moment of elation when the critical paragraphs were voted through.

Shortly afterwards the Danish Socialist President of the European Parliament's delegation to the United States Congress asked me to go with them to explain the Parliament's proposal for a mutual EEC/USA reduction of subsidies to the Americans. I explained the Parliament's proposal to Secretary for Commerce Baldridge, who thought it a splendid idea, then to Secretary for the Treasury Regan, who was beginning (1983) to run up an unhealthy deficit, and he, seeing the budget savings, wondered why no one had thought of it before. Even Secretary for Agriculture Block was in favour of it, so long as we didn't quote him to the farmers.

Then the Congress took us in buses into deepest Virginia to The Homestead, the most sumptuous hotel most of us had ever stayed in, which cost us twice our daily allowances. When the Congressmen from the farm states attacked the CAP and all its iniquities, I explained our proposal for a mutual reduction of subsidies. I said that the initiative ought to come from America whose farm lobby was far smaller than Europe's. We would never get the European governments to propose it, but if America took the initiative, we would in the end be forced to respond. It took them five years, but in 1988 they played back our proposals for a mutual reduction of subsidies. Then after another five years, Europe agreed too – but that cliff-hanger is another story!

Visits like this were special moments in a long continuous grind, flying in and out of Brussels every week and in all weathers, flying to Strasbourg once a month in the ancient and cramped Caravelles and, once there, endless flows of paper, long votes in the oppressive atmosphere of the Strasbourg chamber and a steadily mounting correspondence when we got home.

But at least in the REX Committee we felt that we were doing a worthwhile job. Those were the days of 'Euro-sclerosis' when there were no initiatives from the Commission and certainly none from the Council. It was we, the elected members, who were taking the initiative. If we got agreement in our Committee, helped by the '*Gutes Zusammenarbeit*' between Heide and myself, the Parliament followed; then Willy Hafferkamp would usually pick it up and get Commission agreement; on foreign trade, the Council normally agreed with the Commission. We were also greatly helped by Willy Hafferkamp's brilliant Director General, Roy Denman, who took the burden of most of the negotiations from his laid-back Commissioner. But what helped most of all was that the Community, which negotiated for the ten member states, was the most powerful trading block in the world.

Where, for most of my public life, I had found the British interest frustrated, now, suddenly, I found that the collective power of the Community could carry it.

There was no recognition of this back home. I once persuaded the Conservative back-bench Committee of Trade to ask Roy Denman to talk to them. But, at the appointed time, no one came to the meeting room. Finally a member dashed in apologetically to say that he was so sorry, but they were all in the Chamber questioning the Secretary of State for Trade. I saw John Nott shortly afterwards and said how odd it was, since it was not he, but Roy Denman, who negotiated foreign trade now. He said, 'You know it and I know it, but I'm certainly not going to tell that to the House of Commons.'

We had the same difficulty with the media. To those of us who had been accustomed in our previous jobs to get some national coverage, the result was as dramatic as the sudden slamming of a door. I wrote to George Howard, now the Chairman of the BBC, and he arranged for me to see all the BBC news and current affairs editors at one of their fortnightly meetings at Television Centre in Shepherd's Bush. My eloquence made not the slightest difference. Journalists' capital was tied up in their British contacts so that when anything arose in Brussels, the political journalists rang their contacts in the House of Commons and Whitehall, and their contact's answer was printed, whether they knew anything about it or not.

One odd consequence was that we did not have the usual critical public scrutiny of all we said and did. We were cocooned against all the slings and arrows of political life. And, for lack of material, there was no criticism in the constituency either and we were treated almost as non-partisan figures. This might make for a quiet life, but politicians should be accountable and the lack of public debate was unhealthy.

We also had the problem at home of the size of our constituencies: half a million voters, covering six or seven Westminster constituencies. I tried to spend a whole day in each Westminster constituency at least three times a year, visiting sixth forms, local industry, farmers, party meetings, local press and radio, and constituents who had written in with a specially knotty problem. Local radio was a great help, especially the opening of BBC Radio Cambridgeshire and, as successive assistants got more skilled in their press releases, it became natural for both local press and radio to ask for comment.

Because the constituency was so big, I decided to keep an office in Cambridge, to which there was easy access for constituents, rather than in Brussels. I was also greatly helped when Emily Blatch, who was then leader in the County Council, offered me, with the agreement of the other two parties, an office in the Shire Hall. This made my assistant part of the Shire Hall staff, with access to all their knowledge and skills and they to hers.

I also had a series of excellent assistants, who were both sympathetic on the phone and very skilled in dealing with all the problems. Rachel Barker went on to the Foreign Office – after a 'trawl' for five posts which brought over a thousand applicants – and she has done brilliantly. She married another diplomat and an enlightened Foreign Office has sent them abroad on postings together. Mary Mansfield, the most highly organised, left to be, appropriately, a management consultant, and Debbie Moss, whose gentle Scots accent concealed a sharp intelligence and quiet determination, went on to a job in the Commission's office in Budapest. Ann McLauchlan, who came after five years as a journalist in Central America, went on to do a Stage (apprenticeship) in the Commission.

While the British establishment treated Europe in general and MEPs in particular as an unfortunate necessity, to be ignored if possible and, if not, sent round to the tradesman's entrance, I was greatly encouraged and helped by successive constituency chairmen and officers. My first Chairman, David Sells, had been Chairman of the National Union and knew Peter Thorneycroft, then Party Chairman, and all the other party chiefs. Francis Pym, in the cabinet until after the 1983 election, was also sympathetic and accessible. David Sells was followed by two successive Chairmen, David Weigall and John Martin, both of whom were supportive, encouraging and extremely helpful. I couldn't have had better backing from them or from the Constituency Council. It was a secure base to which to return from the political roughhouse and a warm and friendly counter-balance to the mood at Westminster.

Westminster took its tone from the party leaders. Michael Foot, who took over from Jim Callaghan, was so anti-European that he split his party, and Roy Jenkins, David Owen, Shirley Williams and Bill Rodgers all left the Labour Party and formed the Social Democratic Party. In our own party Mrs Thatcher still paid lip service to Europe, but her real feelings were not concealed from those around her or from the press. The need to increase the Community budget to fund the Common Agricultural Policy gave her the lever she needed to adjust Britain's contribution to the budget. The need for unanimity to raise the budget limit gave her the big stick, so she could have spoken softly if she chose. That would also have been wiser and, since it would not have backed other governments into a corner, more effective. But it was her disastrous policy of letting the pound rise and rise which turned the European market from an opportunity for exports into a threat to jobs from the rising tide of cheaper imports. So public support evaporated.

The arrival of Mrs Thatcher in Downing Street coincided with the arrival of North Sea oil and, with it, came the invisible but powerful flow of oil revenue which enabled her to break all the iron disciplines that had governed the actions of her predecessors and which have, once more, had to guide her successor.

The oil revenue allowed the pound to rise, reducing the costs of imports and curbing inflation without any need – as I had forecast – to consult the unions or to mind what they thought about the sharp reduction in income tax and the equally sharp rise in VAT. The monetarist rhetoric said that interest rates could not be reduced to bring the pound down, because this would increase the money supply. Gradually, as control of money supply turned out to be no more than another failed instrument, the rhetoric subsided, but not before British industry had been irreparably weakened.

The Exchequer financed the tax reductions, and paid the huge bill for keeping three million jobless from taxes on oil revenue. The hard currency savings on oil imports kept our trade in balance, despite the loss of industrial exports and, most decisive politically, it was the oil revenue which allowed Mrs Thatcher to let consumption rise, with record increases in real (post-inflation) earnings from 1982 to 1988. There has never been such a pre-election pay-out as there was before the 1983 and 1987 elections and there never will be again.

She was, of course, greatly helped by her opponents, General Galtieri's Falklands folly and Arthur Scargill's coal strike, called without a ballot, despite government's strategic stockpile, and in the summer when demand for coal was low. Most important, the lurch to the left split the Labour Party.

She avoided like the plague the only policy which would have introduced any discipline: the fixing of the pound into the European Monetary System. Against the repeated requests of her Chancellor, Nigel Lawson, which were backed by his predecessor, Geoffrey Howe, she only conceded the point with the disappearance of both the oil surplus and the remaining reserves which it had earned, and with the arrival of huge internal and external deficits.

This malign policy, wrapped in free-market monetarist rhetoric, destroyed all I had worked for in fifteen years in public service. There was little that a newly elected member of the European Parliament could do about it; but what I could, I did.

Francis Pym was our local MP and the only cabinet member in the constituency, so I went to see him with David Sells. He was very sympathetic, a leader of the group known by Mrs Thatcher as 'the wets', but as Secretary for Defence, he was not on the economic policy committees. There were other 'wets', Jim Prior, Peter Walker, Christopher Soames and Ian Gilmour. She sent the most powerful, Jim Prior, to Northern Ireland, and sacked Christopher Soames and Ian Gilmour. She also sacked her weighty Party Chairman, Peter Thorneycroft. When she had won another election, she sacked Francis Pym and she sidelined Peter Walker. And, as we ran out of money and Geoffrey Howe and Nigel Lawson both pressed her to fix the pound, she sacked them too.

MEPs were allowed no political influence. All fraternisation between Conservative MPs and MEPs was heavily discouraged (with assistance at Westminster from an anti-European Labour Party). Unlike MPs' assistants, we were not allowed passes to the House of Commons. Where all our Continental colleagues had privileged access to their national parliaments, we had to queue up behind the tourists to go through the security check and, once in and without access to an internal phone, we had to queue again for the attention of the Sergeant at the desk. So, with plenty else to do and little time in London, most of us gave up.

From the beginning, I concentrated on the one economic discipline available, fixing the pound in the EMS. The European Democratic Group (EDG) approved the policy and Fred Warner, John Purvis and I put our case to the House of Lords Committee, chaired by Leslie O'Brien, the previous Governor of the Bank of England. They were a powerful group, including one other ex-Governor, one special adviser to the Bank, Douglas Croham (formerly Allen), an ex-Permanent Secretary of the Treasury, and others as knowledgeable and as sharp in cross-questions. They gave us a hard time, but when they reported, they supported our case. They were followed by the *Financial Times* and almost all informed opinion, including Nigel Lawson, when he came back to the Treasury as Chancellor. But Mrs Thatcher was adamant, holding grimly to her opinion, even when in a minority of one in cabinet committee, until all the damage was done and we were left with a gravely weakened manufacturing industry and a huge trading deficit.

Other European countries were also affected, though not so dramatically, by recession following the shock price increases by the oil producers. Though the other Community countries had to pay more for their imported oil, they had the new currency stability given by the EMS and, in most cases, a far stronger industrial base from their longer membership of the Community. But unemployment was rising everywhere.

So I began to think of what we could do to get the European economy moving. In January 1983 Piet Dankert was elected President of the Parliament in succession to Simone Veil. He was a young Dutch Socialist and open, I thought, to a new initiative. I joined him in our small self-service restaurant in Brussels and asked him if he would back a group of the Chairmen of the Parliament's economic committees in getting together some economists to propose a programme for economic recovery. He asked me to come to see him formally and when I did, he agreed.

I asked the Chairmen of the other four economic committees, Jacques Moreau (Socialist), Hannah Wurtz (Christian Democrat),

Michel Poniatowski (Liberal) and Pancrazio de Pasquale (Italian Communist), representing, conveniently, the five major political groups in the Parliament and the four largest countries. The Parliament's governing council authorised us to go ahead and I was appointed rapporteur.

We decided that we must all agree on the names of the economists. Michael Emerson, the Commission's chief economist, gave me a lot of names with his assessment of each of them; but we had great difficulty in finding names on which we could all agree.

Finally the Director General of Neddy suggested Jim Ball of the London Business School and he took it on, helped by Jim Drew, later head of the Commission's office in London.

At the same time the Chairman of the Economic and Monetary Committee, Jacques Moreau, proposed Michel Albert, formerly Chairman of the French Commissariat Général du Plan. I think Jaques Delors, Jacques Moreau's predecessor as Committee Chairman, and then French Finance Minister, had suggested Michel Albert, but I still had to go to Paris to persuade him. Finally he too accepted.

So we now had two names, one nominated by a Conservative and one by a Socialist. We also had a third, of high reputation, nominated by de Pasquale and so we agreed that we had a team. Then, catastrophe, we found that de Pasquale's nomination was a member of the Italian Parliament on the Communist list and Hannah Wurtz absolutely refused to have him. But he had already been asked, honour was at stake and de Pasquale insisted. Jacques Moreau said morosely, '*Il est bloqué.*' But I would not give up.

We finally agreed to appoint the Italian and also a former Managing Director of the IMF as advisers to the economic team. Honour was satisfied. I phoned Michel Poniatowski, our Liberal member, who had some time before suggested a French professor no one had heard of, and said we had a balanced team, so did he insist on his nomination? He said of course not and so we had agreement.

The Albert/Ball Report was a seminal document. Before it, governments knew no other way out of a recession than to borrow and spend on public works. Albert and Ball pointed out that if the Germans had failed just a few years before, no weaker economy could succeed. But they also pointed out that successive efforts at expansion based on government spending and borrowing had now put a totally unacceptable burden on the market sector and, even if we could act together, we faced a law of sharply diminishing returns.

Instead they supported the case made by industry, that the Common Market had ceased to be common. Each country was raising new trade barriers by changing national health and safety standards to suit domestic producers and to limit imports. They called this 'non-Europe' and spelt out the catastrophic costs. Their key proposal was to sweep away all remaining barriers to trade, an irrevocable removal of all barriers to set the fly-wheel of the Community's internal trade spinning once again.

Once or twice they arrived at an impasse. I would get a frantic phone call and would try to help. But they were a well-matched partnership. Jim Ball was a tall pipe-smoking English professor, quietly demolishing the pretentions of reflationary packages; Michel Albert, small, bespectacled and voluble, introduced the new ideas and gave them the winged words which made them carry.

They carried far and wide. The press conference in Strasbourg, chaired by Piet Dankert, was packed, with forty TV cameras all along the back wall – only one from Britain. The press coverage was formidable in every country – except Britain.

After a bit of manoeuvring, which gave them the Chairman and rapporteur respectively, the two big political groups swung behind the proposal that the Parliament should set up a large special committee. I sat on this, with the other founding Chairmen. We had hearings with Ball and Albert and a big hearing in Paris at which Jacques Delors gave evidence, together with representatives of the European employers and trades unions. The trades unions had, until then, thought that the best way to conquer unemployment was to limit hours and share jobs. The employers' President said, 'You do not get richer by working less.'

The Committee endorsed Ball and Albert and so did the Parliament, though the Socialists abstained because the Christian Democratic rapporteur would not put in something on a social dimension – an argument which was to recur. Then we fought the 1984 European election and the manifestos of all the major

172

parties supported the abolition of internal barriers and the creation of a completely open European market.

After the election I was at the annual colloquy between the Parliament's Enlarged Bureau and the Council of Ministers. Pierre Pfimlin, former French Prime Minister, long-time Mayor of Strasbourg and our new President, thought we should make the need to abolish all trade barriers our centrepiece and asked me to speak on it.

The Council, the Community's final legislative authority, is a curious body. It is supposed to consist of all the foreign ministers, but on that day I only counted two, the Irish Peter Barrie, who was presiding, and the Danish Ellerman Jensen. The rest were either junior ministers, like our own Malcolm Rifkind – who left early for a dinner in London – or ambassadors, listening politely but cynically to the latest political brainwave. Finally Peter Barrie, feeling no doubt that there should be some reaction, said with some slight surprise in his voice, 'That sounds like a remarkably good idea!'

The new Commission took it up with enthusiasm. The new President, Jacques Delors, put all our proposals into his first Commission programme in March 1985. I had to respond for the EDG and thanked him most warmly for accepting all the Parliament's proposals. He said that they were his own ideas; but he came to office with the political ground well laid and all political parties and governments by then ready to run with it.

The British government was especially enthusiastic and the new British Commissioner, Arthur Cockfield, was given the job of carrying it out with the target date of 1992.

Although all the barriers did not disappear until 1992, the process began at once. The signing of the Single European Act ended the years of 'Euro-sclerosis', trade improved and Britain, the pound once more competitive, benefited most. Our unemployment came down rapidly until, four years later, Europe ran into the buffers of Germany's high interest rates.

Chapter Eleven

BUILDING A DEMOCRATIC EUROPE

In the 1984 election the Labour Party were fighting an election for a European Community they did not believe in and they could not get their vote out. We dropped from the 'avalanche effect' of 60 seats in 1979 to a more normal 45. Labour went up from 17 to 32, which their leader Barbara Castle bravely claimed as a victory. But with 45 to Labour's 32 there was no doubt about the second defeat of the anti-Europeans and, before the next election, Labour was to change its mind. At the count I tried to console a gloomy Andrew Duff, who had just failed to beat Labour, a sign of the decline of the Liberal/SDP Alliance. And, with our voting system, the Liberals, once again, got no seats at all.

In the second Parliament I was made a full member of the delegation to the US Congress. Except for European election years, we met twice a year with our opposite numbers, January in Europe and June/July in the United States.

The first meeting was in June 1985 and, because of our complaints about the cost of our last meeting at The Homestead, we were taken instead to West Point Military Academy, where we sat on hard seats, but lived within our means.

We flew from Andrews Air Base in Washington to a nearby airfield, where we were met by the Superintendent of West Point. He was immensely proud of his famous institution. As he leant over the chapel's organ console, he said, 'This is the biggest organ in America; let 'em have it, organist!'

He told us of all the famous generals who had trained in West Point, including the Civil War generals on both sides; took us

174

up the Hudson in his launch; to an open-air concert with the great river as a backdrop; to a splendid reception in his lovely eighteenth-century house and to lunch with the cadets. We were told that there was a high rate of drop-out by first year students, and Elizabeth asked the senior cadet sitting next to her what the first year was like. He paused and said, 'Hell, ma'am.'

Meantime the main issue was President Reagan's proposed 'Star Wars' project, aimed to secure America against nuclear attack with a shield of anti-missile missiles. It was said to need fifteen years to perfect, which would, we thought, encourage the USSR to build enough missiles to swamp the system. The Democratic Congressmen clearly did not believe in it. The Senate gave us a lunch at which I put some of our doubts to Senator Lugar, who was our host. He gave the set answers, but was fiercly attacked by Senator Biden before managing to cut the discussion short. By the time we got to the Pentagon to talk to Secretary of Defence Weinberger, we were well briefed; but the unanswerable point was put simply by Didier Motchane, who looked everyone's image of a French Socialist intellectual, with a mop of unruly hair and thick glasses. He said, 'There is an intellectual fault in your Star Wars, Mr Weinberger.'

'Oh yes – and what's that?'

'You do not know whether it will work until you push the button and by then,' – a Gallic shrug – 'it is too late!'

After the 1984 election Henry Plumb asked me serve on the Budgets Committee. The Parliament and Council are the joint authorities controlling the Community's budget, and the work of the Budgets Committee is tough at the best of times. But these were the worst of times.

The American dollar, raised to giddy heights by President Reagan's high interest policy, now started to sink to a more normal level; but, since farm products were traded on world markets in dollars, their price on world markets started to fall too. The Community was committed to selling its surpluses on world markets at whatever cut price was necessary to shift them, so the subsidies started to rise steeply and the Community budget began to run out.

It could not go on and eventually there was a 'reform', which consisted of finding the extra money on the understanding that

that was an all-time limit. I hoped for better things when the British government took over the Presidency of the Council and at a meeting at No 10, I pressed the Prime Minister to put it on the agenda at the London meeting of heads of government, which she was to chair. I was even supported by the Party Chairman, Norman Tebbit. But nothing happened. Every president in office wants the summit in their own capital to go well.

Around this time Tom Spencer, who had lost his seat in Derbyshire at the 1984 election, suggested that we start a cross-party group for a real reform of the CAP. With the intolerable rise in the cost of the CAP and the lack of any reform which did not depend on mere promises to be good, the idea appealed especially to members of the Budgets Committee. So we set up a group, supported also by members of the trade and environment committees, and others with reforming interests. It was given the innocuous name of 'The Land Use and Food Policy Group', but was soon known by the rather ugly acronym of LUFPIG. Jean Pierre Cot, Chairman of the Budgets Committee, joined us. We had members from all the major parties and from most countries.

We met initially as a dining group, organised by Doosie Fodal, able assistant to Gijs de Vries, a brilliant young Dutch Liberal, and invited the Budgets and Agriculture Commissioners to dinner as well as a whole series of experts. And, at Jean Pierre's suggestion, Jacques Delors asked us to lunch at the Commission.

But it was clear that, in some way or other, we had to match the resources commanded by the Agriculture Committee, dominated by the farm lobby and straddling all access to Parliamentary funds. Through their seminars on Europe, Tom and Liz had some good connections with the British food industry, and several food companies promised to back us. The conservation lobby were on our side, so we also got support from the Worldwide Fund for Nature and from the Royal Society for the Protection of Birds, whose headquarters at Sandy were now in my slightly redrawn constituency. That gave us enough money to take on a part-time researcher and organiser. Doosie Fodal suggested another Brussels consultant, Jane Kelsey, whose boss agreed to let us have her part-time. Jane was young and enthusiastic and soon became the hub of the whole enterprise, able to keep our first sponsors in touch, to find new ones, to give us realistic briefs which enabled us to ask awkward questions, and to keep fresh ideas flowing.

In the second Parliament, I found myself with a job which was in the mainstream of British politics, but which had little to do with the European Parliament.

When Mrs Thatcher banished Jim Prior to Northern Ireland, he had set up an elected Constituent Assembly to propose its own constitution for the province. John Hume's SDLP did not take their seats, complaining that its remit was limited to an internal settlement and that there was no 'Irish dimension'. But the other three parties set to work, the Alliance Party making many of the points which the SDLP would have made.

By September 1985 Jim Prior had gone, as had his successor Douglas Hurd, and the Assembly had got bogged down. Martin Smyth of the Ulster Unionists asked me whether I would act as interlocutor. I consulted Ian Paisley, who thought I should accept. I told John Hume that I would not do it without his agreement and, after thinking long and hard, he said, 'If it saves one life it is worth it.'

So I found myself in the old Prime Minister's office in the south-west corner of the main floor of Stormont, seeing the parties one by one. It was one of the toughest ten days of my life; but the steering committee, sitting in the old Senate chamber, finally came to an agreement, which was passed by the Assembly with a very large majority.

In those ten days I learnt what could and could not be done about the province's future. The big breakthrough was the agreement by the Unionists on an Assembly in which the minority parties with a third of the votes would be able to block the majority. There would be no return to the old Stormont. The second point was that all three parties (except the SDLP who were not present) agreed on the need for an elected Assembly.

Although the government received the document sent from the Assembly as a basis for discussion, the SDLP's preference, an Anglo-Irish Agreement, was now too heavily negotiated for the British government to turn back. The Irish government had kept John Hume in close touch with the negotiations, but the

British government had decided to play it 'close to the chest' and the Unionist parties were not consulted. When, towards the end of the year, the Taoiseach and the Prime Minister signed the Anglo-Irish Agreement at Hillsborough, the Unionists were outraged and broke off all relations. They would not speak to any member of the government at Stormont, nor would they attend any function at which a minister was to be present. They said that democracy was the rule of the majority with, so far as possible, the consent of the minority and that in our unwritten constitution, that meant that the minority should be consulted on matters vital to their interests. It was unprecedented that a million citizens should not be consulted. Had it been a million Muslims, they would have been told what was proposed. And it was absolutely unprecedented to make a constitutional change without consultation.

I spent some part of the next four years in a shuttle between governments and parties – greatly helped by colleagues from both Northern Ireland and the Republic in the European Parliament – to try to get something back on track. The Irish government were worried about the Unionist hostility and recognised that, in an island of four and a half million, a million Unionists had to be accommodated. I was told, 'We'd sooner deal with them directly, for we think we understand them and we hope they understand us. But we have to deal dog-leg through the British government, which understands neither of us.' The Anglo-Irish Agreement allowed a Northern Ireland Assembly to take over the British end of the Agreement and that seemed to be the best final outcome. It gave the Unionists the Assembly they wanted and a relation with Dublin which did not concede sovereignty. The British government did not have to go back on the Agreement.

The following year I proposed this in private and in a public – and well-publicised – speech at Queen's University, Belfast, flanked by an armed policeman in a flak-jacket. I consulted everyone beforehand and there seemed to be a broad agreement, but, though there was consensus for twenty-four hours, there were those who wanted to provoke disagreement and others, who should have known better, who allowed themselves to be provoked.

At its heart, the problem of Northern Ireland is a problem of two beleaguered minorities, the Nationalist minority in the north and the Unionist minority in the island. To have peace, both need to be respected and both need to feel secure. After three and a half years, the Unionists started to talk to Peter Brooke, who managed to start 'talks about talks'. But these were not the unconditional talks which everyone had been promised. The internal settlement could not get too far without an external settlement; the Secretary of State could not chair the talks with the Irish government; some international figure had to be brought in whom everyone had heard of but who had never been involved before!

Unsurprisingly the Chairman who was found was no such paragon. Ireland is a very open society and I had blow by blow accounts of the talks, which finally ground to a halt. The Unionists stuck to their proposal for an Assembly. It could not produce a government, but it could work, like the European Parliament, through committees, with the committee chairs shared proportionately to the size of the parties. So far as the parties could agree, the British government would almost certainly act on the advice of the committees; where it could not, it would continue to make its own decision, knowing the considered views of all the parties.

The SDLP compete for the minority vote against Sinn Fein and the Alliance and are themselves an uneasy partnership of rural and Western with working-class Belfast. So they found it harder to agree on their own proposals, but their eventual objective appeared to be commissioners nominated by British and Irish governments. It seemed to me that, without the traditional and well-understood basis of elected and accountable politicians, this gave none of the well-tried and traditional democratic methods of dealing with all the disagreements inherent in the political process. Even an alliance with a Sinn Fein dedicated to peace would not overcome the inflexibility and remoteness of commissioners. But the greatest problem was that it would be impossible for Unionists to sell to their own supporters a deal done with an alliance of SDLP and Sinn Fein.

So, in early autumn 1993 I advised the British government that the only deal which could stick was one which they negotiated directly with the Irish government and I gave the same advice to the Unionists. I told the Irish government that the Unionists wanted to make sure that co-operation with the Republic was on the basis of co-operation between the elected and accountable representatives of the Dáil and a Northern Ireland Assembly. We agreed that the cross-border issues, such as waterways and tourism, were not difficult to deal with.

The government were clearly coming to the same conclusions, since the Taoiseach and the Prime Minister made the Downing Street declaration in November 1993 and in late summer 1994 Sinn Fein proclaimed a complete cessation of violence, followed shortly afterwards by the 'Loyalist' paramilitaries. We hope and pray.

In 1984 a Greek pastor, Costas Macris, and two members of Youth with a Mission (YWAM) had been sentenced by a Greek court to four years in prison under an old law against proselytising. I was asked to help them, so my Budgets Committee colleague Timios Christadoulou (later Governor of the Bank of Greece) arranged for me to see the Archbishop of Athens. A Socialist colleague on the US delegation, Tony Lagakos, fixed an appointment with the Minister of Justice.

The Socialist government were committed to repeal the legislation, but the Greek Church, guardian of the Greek identity through four centuries of Turkish occupation, had strong political support in Greece. So I went, with Timios Christadoulou, to see the Archbishop first.

We had a warm and friendly conversation. I said that this little-used law was directed against sects and there were, of course, some anti-social and even dangerous sects, but the European Parliament had concluded that citizens were best protected by the ordinary law and that a specific law against sects was unnecessary.

I said that in any case Costas Macris was a Presbyterian, the national Church of Scotland and the Netherlands, and the second largest in the United States. The two YWAM workers were Baptists and that was the largest Church in the United States. Neither could possibly be called sects.

The Archbishop said that he accepted that the Presbyterians were not a sect and, with a smile, he would for my sake accept the Baptists also. If my friends in the Protestant Churches in Greece

180

wanted to meet him to talk about their relationships, he would be very glad to do so.

I told the Minister of Justice that I had seen the Archbishop and that if an appeal court overruled the judgement of the lower court, I did not think there would be any trouble from the Church. Since his government was committed to repeal the law, I was sure that he would wish the judgement to be reversed.

In the event the case did go to appeal, the judgement was reversed and, though the Socialists lost office before repealing the law, my Greek colleagues told me that the Appeal Court decision had now set a precedent and that there could not be a successful prosecution under that law against the Protestant Churches.

I had less success in my meeting with the Protestant Church leaders. They were deeply suspicious of the invitation by the Archbishop and, though I pressed them, then and later, they never took it up.

That October I had an invitation to speak in Paris on the three-hundredth anniversary of Louis XIV's revocation of the Edict of Nantes in 1685 – after which most French Protestants, the Huguenots, went into exile, at great cost to France and equal benefit to Prussia, the Netherlands and Britain.

Paris was at its best in the early autumn sunshine, and Elizabeth and I wandered along the bookstalls by the Seine, visited La Chapelle and Notre Dame, and strolled by the cafés of St Germain in the evening.

President Mitterrand opened the proceedings, the first French head of state to address its Protestant community. He followed a rather dull pastor, with a speech which had no spiritual content but which brought the assembly alive by its verve and sense of occasion.

I was anxious to make the address in French and not through interpretation, so I had all the text checked; but when I read it through to Elizabeth, my English accent was so strong that we both had to laugh. I tried it again and we decided that I should go through it a third time with a French friend, Daniel Brech. When I asked him for his verdict, he said cryptically, 'Well, they will certainly understand you!'

In the event I followed a distinguished liberal professor whose message was full of nuanced doubt. By contrast mine was an appeal to remember that the Christian faith was eternal, the same today as when it inspired the Huguenots to their great deeds: '*le même Dieu, le même Seigneur, le même Esprit*'. I was so carried away by the message that the accent did not seem to matter either to me or to the audience. My colleague, Christine Scrivener, was warm in her encouragement and I was content. We brought back as a souvenir a beautiful porcelain Huguenot cross which still hangs outside our library door at home.

In January 1987 Henry Plumb was elected President of the Parliament by five votes. He was backed by the centre-right, which had only a slim majority and we needed all the votes we could get. But it was worth the effort, for Henry made a great President. He was reputed for his English 'fairplay' and was helpful and accessible. He also did a splendid job in representing the Parliament in Europe and the European Community on the world stage. In Siena the whole town turned out to greet him. In Canton a hundred thousand in the football stadium cheered him. He was the first President to be accepted at the summit meetings of European heads of government – but not accepted by all. After a brush-off from Mrs Thatcher before one meeting started, he sat down beside Chancellor Kohl, who was chairing. Kohl looked across at the British Prime Minister and said to Henry, 'She wants to put you in the Tower of London and feed you on bread and water – black bread!'

On the President's official visit to London, Mrs Thatcher introduced him curtly, 'You'll have heard of Henry Plumb, a former President of the National Union of Farmers.' About an hour later the press asked him what his relationship was with her and he said, 'She is one of my Prime Ministers.' On tour as President, he found himself billed to speak at coffee mornings of a dozen ladies. His lowest point was a visit to a small Welsh town where the local MEP, not finding any meeting organised, went into a garage, seized two feet sticking out from under a car and pulled out the mechanic on his trolley. Despite all this he promised to come to speak for me in Peterborough and we showed what could be done. Between the Chamber of Commerce, the Development Corporation and the East of England Show, we had a packed audience of four hundred for a lunch and Henry certainly rose to the occasion.

Had the pound been fixed to the EMS in the mid-eighties, the immense damage done to the British economy by the hard pound in the early eighties might have been repaired. Nigel Lawson had allowed the pound to fall in line with the dollar, in which we buy so many of our imports. So, uniquely and unrepeatably, British exports had become more competitive in our main market, the EC, without the risk of inflation from higher-cost imports.

I went with two colleagues to see Nigel Lawson to make once more the case which we had made to his predecessor. We now know that that was his view too, but that he was overruled by Mrs Thatcher. It was a tragedy. Inflationary expectations were so built in to wage bargaining that, despite this one-off opportunity, it was not possible to persuade negotiators that wage awards should come into line with the new low inflation rate of under 4 per cent.

The Ford of Britain top management came out to Strasbourg and I made the case to them. They said they were in the business of making cars and if their workforce expected inflation to rise again, they had to accept it. I also spoke at the annual dinner of ACAS and the Institute of Personnel Management, where the case was rejected on the same logic. It was clear that only the external fixing of the pound could get us off the wage-price spiral, and so it proved. Wage awards averaging 4 per cent a year in real terms for four years won the 1987 election, but we had spent the oil revenue and now we were on our way through the reserves. In 1985 a Committee of the House of Lords, chaired by Toby Aldington, had given a strong and considered warning, but it was ignored.

Everyone now agreed that free movement of goods, services, capital and people was a great idea, and once the legislation was through, we began to look at all the consequences and what else, if anything, needed to be done. The Commission asked a retired Director General, Ceccini, to do a study and gave him a generous budget. I was asked to do the same for the Parliament's Institutional Committee, with no budget at all.

With a constituency of small high-tech businesses, which could sell across Europe, but which found money-changing too risky and expensive and Customs papers too much of a hassle, I was sure that the traffic along the newly opened Euro-route would be from small businesses. It cost them up to ten times as much to change money as the multi-nationals and they did not have their well-staffed departments to deal with all the documentation.

One constituent wrote to complain that he had taken his latest high-tech product to a trade fair in Amsterdam, together with a tax-exemption document to say that it was an exhibit and not for sale. But the Customs at Calais said the document was invalid and he had to pay the tax; also on the Belgian frontier. That disposed of his spare cash, so he had to wait a couple of days in Belgium for the money to pay the Dutch frontier tax and arrived at the exhibition half-way through, determined that exporting was not worth it. Big companies would have known at once that the Dover Customs had stamped the document in the wrong place, but he didn't. (We got all his money back with profound apologies from the head of Customs.)

Ceccini by contrast spent a lot of money on a survey of the multi-nationals, who were set up in every country anyhow and they told him that 'with them' open frontiers would simply lead to rationalisation. When he had realised his mistake, he came to the same conclusion as we had done and events have borne us out. Over five years, the rate of unemployment in the Community dropped sharply until stopped by Germany's high interest rates. That was the first object of the exercise and it was achieved.

Our second conclusion was that the biggest gain of all would come from concerted economic policy. Ball and Albert had pointed out that if any one country eased credit to keep their economy going, then it simply sucked in imports from the rest, ran a trade deficit, weakened its currency and had to stop. If the German attempt to succeed the US as the motor economy had failed under Schmidt, who else could do it? But if the EC could all move forward together, the gains in output and employment would be enormous.

That led to a third conclusion. Twelve countries now had to defend twelve separate exchange rates out of twelve separate reserves and, in the free competition in an open market, some would be gainers and some losers. But we now had, at British insistence, free movement of capital as well. There would come a morning when some country in trade deficit would wake up to find that it had lost half of its currency reserves before breakfast – which is exactly what happened on 'black Wednesday', when the pound was forced out of the EMS. So we concluded that the open market needed a much stronger currency union.

Since we would have impossible tensions without a concerted economic policy and great gains with one, and since we needed a more powerful monetary framework, the Parliament concluded that we needed an equally strong framework of open political accountability. It was no longer good enough to make decisions behind the closed doors of the Council and tell people that it was for their own good.

My own conclusion was that the European Parliament could not take over that task alone. We needed the support of a second chamber composed of members of national parliaments. They did not need a vote, since they had one in their national parliaments, when the legislation arrived there; but if they could go through the same process of examination in a chamber with the same mix of nationalities and parties, then they would know what could and could not be done at a European level and could hold their own governments accountable. I could not carry my colleagues on this particular point, though Michael Heseltine took it up and put it in his book on Europe shortly afterwards.

The idea of the single market emerged from the European Parliament. Boz Ferranti's Kangaroo Group promoted it among the business community and it had wide and enthusiastic acceptance. By contrast, the Maastricht Treaty emerged from the private negotiations of the Council and was based on the Delors Report, composed of a Committee of Central Bank Governors. It leaned too heavily on monetary union and ignored the potential dynamic of economic union. It was also flawed technically. It proposed to make the change to a stronger monetary union along the stepping stones of the weak EMS, which, not surprisingly, gave way. Its reason, that this gave time for adjustment, ignored the lesson of the EMS, which was that it was membership itself which compelled spendthrift governments to adjust.

Small wonder that the first Danish referendum was against the Maastricht Treaty, that it only just scraped through in the French referendum and that it took a long hot summer to get it through the House of Commons. I voted for it because it gave a German commitment to Monetary Union, without which Europe would become a Deutsche Mark zone. But it showed that a democratic Europe of 350 million could no longer be run by private conclaves of full-time bureaucrats and part-time ministers. The enlargement of the European Union, especially in deeply democratic Scandinavia, makes the case even stronger.

None of these vital issues was debated in Britain. Instead, with a growing internal and external deficit, borrowing billions a month to keep afloat, and with rising inflation, we were treated to the rhetoric of Mrs Thatcher's speech at Bruges and then the successive sacking of her Chancellor and Foreign Secretary for their impertinence in trying to keep her feet on the ground.

The peculiar perversion of the Bruges speech was the way in which it conjured up non-existent foreign threats. When things go wrong at home, it is an old and sinister political trick to blame a foreign enemy. There are indeed threats to the British identity. But they are all internal and have far more to do with the collapse of the moral order and the rise in materialism than with currency or with health regulations on the contents of sausages. And wrapping the Union Jack round the currency conceals the harsh fact that it has lost over nine-tenths of its value since it first bore the Queen's head. Indeed the Queen might well ask for her portrait to be removed from such a debased coinage.

Nationalism, as we Ulster Scots know, is a dangerous genie which cannot easily be returned to the bottle. A self-assured England has never felt the need for it. But now it is common to hear on the doorstep from people who have never been to France that the French are our natural enemies and to see their disbelief when you tell them that that is not your experience. The Bruges speech licensed the foreign-owned press to pursue jingoistic campaigns which have no place in a civilised society and gave credibility to a minority in Parliament to echo the nationalist rhetoric.

Perhaps we should look at what we are defending. As I prepared a report on the European constitution, and looked at the democratic constitutions in Europe and America, I began to realise the utter inadequacy of our own unwritten British constitution. True, the precedents on which it was built go back to the English Revolution of 1688 so it can claim to be the first. No doubt that is why we never bother to look at the improvements of the later models. Never mind the feeble brakes, what Rolls and Royce produced is good enough for us. But there are, in those later constitutions, safeguards to the citizen which are wholly lacking in ours. Ours, unlike all later models, starts from the viewpoint of government, not from that of the citizens. Our rule is that 'The Queen's government must be carried on.' Carried on regardless of what? Because we start from the top down and not from the bottom up, our unwritten constitution consists of periodic concessions from government to people made under political pressure. We have never had to look systematically at the balance of powers and the protection of the citizen.

All other democracies today have written constitutions, often supported by a bill of rights and with a court to decide constitutional issues. We boast of the flexibility of an unwritten constitution, but flexibility favours those in government who know how to operate it, rather than the citizen who does not. In all European democracies except Britain, it is impossible for a government to be formed which represents only a minority of the voters. In most countries there is a regional government, which is entrenched in the constitution. The government of Paris cannot be wound up as was the GLC by our government. In a majority of countries there is a democratically based second chamber, usually based on representation of the regions. In many countries, parliament has a fixed term, so that governments cannot call elections when there is the best chance of re-election. Most countries have central banks with a great deal more independence than the Bank of England, so it is harder to debase the currency for political advantage. And many countries have a separation of both powers and office-holders between government and elected representatives, so that government cannot bribe their elected representatives as they can and do in Britain, with promises of political power.

That is a formidable list. A stronger European constitution

would fill some gaps, but if we do not want to rely on that, then it is time we reformed our own constitution.

While I was drawing up this report, I was still a member of the US delegation and it was a great help to see first-hand how another democracy ran its affairs. On the bi-centennial of the Constitution there were a good many useful accounts of the origins of American democracy. I preferred the European system in which the chief executive is elected by those who have to agree to pass the laws that his or her administration put forward. But otherwise I thought the American balance of powers and interests a good model for Europe.

On the US delegation we also continued to talk about agriculture. Dame Shelagh Roberts had succeeded me as President of the Foreign Trade (REX) Committee and in 1986 they updated our resolution of three years before, calling for the mutual reduction of farm subsidies on both sides of the Atlantic to be locked into the new round of GATT negotiations. She joined the US delegation on our visit to Washington in the summer of 1986 to give, once more, a firm and practical answer to the American complaints.

We had our own complaints too. We were very critical of the Reagan administration's support of the 'Contras' in Nicaragua, though we knew nothing of the 'Iran-Contra' affair. We were told that this was America's back-yard and that if we were in the South-west we would begin to appreciate all this.

So after Washington we went, this time, to Santa Fe, the capital of New Mexico. When we got there we asked how near we were to Nicaragua and were told it was 3,000 miles. Some back-yard! The plane-load of Congressmen and another of European politicians arriving in this tiny state capital made a big splash. The school orchestra was on the tarmac to greet us, the Governor gave us a barbecue and we were despatched in buses up the valley of the Rio Grande to an Indian reservation in Taos. And between times we argued with each other in the State House.

Next year the main argument was about the subsidy to the European Airbus and of course we had to go to Seattle, the home of Boeing. Boeing gave a dinner with a thousand or so of

Seattle's leading citizens and the Governor made a speech. Our argument was that the loans to the Airbus were not a subsidy and, in any case, the huge American defence budget gave the US aircraft industry an indirect subsidy with which we could not compete. In the end we decided not to fall out about it.

In 1988, it was the turn of Minneapolis, containing the district of Republican Congressman Bill Frenzl. Cargill, one of the world's biggest grain merchants, gave us a dinner in the garden of their HQ outside the city and Bill Frenzl introduced me to one of their Vice Presidents. I told him that I was Chairman of a cross-party group for the reform of the CAP and that, because the farm lobby dominated our Agriculture Committee, we needed outside funding to be able to put forward alternative views. I said that we were already funded by companies like Unilever, but we thought it would help to have the support of a multi-national with American experience. He was very helpful, and Cargill joined the European food companies and conservation groups who already sponsored us, so that we could now have Jane Kelsey as a full-time administrator and spend some money on outside research. That year the American administration had, at last, five years after my resolution and two years after Dame Shelagh's, made proposals to the new GATT round of talks for a mutual reduction of subsidies, bringing both EC and US near to the awkward domestic political decisions.

Our three days with the Congressmen usually came after a briefing from the EC Ambassador and a visit to the Senate, where they gave us lunch and received us on the floor of the Senate Chamber which, with only a hundred members, had a rather intimate atmosphere. Then we visited Administration, Commerce, Treasury, Defence, the Federal Reserve Bank and the National Security Council – which last, under the Reagan Presidency, we found most worrying.

So, before we talked to Congress, we were well briefed. The best and frankest briefing was from Roy Denman, former European Commission chief trade negotiator, who was now in Washington as EC Ambassador. He was an important figure in the capital and everyone who was anyone came to the reception which he gave in his small garden.

The European Parliament's access to Congress is unique and

not available to any national government or parliament. Congress recognises Europe as an equal and powerful partner in most major external problems, so it has to give the relationship time and thought.

We made good friends too: Bill Clinger from Pennsylvania, Ben Gilman from New York, Doug Bereuter from Nebraska and, on the Democrat side, Sam Gibbon from Florida (formerly the Chairman of Ways and Means), and Tom Sawyer from Akron. And, since they brought their wives and there was a demand for matching English-speaking wives, Elizabeth always came with me (at our own expense) and became, gradually, the interlocutor for the European wives. 'Elizabet, the building they are showing us is not really old at all, tell them we want to go shopping.'

Each January they came to a European capital. After Dublin in 1986, the delegations met in Madrid in 1987, Bonn in 1988 and Paris in 1989, following the Presidency of the Council. In Bonn, after a series of discussions and debates with German ministers, including a very lively debate with Martin Bangemann, we went to see President von Weizsäcker, one of the wisest politicians I have ever met.

In Paris we had lunch at the Quai d'Orsay and I sat at the table of the Permanent Secretary, the personification of the worldly wise French diplomacy of our imagination. Jean Pierre Cot took two or three of us round the French Parliament, where public access is confined to one outside door which goes straight up to a narrow gallery. Jean Pierre explained that this restricted access had aimed to protect them from the citizens of Paris, who, when they got excited about an issue, used to rush across the bridge into the Parliament to browbeat the Deputies.

Whatever the Americans say about the 'special relationship' with Britain, it is very clear to me, from ten years of close association with Congress, that the Americans are, above all, realists. They want to deal with equals. And, though the EC is not – and probably never will be – a United States of Europe, it is with the EC and not the member states that they want to deal. And, because they want to deal with a body politic which can deliver its end of the agreement, they want the EC to be more coherent and not less.

America is a friendly power, but it is nevertheless a power

and we need equal negotiating strength to deal with it. We talk about Britain 'punching more than its weight', and we have had excellent ambassadors, like Nico Henderson during the Falklands war. But Nico was quite exceptional; we cannot rely too heavily on individuals. So to look after our interests where they conflict with America's or to check an inept or inexperienced American administration from dangerous if well-meaning folly, we need the constant weight of the whole European Union.

On 1 July 1987, aged eighty-six, my mother died, sitting on the sofa in John and Elizabeth's house in Leamington.

With her strong Christian faith, she had a profound influence on my life. Whatever the immediate cause of my Christian commitment at the age of nine, her teaching and example must have been behind it. My father had humour and charm, but she was the steadying influence. She was a great woman of prayer and included all the family, children, grandchildren and, finally, great-grandchildren. At Ballin a Cor and at Rosapenna, she was enormously hospitable and had a wide range of friends; but she was not entirely happy in the *Vanity Fair* of Rosapenna and much more content when she and Father moved to England, near her children and grandchildren.

Chapter Twelve

EUROPE WIDE AND FREE

Despite Mrs Thatcher's Bruges speech the previous October, the Conservative manifesto for the European election in June 1989 was pro-European. The Labour Party had at last regained their belief in Europe, a speech to the Labour Party Conference by Jacques Delors playing some part. But the leader of the Labour group in the European Parliament was an unreconstructed opponent and we looked forward to exploiting that contradiction.

However Mrs Thatcher took strident charge of the campaign and the public impression was that it was the Conservative Party, not Labour, who were divided. On the streets the pro-Europeans told us, 'We'll never vote for you again until you get rid of that woman.'

The anti-Europeans were equally clear, 'Maggie's absolutely right, we're not going to vote for Europe.'

So we lost both wings of the party and 13 seats (equivalent to about 70 Westminster seats), going down from 45 out of 78 British seats to 32, with Labour going up from 32 to 45. This turned the narrow centre-right majority in the European Parliament into a narrow majority for the left. With poetic justice the right-wing nationalist 'Blue Circle' faction in the Conservative Group was literally decimated, losing nine of its ten members.

I went to see my one Cambridgeshire colleague in the cabinet, John Major, who had been appointed Chief Secretary to the Treasury after the 1987 election. He had done well as Chief Secretary and was rightly proud that he had settled two budgets with all the spending ministers without one appeal. I was strong in my complaints. He said that he would pass on all I had said to the Chancellor, and I should come to see him again and brief him on Europe. Before I could do this, Geoffrey Howe had been moved from the Foreign Office to be Leader of the House and John was the new Foreign Secretary.

Then, after the party conference, Nigel Lawson resigned as Chancellor and John was the new Chancellor. The old man with a gammy leg who took me up to see him in the Treasury said, as we turned into the long north corridor, 'There's your man,' and stumped away again. In the distance were three young men in shirtsleeves and, getting nearer, I recognised John as one of them. This time he seemed not to need any briefing from me on EMS or anything else. He knew what he wanted to do and I was sure that he would do it. But he was still the same easy and friendly colleague, totally unaffected by his sudden promotions.

The EDG felt the loss of its members. Before the election the Spaniards had left us for the predominantly Christian Democrat European People's Party (EPP), because they could not fight the election allied to Mrs Thatcher's party. And, because of the Anglo-Irish Agreement, our Ulster Unionist, John Taylor, had also left. Our Danish colleagues had lost two of their four, so we were down to a group of thirty-four instead of sixty-six, losing almost all our political leverage unless we too could join the EPP.

However we were entitled to support from other groups for a Vice President of the Parliament and at the first group meeting there seemed to be a feeling that I should be our nominee. It was not an office I had sought, but it seemed to be a worthwhile job and one which colleagues wanted me to do. So, on the Monday of the first Strasbourg week, I was nominated as a Vice President; I was elected in the first round on Tuesday, and on Wednesday, without time to study the rule book again, I was chairing a packed chamber for the crucial votes which decided the competencies of all the committees.

There was a conflict on competencies between the Agricultural and Environmental Committees, with the environmentalists wanting to take again a vote which they had missed in error and the farm lobby in uproar the other way. I allowed points of order to

193

run on instead of using the rule book at once and then supported the emerging consensus with my own firm recommendation that if there was now unanimity, we should take the vote again – which we did. Presiding over twelve nationalities and seven political groups is no sinecure, but having survived that baptism of fire, I felt more confident in the chair.

Enrique Baron, whom Henry Plumb had defeated so narrowly two and a half years before, had been elected President and we developed a good relationship. He did not have anything like Henry's self-assurance or ease of manner, but he was a hard-working and conscientious President. At that time the President and Vice Presidents sat as the Parliament's Bureau handling the administration of the Parliament, and were joined by the Presidents of the political groups in the Enlarged Bureau for the more political decisions. Since then the Enlarged Bureau has been abolished and the Group Presidents now take the political decisions alone.

Valéry Giscard d'Estaing, former President of France, was a new member and was elected President of the Liberal Group. He brought a shrewd judgement, put his points with elegance and wit and, on the Enlarged Bureau, we often found ourselves in agreement. He grew increasingly friendly, maybe with some alliance in mind between us and his French colleagues, who were then allied to the Liberal Group. He gave an exploratory dinner, insisting that in the general discussion the French spoke English and the English French. Eventually they left the Liberals to join the main centre-right group, the EPP, and we followed them.

Since John Martin, my constituency Chairman, wanted a really big name for a constituency dinner, I invited Giscard. I had been told that he often accepted and then, at the last moment, couldn't come. Not until we heard that his car had passed the Stansted turning did we really believe that he would arrive. I had asked Michael McCrum, the Master of Corpus, to be host. As he was a former Vice Chancellor of Cambridge and Headmaster of Eton, I felt that the protocol was in a safe pair of hands.

The head porter was on the door with his top hat; so were radio and TV. Michael McCrum and I escorted Giscard to the Master's Lodge and then to the reception. At dinner he asked me what he should say. I said, 'Tell them not to worry so much about

Europe.' He said that we two old nations understood each other; no European Union was going to affect our national identity, developed over all those centuries; a Frenchman would always be a Frenchman and an Englishman an Englishman, so who could want or even imagine anything different? It went down well.

At the beginning of this third Parliament LUFPIG decided that we now had enough support from sponsors to commission a group of agricultural economists to propose a fundamental CAP reform package. Ray MacSharry, the Agricultural Commissioner, asked one of his senior officials, Graham Avery, to help us. With his advice, we agreed that John Marsh from Reading University would be the best Chairman and we asked Stefan Tangermann (Germany), Louis Mahé (France), Secundo Tarditi (Italy), Brynn Green (UK) and Brendan Kearney (Ireland) to make up the group.

In the summer of 1990 the GATT talks began to run into difficulties over agriculture and when we met Aart de Zeeuw, the Chairman of the GATT agriculture working group, it was clear that the whole trade round would be in deep trouble if there were to be no agreement on the CAP. It was also vital that any reform package should be locked into the GATT agreement, so that the reform was permanent.

At the end of July the economists came together in the Hague; Jane Kelsey and I briefed them. Until then there had been no published figures on the effect of a CAP reform. We told them that we needed to know how far the subsidies would have to be reduced to bring EC internal prices and world prices into line, how much this would save the EC budget and and how much of this would in turn be available to compensate the farmers. We had been told that the best economic model in Europe was in Louis Mahé's university, Rennes, and he undertook to work out the figures.

In October they all came to Brussels with their initial papers and we looked together at the effects of change, the availability of other jobs, the changes to the environment and the need to pay farmers to protect it. We also looked at how best the saving could be used to compensate farmers. We were sitting under a picture – *Tom's Place* – of a poor Irish farmer, which reminded

195

us of the bleak outlook for the marginal farmer in areas where there was no other employment.

The faxes flew until, finally, the team had a report to present to Ray MacSharry in Strasbourg and at a press conference following. The main message of the report was that the reduction in subsidies needed to bring EC and world prices into line would enable farmers to receive full compensation for the loss and as much again would be saved on the Community budget. Ray MacSharry was very receptive and it was on those lines that he based his own 'reflections' in the following February.

Our press coverage was wiped out by the resignation that day of Mrs Thatcher; but gradually the ideas in the report began to infiltrate the press. Stefan Tangermann had made a specially attractive suggestion: that there should be annual compensation for fifteen years, but that if a farmer wanted a capital sum to pay off debt, to set up in another business, to take over another farm or to retire, then the annual payment should be in a form of a Community bond, so that it could be sold on the market for the needed lump sum. This was too controversial for MacSharry to use except in one sector – he had enough of a fight on his hands – but it was, in our view, better than 'set-aside' and its time may come.

That was the easy part. In the following month the GATT negotiations broke down on the issue of agricultural trade. Through 1991 we had to work on the Parliament's own report and MacSharry had to work on the member states in the Council.

Our problem in the Parliament was to remove the domination of the Agricultural Committee on an issue which went far outside their competence. It was agreed on the Enlarged Bureau that the Budgets, Environment and Foreign Trade Committees, whose Chairmen were all members of LUFPIG, should co-operate and that each should have equal weight with the Agriculture Committee in drawing up the final reports.

Throughout the year, I had to defend this position on the Enlarged Bureau, mainly against attacks by the EPP (Christian Democrats). Each committee held its own hearing and worked on its own contribution, but they had great difficulty in persuading the Agricultural Committee rapporteur, Reinhold Bocklet, to take any account of their views in his report. So we set to work to amend the Bocklet Report.

There was strong support in the Socialist Group, the largest in the Parliament, as well as in the overwhelmingly British EDG (Conservatives), for the amendments to bring the views of the other committees into the final report. But in a preliminary vote the French Socialists had voted against the Socialist whip and with the farm lobby. So Terry Wynne, Budgets rapporteur, a Socialist member of LUFPIG (and later my successor as Chairman), organised a sudden call by twenty-one members in the middle of the debate to take the report off the agenda. I was warned of this, as the Vice President likely to be in the chair, and consulted the clerks, who confirmed that the motion would be allowable. As it happened I was not in the chair, so I told our Group spokesman and we both went into the chamber with some others from the Group to support Terry.

It caused consternation, not only in the farm lobby, but in the EDG, where we were in the final stages of our application to join the EPP (Christian Democrats). But the risk was worth taking, for when the report was finally restored to the agenda, the Socialist Group vote was solidly behind the amendments and the Parliament voted for reform. As footnotes, Reinhard Bocklet left the Parliament to become Minister of Agriculture for Bavaria and we joined the EPP on schedule.

Meantime, very anxious that the US Congress allowed continuation of the President's 'fast track' mandate to negotiate the GATT, I had paid a visit to Washington at the end of July to ask them for patience while we got the necessary internal agreement in the Council of Ministers.

Andreas van Agt, the EC Ambassador, was extremely helpful, arranging for me to see all the key people. Kiki de la Garcia, Chairman of the House Agriculture Committee, gave a lunch and was very friendly and supportive; Senator Leahy, Chairman of the Senate Committee, was friendly, though his chief of staff was not, the Senate having a disproportionate membership from farm states. We saw the Departments of Agriculture and Commerce and I spoke at a lunch for the major companies trading in farm commodities. I also got to a much wider audience on the radio network which reaches about forty stations covering the farming community and had half an hour's interview which went coast to coast on the Capitol's own TV station, C-Span.

The Americans were very patient. They not only waited the six months which I asked; it was eighteen months before the Blair House Agreement, which embodied the final settlement. Before the European side was agreed, Ray MacSharry had to resign as the European negotiator and be reinstated on his own terms, and John Major had to detach Chancellor Kohl from the French. Before the agreement was ratified, Congress had to extend the 'fast track' agreement (which prevented them from unpicking it) and America had a new President. In Europe, France held out until the very last moment. Finally our aim was achieved and we had a GATT settlement locking the CAP reforms into an international agreement, which could no longer be changed, however great the pressure from the farm lobbies.

Fortunately I had no difficulty at all with my own farmers. I met with the two NFU branches in Cambridgeshire and Bedfordshire and explained the reforms, including our own proposal for a bond which would be saleable for a lump sum. They asked me to go to the NFU and tell them our ideas. Their NFU Council member came with me as did Henry Plumb, who later persuaded the House of Lords to accept the idea of a flexible compensatory bond.

In February 1990 I paid a visit to Turkey at the request of the Evangelical Alliance, who had had appeals from Protestant Churches whose services had been broken up by police, on the grounds that the hotel conference rooms in which they usually met were a 'public place', where religious meetings were prohibited. Mike Morris of EA came with me and also an excellent interpreter.

The very helpful Turkish Ambassador to the EC had arranged for me to see the Turkish Deputy Prime Minister, Professor Ali Bozer. But I spent Sunday in Istanbul to meet representatives from ten churches in Western Turkey, because most of the protests had come from expatriate church members and I wanted to make quite sure that the Turkish Christians themselves were quite sure that they wanted to raise their profile in protest. We had a good discussion and when they had thought about it, they agreed that it was the right course. Next day I had an early meeting

198

with seven churches from the Ankara region and, again after a thoughtful discussion, they came to the same conclusion.

The Turkish government could not have been more helpful. The Deputy Prime Minister explained the reason for the prohibition of religious meetings in public places, and I could well understand it. Turkey had open frontiers with Iran, Iraq and Syria, all full of fundamentalists for whom a public meeting could quickly turn into a huge political demonstration.

I said that Turkey was a secular state where everyone was free to worship; so, if a conference room in a hotel was a public place, the government should tell these small Protestant Churches, which did not have enough money to put up buildings of their own, where they could worship within the law. I said that in the present uncertainty, the Churches were far more frightened of the police than of the government in Ankara and that was not healthy. The thought that we saw the police as capable of undermining the authority of the government struck home and I was passed on to the Justice Minister to work something out.

The Minister of Justice was a rough and genial politician from Eastern Turkey. He said he had heard of Catholics and Orthodox Christians, though never of Protestants, but, 'As we want to join Europe and half of you are Protestants, we had better look after you.' But why, he asked, could the Protestant Churches not use some of the redundant Catholic or Orthodox churches? I said that we Protestants were like the Muslims; we did not like all those images, and preferred plain churches. He said that in that case the problem was solved; we should borrow the mosques! On second thoughts he could not offer the mosques, since government did not own them.

In the end we left it that the government would get in touch with the Protestant Churches and come to an agreement as to where they could meet without infringing the law against religous meetings in public places. I reported this back to the Churches, who had been praying while I was talking with the government, and they were content.

The European Community Ambassador, Jan Van Rij, was also very helpful. He briefed the twelve EC Ambassadors and when, next day, some of the papers accused the Turkish government of making exceptional concessions to Christians, he persuaded the government to ignore it. I understand that the agreement finally reached was that the Protestant Churches were to tell the local authorities where they were meeting and that this would cover them against any harrassment. So far as I have heard there has been no further trouble.

Though I may have risked the wrath of the EPP farm lobby, I did make a contribution to the merger of our small group with the EPP, which gave us much needed leverage in the Parliament. I went, with others of our Group officers, to see Chancellor Kohl. The glass and concrete Bundeskanzlerai makes 10 Downing Street look positively twee and the Chancellor was on the same massive scale as his chancellory. He told us that we must be patient, that the Rhine takes a long time to get down to the sea. We said that we did not have much time. European Union had a timetable and until membership of the EPP gave us some influence in the European Parliament's debate, he could not expect us, as politically powerless MEPs, to have any leverage in the debate at home. After our visit he put the whole of his considerable political weight behind our application for membership.

Although the EPP was an alliance between six national Christian Democratic parties and five others which were not, the Christian Democratic influence was paramount and it was considered that EPP policies should reflect a Christian viewpoint, even if tempered to the views of secular society. But in Britain we believe in separation of Church and state, and the Dutch especially thought that this made us incompatible partners. With the support of one of our Jewish colleagues, I led our side of the negotiation on this religious problem, sent off with the cheering comment that it was the single issue which could sink the entire negotiation.

My opposite number was Aire Oostlander, a Dutch Christian Democrat, who was strongly opposed to our joining. I pointed out that Britain was not a secular state. Our Queen was the head of the Church, so, under our constitution, given us at the English Revolution by William of Orange, a Dutch king, no party could claim to be the Christian party.

The Greek EPP member of the small committee supported me, saying that that was very much the position in Greece.

The Orthodox Church was recognised by both main parties, but neither of them could claim it. And the German member had clearly been briefed by her German colleagues. So the committee agreed, with Aire Oostlander recording his solitary vote against.

When the thirty-two British Conservative members joined the EPP in January 1992 for the second half of the Parliament, we and the thirty-two Germans were equal largest national sections and had a strong identity of interests. We British were also better than most in attendance, in voting and in debate within the EPP, so we had, once more, a strong influence in the decisions of the Parliament.

The third Parliament had begun with the fall of the Berlin wall and the new freedom of the countries of Central Europe. President Baron convened successive meetings with the heads of the newly liberated states: President Walesa of Poland, President Havel of Czechoslovakia and Prime Minister Antall of Hungary. All of them had inherited bankrupt economies and needed our help if they were to preserve their new democracies. But they were in a better state than the Soviet Union itself and they worried desperately about what would happen there. Lech Walesa said, 'If it breaks up in the East and the refugees pour across our frontier, there is nothing we can do; we will simply pass them on to you.'

I went to Budapest with our new delegation to the Hungarian Parliament. We were led by Otto von Habsburg, an MEP for Bavaria, but, more famously, the eldest son of the last Emperor of Austria-Hungary, who remembered his father's coronation in Budapest in 1917. He had been very active in the restoration of Hungarian democracy and it was a great moment as we walked up the ninety-eight red-carpeted stairs of the grandiose Hungarian Parliament and into a rapturous reception from a full chamber. We were all welcome, but there was no doubt that Otto was the man of the hour. He was the Hungarian link with a past in which they could still take pride.

But outside the euphoria of the newly gilded Parliament, life was grey. They had to make huge changes and hardly knew where to begin. They had 18,000 teachers of Russian which no one now wanted to learn but hardly any teachers of English and German, languages now desperately needed since no one in the outside world spoke their own unique and difficult tongue. More critical to the future, their industry had no experience of the market economy, their managers and workers no experience of the disciplines of competition. We met the trades union leaders, old and new, Otto acting as interpreter. The old had a lot to forget, the new had everything to learn. But in Hungary they had at least made a start. They had commercial laws and a banking system, the basis for Western industrial investment. And the three countries on our immediate border were an obvious priority for the aid of the European Community: 350 million could clearly help 65 million.

Then, after the failed coup against Gorbachev, the Soviet Union began to break up. They were 285 million, a different scale and a far worse problem. Our natural instinct was that aid to them would be throwing money down a black hole. They had not had a market economy since 1917; three whole generations had been brought up on a command economy. There were no merchants who knew how to put together buyer and seller, no bankers who knew how to tell a good loan proposition from a bad one and, unlike Central Europe, an industrial base totally distorted by the huge defence industry which they could no longer afford.

In the second half of the Parliament, when the Soviet Union broke up, I was Vice President of the Foreign Affairs and Security Committee. Russia and Ukraine were still nuclear powers and as we studied the possible outcomes, the political risks of doing nothing began to loom far greater than the financial risks of an aid programme. We decided to have a hearing on aid to Eastern Europe and I was appointed rapporteur. In the end we had to have two hearings, and I had to pay two visits to Russia and two to the United States.

The Soviet Union had a unique and unprecedented problem. It collapsed when its civil industry could no longer pay for its defence industry. Every new generation of weapons in the cold war was several times as expensive as the last. The cost was still only a fraction of the total output of Western industry. But in the Soviet Union, the cost was eventually more than half of their industrial output.

My first visit was to St Petersburg, where they told me that

70 per cent of the workforce was dependent on the arms industry. In Moscow I found that most major cities had the same dependence, and that the secret defence cities in the Urals were totally dependent on defence. The social safety net in every city depended on industry and so, if the defence industry were bankrupt and the workers thrown out on the streets, there was no social safety net.

Faced with this dangerous problem, Western governments had nevertheless made the political decision to channel aid to the former Soviet Union through normal loans from the International Monetary Fund and the World Bank. Since these institutions had in turn to borrow the money they were to lend, all but a miniscule fraction was on their usual terms and conditions, which required that the money would not be lent until inflation was brought under control.

But the Russian and Ukranian governments did not have the resources to convert their vast defence industries to civil production, and so, despite all their promises to the IMF and the World Bank, could not bring inflation under control without outside help. Meantime, inflation enabled them to spread the misery and avoid the crisis of millions of defence workers out on the streets.

All this became very clear at the first hearing. The Russian government, represented by Deputy Prime Minister Shockin, maintained that they would meet the IMF criteria; but the members of the Russian Parliament clearly did not believe a word of it, nor did the Western economic experts. Western industry would not invest in Russia or Ukraine until the uncertainty was resolved. So in September 1992 the Parliament passed a unanimous resolution asking for a rethink.

By the end of the year it was clear that nothing was going to happen and we decided to have a second hearing; I was, once more, rapporteur.

It was by now clear that the political reason for proposing that aid should be channelled through the most unsuitable agency of an international bank with a three-star credit rating was to keep aid off national budgets. And yet there were enormous physical resources and human skills in Eastern Europe, if only they could be organised. The Russian natural gas reserve alone was capable

203

of paying for the whole reconstruction programme and more. So we began to look at it like bankers setting up a viable deal, where no one lost and everyone gained. The resources of America's West had given America its dynamic century of growth. The same could happen in the European East.

We were increasingly conscious too of the need to find other work for the Western defence industry, whose output was geared to the massive strike and counter-strike of the cold war and was quite unsuitable for troubles like those in Bosnia or Somalia.

So we thought that we would use the second hearing to test a model for aid, which would help to convert both Western and Eastern defence industries at the same time. We would need a framework, like the OEEC (now OECD) of the Marshall Plan, at which donor and recipient countries would agree together on the industrial investment which could turn their economies round fastest. Mending the Russian oil pipelines, for instance, would have a huge immediate payoff; so would investment in food storage, processing and distribution. Electronic communications would be needed for a functioning market economy.

The new OEEC might then commission projects for the hardware, with priority to Western companies or districts suffering from defence cuts, the equipment to be put in place by East/West joint ventures. This take-up would allow both defence industries to be run down faster and the cost would be offset by the lightening of the defence budget. The joint East/West agreement should also cover the legal framework needed to protect Western companies working in Eastern Europe.

Booz Allen's Washington office, specialising in defence, asked the opinion of their defence clients, who thought it feasible, and Michael Emerson, now EC Ambassador in Moscow, introduced me to a Hungarian-born German, Peter Sipos, who knew the Russian defence industry well. He organised a remarkable all-day seminar in Moscow for most of the leaders in the industry. At the end of it the Russians, though reluctant to admit the need for Western help, agreed that it was feasible and should be done.

I consulted two old friends who had been officials in the Marshall Plan, and the UN Economic Commission for Europe had done a paper which said that a Marshall Plan for Eastern Europe was both feasible and necessary. The Stockholm International

Peace Research Institute told us that NATO was still spending $100bn a year on new weapons and a further $50bn on weapons research, so there was clearly leeway in defence spending to find the $15bn which was the World Bank's unofficial estimate of the minimum needed to preserve democracy in Russia.

The hearing found along these lines and the European Parliament, once more unanimously, passed a resolution incorporating the findings.

On my second visit to Moscow, Michael Emerson took me to the MiG headquarters. We were training them to sell in Western markets and they had asked to see him. It was like an old Lancashire cotton mill. Great gates swung open as we rounded the building and then swung shut behind us again. We went up wooden stairs to a long room which gradually filled with men who were tense and angry.

They had made a bid for tail fins to the French company, Dassault, which looked as if it might be successful; they had to be to Western specifications, which, in itself, was no problem; but that needed a test rig costing $1.5m and neither they nor the Russian government had the money or credit to raise it. We were training them, but our aid programmes did not cover equipment, so they could not put their aid into practice; what did we think we were up to?

We watched the workers streaming out of the plant through the Moscow slush. They were entirely dependent on us and we were doing nothing for them. Two veterans showed us with great pride round the MiG museum. This was the company which had taken on the Luftwaffe, saved Moscow and driven the invaders out of Russia. There were photographs of their wartime planes, and their flying aces with their medals and awards. I thought what a dangerous thing it is to wound the pride of a great nation.

In the top echelons of the European Commission it was admitted privately that the IMF strategy concocted by the group of seven richest nations (G7) would not work. But President Delors sat with the seven heads of government on the G7 and his formal reply was along the official line. No single European government could act without a lead from the Americans, who made two thirds of the weapons, so, supported by the Parliament delegation, I talked to our Congress colleagues again. They agreed with the logic of our view, and the Chairman of the House Foreign Affairs Committee said that, because of the dangers, aid to Russia should be the first priority. I also talked to Sam Nunn, Chairman of the Senate Armed Services Committee, and he agreed with our arguments. He pointed to the Nunn/Lugar project, which did what I had suggested on a very small scale, but said that anything more depended on the fragile coalition which had put it through and he needed a firm lead from the President. That lead never came.

There was an attempted *putsch* by the Russian Parliament, which was besieged and destroyed. Then there was a referendum which President Yeltsin barely won and an election to a new Duma, where an extreme nationalist, Zhirinovsky, emerged as the leader of the largest party. The G7 argued as to whether the Russians should receive even the unconditional $1bn.

I made a final appeal to Congress at our meeting in Athens in January 1994 and, once more, they were with me, but did not see what they could do.

After that the June 1994 European election was looming and my time was running out. It was a large project which needed the kind of concern for former opponents and the generosity of spirit that had produced the Marshall Plan two generations before. I could only conclude, sadly, that the countries of the Western world had forgotten the lesson of Versailles: that the victors should not endanger the economy and insult the dignity of a proud nation in its defeat.

I had decided that fifteen years in the European Parliament was enough and that there was other work to do. I had, of course, many regrets when I hung up the headphones for the last time. There is a tremendous cameraderie among members of Parliament, all of whom have an exactly equal right to be there. And there was an especial cameraderie among the founding members. We had been through tough times together and we all knew each other well, with all our strengths and weaknesses. No one, whatever their temporary office, was allowed to get above themselves. It's tough to leave so many really good friends behind.

And, back home, the constituency, your own patch of England, for which you carry personal responsibility, brings a strong sense of identity. Whatever the projects in the Parliament, the real job is that of representing your own people. I enjoyed being the member for Cromwell's country and, for ten years, Bunyan's country too. It is Cromwell country still, a people of great independence; from the Fens in the north to the small and equally independent high-tech companies around Cambridge, they are all their own people, beholden to no one.

Every corner brings memories: questions from bright sixth-formers; walking round shop floors; trying to understand the language of the computer experts; wine and cheese parties on dark nights in village halls; the wide horizons of the Fens, with their long straight drains; five generations of undergraduates at my old university and, not least, farmers' meetings, never sure whether they believe you or not.

The European Parliament is much nearer in style and purpose to the Congress of the USA than to Westminster. As in the American constitution, there is complete separation of powers between administration and legislation. Neither the US Congress nor the European Parliament are stepping stones to power. We are there to represent those who elected us, period. We cannot be bought by promises of office or honour. We cannot be relegated to the back-benches, for there are none.

What mattered to me was what my own folk thought back home. That makes for the kind of independence in an elected representative that we seem to have lost in the Commons.

But we do not get the extreme partisan spirit of the Commons either, for no one single party has a majority. So we have to spend our time being nice to our political opponents in order to try to persuade them to vote with us. Power in the European Parliament comes from the ability to work together and not from the ability of extremists to hold a government to ransom. It seemed absurd to us that in a Commons which was overwhelmingly pro-European, a few anti-European extremists should be so dominant. It should not surprise anyone that, faced with problems in the real world, it is easy for people from different political parties to come to common solutions. I found no problem, as Chairman of LUFPIG, in working with Socialists like Ken Collins and Terry Wynne or Liberals like Pat Cox and Gijs de Vries. We all had the same objectives; we

207

all respected the special needs and attitudes of our colleagues' different parties.

There is no doubt that Senators for Texas speak for the citizens of Texas who put them there; but there is no doubt either that the hundred Senators in Washington speak for the United States. And so it is in Strasbourg. The Parliament collectively feels bound to work for the interests of the European Union; whereas our co-legislator, the Council of Ministers, being a part-time, very temporary and second-priority activity for each member, does not have the time, energy or knowledge to do more than deal with what is put before them. That is why Maastricht was a mess, why they dare not open their debates and voting record to public scrutiny and why the Parliament feels a special responsibility for the political direction of the Union.

It is this sense of responsibility which makes us anxious to try to find agreement; to find ways of doing things together which will help us all whilst allowing for special cases and special problems. And those detailed negotiations give us a sense of what can and what cannot be done. National interests are made up of a balance of regional and sectional interests, all of which cross frontiers. On agriculture, Northern Ireland has far more in common with the Irish Republic than with Great Britain. The industrial interest is far more important in Germany than the farm interest; but at a critical point in the GATT negotiation, it had to be encouraged to speak up for itself as it eventually did, with decisive effect.

It is to get this feel for the balance of interests, of what is politically possible, that I believe we need to have a second chamber in the European Parliament for members of national parliaments. It is only when you are in debate with different parties from different countries that you can get a feel for what can and cannot obtain a majority. National parliaments have the formal power to smash a carefully structured European policy. To prevent their doing this, governments keep them in ignorance and then present them with a *fait accompli*, daring them to turn it down. That is neither a stable nor a democratic system and one day it will have to be changed.

We in Britain will one day have to take the European Parliament seriously. In every other country there is a free flow of leaders between national governments and the European Commission and Parliament. Jacques Delors was an MEP, then French Finance Minister, then President of the Commission. Simone Veil was a French minister, then an MEP and is now a minister again – and so with all the other countries. But no British minister has given up the Commons to be an MEP; no British MEP has become a Commissioner. One day a British ex-MEP may be in the cabinet, but only after serving due apprenticeship in the Commons. Like a lot of other attitudes, that does not serve the British interest.

Those of us who live in a warm and active family circle, spanning the generations, are especially conscious of what so many others today are missing.

Elizabeth's mother, Bethan Lloyd-Jones, lived with us and with her other daughter, Ann, until she died at the age of ninety-two, in full possession of her faculties and able, to the last, to tell us what to do. She was a great character. Our children, challenged to decide whether their grandfather (*Dadcu* in Welsh) or grandmother (*Gu*) had the last word, said without hesitation that it was *Gu* (on their own parents, they thought it was 50/50).

She retained her beauty and dignity to the end. She had twenty-seven proposals of marriage, of which Martyn Lloyd-Jones was the first and the twenty-seventh. Her father was an eye specialist and among his patients was David Lloyd-George. We still have his wedding present to them. She trained as a doctor, but gave it up, together with a comfortable professional life in London, to marry Martyn and go to live in a small house in Aberavon, where he went as minister. She never had any complaint. She looked after her own mother (known in Welsh as *Mamgu Bach*) until she died in her nineties, and it was inconceivable that we would not keep her with us in the ten years while she was herself a widow.

It was sometimes difficult juggling with diaries, but her company was its own reward. She defended her views stoutly against her grandchildren and I remember her, round the big kitchen table, silencing completely a leading theologian on a point of Christian doctrine. She was unbeatable at croquet and a devoted follower of TV billiards. We have found it hard to watch it since she died.

We were very glad that she saw her first great-grandchild, Bethan's Myfanwy, and we had a four-generation photograph taken. In the silence as her coffin was lowered into the grave on the slope above the Teifi, we could hear Myfanwy's voice, the new generation taking the place of the old.

When Christopher left Oxford, he flirted first with the Bar and then with the BBC, but finally, after taking another degree at Cambridge, he settled to the life of a publisher's editor, persuading, with considerable success, busy people to spend a great amount of their time in writing books for little material reward. He was a great help in deciding the pattern of the Doctor's books; he persuaded Jim Packer to do a series, and Roy Clements to write his first book and, most recently, master-minded a successful bible guide series for house-groups. Then his company was taken over, together with all the books he had commissioned, and his job disappeared. Such is life in Britain in the mid-nineties.

He was in his mid-thirties when in 1991 he married Paulette Moore from Virginia, doing a doctorate in New College, Oxford. The wedding was in the Chapel, no less than five clergy officiating, with a reception in the college gardens.

Bethan graduated from Nottingham, with a year's teacher training in Cambridge. She had lots of admirers and, under strict instructions from Elizabeth, I made no comments on any of them. But at Cambridge she accepted Richard Marshall, a Yorkshire student on the same course, who came and asked for her hand in marriage in the old-fashioned way, and her parents and brothers breathed a huge sigh of relief. They both taught in West London comprehensives, Richard moving up to head of department and Bethan transferring to be a lecturer in King's College, London.

At about the same age that I was advising the Labour opposition on the virtues of little Neddies, Bethan is campaigning on education policies, now hot issues in the political debate. The main difference is that she is a committed Socialist, while I, at that time, was only committed to the views I was putting. At one time, with Christopher a Conservative, Bethan a Socialist and Jonathan a Social Democrat, we had some good discussions round the table in the big kitchen.

Myfanwy is now a thoughtful and very articulate four and Angharad, born in 1992, is now two, almost as talkative, bright as a button and with the strongest sense of humour I've ever seen in any child. They are exhausting, demanding and extremely enjoyable. They certainly keep us young. It is when grandchildren come that you know absolutely without a doubt that there is nothing, however expensive, which can substitute for a family.

Although Jonathan lost a term at school and was late in going to university, he finally got a First at Sussex. He then mortgaged himself to go to Columbia for an MBA, worked round the clock for five years as a consultant with Booz Allen, first in London and then in New York, was finally head-hunted by one of his clients and is now Vice President of Corporate Strategy for a huge telecommunications corporation in Stamford, Connecticut.

In 1994 he married Megan, our second American daughter-in-law, who works for the Baltimore Symphony Orchestra. Her sister Molly and her husband Bill were good friends of Jonathan at Columbia and they now live near them in an old (eighteenth-century) house in Ridgefield, Connecticut.

While being quite content with each other's company, Elizabeth and I would not miss the weekly, often daily, interchange with a lively and warm-hearted family, who do their best to keep us young.

ENDPIECE

After fifteen years in semi-exile, we have come home to a country which seems unhappy and confused. Some of that arises from the political errors of the Thatcher years and I have already said enough about that. Some of it continues because militant Thatcherites hold the balance of power in the House of Commons. It is hard, when there is someone whom you have known well and is now Prime Minister, to be entirely impartial, but I doubt whether, given the Parliamentary arithmetic, another Conservative Prime Minister could have done anything different.

I believe that there are political changes which must be made; there have to be measures to recreate a sense of community in a society where it is everyone for themselves.

In our thousand-year history, we have been held together by the institutions of family, Church and state and, in the last thirty years, the family and the Church have been gravely weakened, leaving the state with the impossible job of filling the gap. So, at the least, the state should look for the help it can get from the intermediate institutions between citizen and government which the Thatcher years have done so much to dissolve.

We need regional government to tap regional loyalties; we need it now, entrenched in a national constitution. We have to encourage the independence of the other organisations to which people give loyalty and which can inspire some social cohesion, such as the trades unions, the professions and the universities. They will not be enough to substitute for the breakup of the family and the decline of the Church, but they will stand in until we can put right what has gone wrong. For something quite fundamental has gone wrong.

I don't think we need to argue any longer that British society really has gone wrong. We don't just have to look at the terrible social statistics. People have started to look back to the good old days, not so long ago, when almost everyone had a job, most people had a home, children stayed at school, the family stayed together and we all looked forward to better times. We look back because we dare not look forward.

When I first went into public service thirty years ago, unemployment varied between a quarter and half a million; now it varies between two and three million. In those days the trades unions used the bargaining power of the strong to help the weak; now the unions are pushed to one side and the powerful pocket what they can for themselves. In those days, the taxes of the rich were used to help the poor, but today's taxes are easy on the rich and hard on the poor. In those days the elected government had some control over the economy; it could pull the economic levers and get results. Now the levers come off in their hands. In those days there was a public housing programme; today there is none.

We have created an underclass again, and right at the bottom of the bottom of the pile are beggars once more on the streets and youngsters living among old winos in cardboard boxes under the arches.

Don't just blame the politicians. They are simply a mirror of the society which elected them and they know that the only thing that really matters in an election is the amount of money we have in our pockets. All parties now recognise that it is the haves who elect them and the have-nots are only a minority. Greed is the logical result of the belief that there is no life after death. We grab what we can while we can, however we can and hold on to it hard.

Thirty years ago there was still some pretence that the Christian faith was the foundation of the moral and social order. Now it is politically correct to hold that there is no absolute right or wrong. Dogma is out and tolerance is in (though we find that tolerance does not extend to those who question that particular dogma, so there a major flaw in the logic of the argument).

The result is moral confusion. The powerful use their power and the weak go to the wall, not just the poor, but the weak-willed, and especially the children, who have always depended on the age-old combination of discipline and loving care given by the family.

Today, with the change in the divorce laws, mothers who feel bound to care for their children are often at the mercy of fathers who do not. The divorce rate has soared and so has the number of one-parent families, 90 per cent of them mothers left behind to look after the children alone. There are estates in our great cities where nearly half of the households are unmarried mothers, where hardly any of the men have a job; the children don't see the point of staying at school or of training. These estates, which have become no-go areas under the effective control of gangs, are where drug-dealing and drug abuse follow naturally. But even more affluent areas are full of confusion and misery, which money helps to hide.

I doubt whether government alone can turn the tide. The political leaders do not know what has hit them. The great changes of the sixties were not meant to turn out like this. The permissive laws on divorce, on homosexual practices, on abortion and pornography, and the removal of the Christian moral law as the basis for our social structure, were all meant to make for a happier, freer society. But that is not how it has turned out.

A chief constable of a big city once said to me that if two parents could not control a couple of children, a few of his men could not control two thousand. The social services have been overwhelmed, but where they can act, they can only deal with the symptoms. If the cause is moral failure, they are gagged. A drugs unit can help people to come off drugs, but cannot give them a moral reason for staying off.

Around the cabinet table, ministers will admit that people are deeply anxious because the social pillars of society have been shaken. In Britain, all down the centuries, the Christian faith has given governments moral guidelines to help them shape legislation and social structures. Now that it is no longer politically correct to have moral guidelines, they do not know what to do.

They see a weak Church, which has gone along with the tide of worldly opinion, whose moral guidance is so flabby that it is no longer respected by the citizens, so it no longer performs its function as the 'salt and light' of society, preventing corruption and showing the way. Yet, feeling that legislation is not enough without moral cement, they are pressed to make the moral arguments themselves. But as the failure of the 'back to basics' slogan showed, they are even less able to inspire moral behaviour than the Church.

We are not yet beyond the point of no return. I believe that the Christian Church can once more inspire the loyalty which has carried it through two thousand years and has won the public argument against Greek philosophy, Roman imperialism and the paganism of the Northern European tribes, including our own. But this loyalty has to be earned, it cannot be imposed. We have to win it, as we have always won it, in the market place of ideas.

For the Christian Church, of course, the first duty is to teach the gospel of salvation, the offer of God's forgiveness for our rebellion, if we will only ask for that forgiveness, and trust in Christ's death to redeem us. That gift of eternal salvation matters more than anything in this life.

But faith without works is dead; we have to show our faith by our works; we have to be concerned, as Christ was and the Prophets before him, for the injustices and injuries of this world, and we must do our best to put them right.

So we will not win this public argument unless words are backed by deeds, by obedience to the second great commandment, that we are to love our neighbours as ourselves. Christ, who gave his life for men and women, when he was here on earth, taught the people, but he also healed and fed them. Because he showed his love by his care for the needs which they felt most acutely, they were prepared to believe him when he told them of a spiritual need which they did not yet recognise. Christians have to do the same.

The damage done by a materialistic and permissive society has created new problems which are too much for the existing social institutions. The Churches and para-church organisations are already at work here and there. I believe that we need to get together in all the major cities to form Christian Action Networks, so that anyone in need can look to a church and be directed to help somewhere in the network. As the networks develop, so we can help each other develop best practice, both locally and nationally.

Before I retired from the European Parliament, the Council of the Evangelical Alliance (EA) asked me to succeed Timothy Dudley-Smith, Bishop of Thetford, as President. I said that I would do it on condition that I would have their backing in trying to organise common action between churches in dealing with the problems, including unemployment, which all of them now have to face.

Our EA team have so far visited four London boroughs: Brent, Hackney, Lewisham and Southwark; and thirteen cities: Cardiff and Swansea in Wales; Brighton, Bristol, Southampton and Swindon in the South; Manchester in the North-west; Birmingham, Coventry and Nottingham in the Midlands; and Aberdeen, Edinburgh and Glasgow in Scotland. Yorkshire and the North-east are due to follow soon. On most of these seventeen visits we found that there were church projects where help could be offered, especially for the young.

The main problem was not that young people did not want work; it was that, after prolonged and unsuccessful efforts to find it, they became so discouraged that they no longer felt of any use to anyone and that it was not worth trying. So we found classes aimed, first of all, to recover their confidence in themselves, then to find out where their interests lay and what they could do and, finally, to teach them how to put in a job application and conduct themselves in an interview. In most projects the success rate was about 70 per cent.

In a Southwark project, teams went round the big estates offering training. They found a heavy goods vehicle driver who said that that was his only qualification and that there just were no vacancies for the job. But when pressed on his hobbies, he said that he was the Secretary of the Southwark Society for Exotic Birds. So, they pointed out, he had organising skills, he collected subscriptions, he bought and sold birds. There was a life outside heavy goods vehicles.

A project in Brent was the only one we found on our visits

which undertook training, with funding by the local council. They concentrated their limited resources on skills in high demand, mainly word-processing. Elizabeth and I paid a quick visit to a project in Belfast where the young unemployed ran their own café and drop-in centre. But there is clearly a limit to the jobs which churches themselves can create.

Much more worrying was the plight of the big estates in cities where whole industries had closed down. We visited estates in Manchester and Glasgow where half or more of the families were unmarried mothers and, where there was a father, he was usually out of work. So children were being brought up in a culture in which regular work had no part and they had no incentive to stay at school or to acquire skills. They had nothing to do and all day to do it in. There was thieving and joy-riding, and the Manchester estate seemed to be a no-go area for the police.

In the Glasgow estate, seven churches had come together to form a community through which the people who lived there could run the estate themselves, and this had been funded by the local council. Morale there seemed to be a great deal better, though the church we visited still had to take some precautions against vandalism.

It is not enough to tell young people brought up on these estates to get on their bikes and look for work. Most don't have bikes, but more important, they have never learnt the social skills needed to be part of a work team; they have no practical skills, nor have they even learnt the minimum discipline needed for any type of work, however simple.

On these estates, the problem of unemployment was, of course, made worse by the breakup of the family. On the Manchester estate, a team of three young Christian workers tried to provide a substitute family, renting a house on the estate, as a drop-in centre, taking the youngsters swimming, to volley-ball and out on the moors.

Too many young people in Britain today have no home at all. Their mother has been forced by her new partner to choose between him and a stroppy and resentful teenager. After a final flaming row, the teenager has left home to to add to the growing number of young homeless. So a major job for the churches in each city has been to find homes for homeless teenagers.

In one church in Penarth near Cardiff, we found the 'uncle' to all the homeless boys sitting in an accessible office just inside the glass doors of the church. He knew the landladies in Penarth and they trusted him not to land them with a wrong one. The church had a fund to cover the first week's rent. Other churches elsewhere had houses for short-term stays. Until they have an address it is almost impossible for these boys to find a job, so a home is the first stage to getting themselves sorted out.

The teenage girls seem less likely to find themselves homeless, but when they do, they are picked up by pimps and are then out of reach; but in Glasgow we found an old pub being converted into a drop-in for teenage prostitutes, a temporary haven out of sight of pimp and client.

The churches try to help the single mothers too and a lot of churches have day nurseries where mothers can leave children while they are at work and where they can talk to friendly helpers about their own problems. We called on one beyond what our taxi-driver called the 'front-line' in Bristol. He would take us no further; it was at the centre of the drugs trade. But, after a short walk, we found a couple running a day nursery.

The drug trade is getting worse, and not just in cities. A senior police superintendent in the Fens took me out to lunch to meet his drugs officer. In the little Fen towns, where there were no buses to Peterborough or Wisbech and little to do, the drug dealers were marketing leisure drugs as an alternative way of escape from boredom. Legalisation might channel the trade away from the pushers into legitimate shops, but no one knows how much the number of clients would multiply or what would be the result of extensive drug abuse in a society where we increasingly depend for our safety on the rigid personal discipline of others.

In Swansea we visited a rehabilitation centre, run by a smartly dressed and very able young man who had been a drug addict himself. In a preliminary visit to Liverpool one church took us to a café with motherly ladies behind the counter, just opposite the corner where most of the drug dealing was done. It was, while it lasted, another way out for those who were just lonely. But the café was repeatedly vandalised and had to be closed.

At the heart of many of the problems was the breakup of the family, and many churches concentrated on counselling couples who were in marital difficulties. Sometimes the problem had nothing to do with relationships; it was debt. They had not counted the interest cost of what they were buying and before they knew where they were, the only solution seemed to be to split up and disappear from their creditors' view. One church had a debt advice centre tactfully concealed at the far end of a bookshop. They reported that among those most likely to be caught out were accountants who thought they could calculate precisely how near they could sail to the wind.

There were two churches in Manchester which had teams who visited those dying of aids whose families and former partners no longer wanted to know them. The most distressing visit I paid was to an excellent aids hospice. They have now had to open an annexe for mothers and their babies, both dying of aids. They do all they can for those who come, but it is a horrible way to die.

So I have a new job, to try to put together Christian Action Networks among the Evangelical churches (my particular bailiwick) in the major cities and boroughs. Each church seems to be trying to do something, but none seems to know what others are doing. We need a network: first to make sure that anyone going to a church can be directed to someone with experience and resources to help; second, so that the local community know where to send friends and constituents who need help; third, so that we can all learn from each other's experience; and finally so that those rich in funds and/or skilled helpers can help those who are not.

In between my last two sessions in Strasbourg, Elizabeth and I visited seven of the ten great Spring Harvest/Word Alive conferences run alongside the Evangelical Alliance to talk about the Christian Action Networks. By contrast to the thin attendance at any political meeting nowadays, there was an average of a thousand at each of these ninety-minute seminars. So there is a willingness in the Church to do what it can for our country today.

But picking up the wreckage is not enough. One way or another, society will insist that we restore a moral order too. All depends on what moral order it is. In the thousand years of our history, we have always gone back to the basic Christian teaching, stripped of additions to underpin all the pretension and power of prelates. Wycliffe and his Lollards before the Reformation,

Hugh Latimer of Cambridge and others during the Reformation, the Puritans a hundred years later, then Whitefield, Wesley and the Methodists in the eighteenth century, and Spurgeon in the nineteenth, all preached the original Christian gospel and the Churches, revived and reformed, set standards for society. The twentieth century has produced its giants too, but none of them has stopped the slide.

We are told that in this multi-faith society there can be no single moral order. But there is no society which has survived without a moral order. If the intellectual leaders undermine the old moral order, people will find a new one. Modern science, which was founded on the Christian view of a unique, orderly, rational, stable and benign creator, will give way to the old pagan beliefs in conflicting deities, disorderly, irrational, unstable and malign. As we pass by the artwork in the airport lounge which reflects today's irrationality, we should be thankful that the design of the aircraft still reflects the Christian view of science.

No one can predict the outcome. We can simply work and pray for what we believe. But time may be short. The intellectuals have not carried the people with them. Political correctness as a guideline has limited popular appeal. Few people want intellectuals telling them what to do. As the social disorder grows, the fuel for a populist backlash grows with it. Politics is edging to the right. The tabloids are playing on a real xenophobia. People want the streets to be safe again, they want their jobs back from those they think have taken them and they want tough punishment for crime.

That is not a position of equilibrium and people will eventually insist on a stable society, however it is achieved. The danger is that some politician will produce a blend of popular morality and a political programme backed with racism in a strong, attractive, nostalgic call to national regeneration, which will appeal to us as Hitler appealed to the confused and demoralised German society sixty years ago. The absence of a British constitution, the unrestrained political power of the House of Commons, the ability to form a government on a minority of votes, the weakness of the Church, even the present unpopularity of the next generation of the Royal Family, all ease the path for a democratically elected authoritarian government.

I have always been far more worried about Fascism than Communism, for Fascism is based on nationalism which has a far broader and deeper resonance. It would be only too easy to recruit our own brownshirts from the young unemployed, as the paramilitaries did in Northern Ireland. No one has shown them love, so why should they show love to anyone else? They have nothing to live for; someone one day may find them a cause, and make them feel that at last they do have something to live for and something to fight for. We have no lack of minorities on whom to blame the loss of jobs and houses, the loss of the old national identity. And the danger is that the backlash would not be confined to the young and out of work. English nationalism has a strong resonance across the social spectrum. It is not limited to the tabloids; there are articles in the respectable press, based as much on emotion and as little on logic. Our Continental friends, especially those who are older, recognise the symptoms only too well.

Even Christians, members as we are of an international Church which prohibits division by race, are not immune, and would welcome the overthrow of the intellectual humanists; would want order in society, the return of family and discipline, the recognition that crime deserves punishment. Many would warm to an appeal to our heritage, reading into it the struggles of a Protestant England against the embrace of Continental Catholicism – we do not have to look too hard for that attitude now. Only too late would we find that we had lost the most important part of Britain's Christian heritage: the freedom of speech which allows us to preach the gospel of Jesus Christ in public.

The Churches should share the blame for any drift to autocracy. By their failure to stand for the historic creeds, they have undermined the Christian moral order, leaving a moral vacuum which the state feels forced to fill. But in Christian teaching, Church and state are separate; it is the Church which teaches what is right and wrong, and on that moral consensus, the state lays down what is legal and illegal. But when the state itself lays down what is right and wrong it becomes totalitarian; for against that there is no appeal of conscience. That is where we are now heading and I doubt whether, at the current rate of destabilisation, we can be sure of more than another decade of democracy.

I believe that only a Christian view of life is capable of holding together the free society which we have inherited. It is not an order to be imposed, but argued on its merits, as the early Christians argued it in the pagan Roman Empire. All Christians should ever want is the freedom to put their case, for we believe that it has an echo in the universal conscience, which is why it has prevailed for over two thousand years and why it is the most widely accepted faith in the world. All the conversions recorded in the New Testament were of people who, like the Roman Centurion, Cornelius, or the Ethiopian eunuch, actively wanted to know about the Christian faith. So a forced conversion is no conversion. Jesus sent out the disciples to preach the gospel, but he told them not to stay in the villages which did not accept it.

But it was not just by what they said, but by what they did that the early Christians won over the pagans. 'Faith without works is dead.' So if our Christian Action Networks can heal where it hurts, they will convince more people than all the intellectual argument.

When I am the elder on the door at Eden Chapel on a Sunday, I find it hard to be pessimistic. Seeing young and old pouring across New Square, to pack our five hundred seats and overflow until the children go out to family bible school, how can one not have hope? The students are not just those brought up in Christian families; many had no faith when they arrived in Cambridge, but a friend brought them. Many resisted Christianity as hard as they knew how; produced all the usual arguments, hardened their hearts, sneered at their Christian friends and yet something inside held them until they confessed that they themselves were the trouble.

Our minister, Roy Clements, understands all this. He himself came to Christianity the hard way, the chief antagonist of all the Christians at school in East London, – until his mother got rid of a door-to-door evangelist by passing him on to her son. The evangelist listened and then suggested that it would strengthen his arguments if he actually read the New Testament. Then he could really pick the Christians to pieces. So he read it and found that it picked him to pieces instead.

He knows all the arguments he himself used to put. He has a doctorate in chemistry and no one is going to tell him that

Christianity and science are incompatible. But, as he leans his six foot six across the pulpit, he knows that what gripped him will grip them, the word of God itself; so his sermons are not his own opinions on what is right and wrong, but an explanation, in today's language for sure, of what Christ has said, what the Apostles have spelt out, with Christ's own authority, about the nature of men and women and the nature of God. They listen for up to an hour and come back next Sunday for more.

It is not a gospel for the British, it is a universal gospel. There are maybe thirty to forty Chinese every Sunday morning. We have a Sri Lankan family, some Koreans, occasional Japanese and lots of Africans. They are a reminder that the Christian faith is universal and growing fast, not just part of our own culture and not everywhere in decline.

Our church is not alone in Cambridge. The Anglican Round Church overflowed and had to move first to the union, then to a bigger church building in the city centre, and now that too is overflowing. Few students go to hear the college Dean down the road who has had such extensive coverage on radio and TV as he tried to explain away the Christian faith.

Fifty years ago, we in the CICCU were a tiny band, fighting the prevailing liberalism of Cambridge. The CICCU today is about five times the size and, at student level, liberalism has almost disappeared. Yet it is the tolerance by liberalism of secular humanism which is responsible for the deserted churches of Britain and for the moral state of the nation. I cannot but believe that the leaders going out from the Christian Unions of our universities today will, under God, turn the tide. Under Douglas Johnson, the IVF Easter conference would be a few hundreds. For the last two years the UCCF had fifteen hundred students at the Easter 'Word Alive'.

Douglas Johnson founded the Christian Medical Fellowship, where Christian doctors tackle all the moral issues raised by new laws and new technology. His successor, Oliver Barclay, helped to form similar bodies for other professions; so there is a growing band of Christian leaders everywhere.

And yet it takes time for changes in the country's intellectual climate to work through. However bankrupt secular humanism may be, its beliefs that there is no God and that there is no absolute right and wrong are what is wrecking society today. That is why what happens in our cities is so critical. The answer may filter down intellectual channels in the end, but today it is Christian love in desperate situations which alone can save our society from collapse and the backlash which would follow.

Appendix

BRITAIN'S ECONOMY

The Sixties and Seventies

In the sixties and seventies Britain had no oil income and very limited currency reserves. The bipartisan objective of economic policy was to reconcile the post-war pledge of full employment with the imperative need for a surplus of exports over imports. Co-operation between government, management and trades unions was thought necessary to that objective.

The first set of figures shows the battle to achieve that aim between 1964, when I first entered public service, and 1979, the last year before the North Sea oil revenue.

	UK current balance of o'seas trade £000s	Unemployment 000s	%	Investment in plant and machinery for manufacturing (1990 prices) £000s	1970 = 100
1964	(376)	381	1.6	6,437	69
1965	(52)	329	1.4	6,985	75
1966	83	360	1.5	7,417	80
1967	(298)	559	2.4	7,428	80
1968	(288)	564	2.4	8,044	87
1969	440	559	2.4	8,375	90
1970	871	557	2.5	9,284	100
1971	1,076	752	3.3	8,741	94
1972	176	835	3.7	7,551	81
1973	(1,056)	588	2.6	7,941	86
1974	(3,378)	585	2.6	9,000	97
1975	(1,674)	936	4.1	8,473	91
1976	(1,116)	1,304	5.6	8,205	88
1977	(284)	1,423	6.0	8,367	90
1978	620	1,410	6.0	9,667	104
1979	(1,670)*	1,325	5.6	10,365	112

Sources: CSO Economic Trends No 326 (Dec 1980); 1994 Annual Supplement (for unemployment); The Economist Diary 1982

Notes:

1. The deficits for 1967 and 1968 were the cause and consequence of the devaluation of the pound in November 1967. In the critical decisions at the end of 1968 the Treasury, having been over-optimistic, was over-pessimistic and did not believe that 1969 would be so firmly in surplus.
2. In 1971, my last year as Director General of Neddy, Britain had a trade surplus of £1bn, but by 1974, the year the Conservatives left office, there was a deficit of £3.4bn (a combination of the Barber boom and the soaring cost of imported oil), from which we gradually recovered over the next four years.
3. *The trade balance for 1979 went into deficit because of imports of about £2bn for equipment for oil production.
4. The year of the referendum on Europe (1975) saw a setback in both exports and investment in manufacturing plant, but in the four years after the 'Yes' vote, exports rose by 26 per cent and investment in plant by 23 per cent.
5. The sharp rise in the unemployment figures in 1975 and 1976 reflects the effect of the first oil shock on an economy with limited reserves, suffering from long exclusion from the EEC and also from the end, in the early seventies, of the post-war currency system, linking the main currencies, including the pound, to the dollar.

The Eighties

In 1979 the incoming government, freed by the oil income from the constraint of the balance of trade, abandoned the post-war consensus and the policy of full employment. The hard pound kept down the cost of imports and, with it, the cost of living. Real income rose to record heights – but at the cost of unemployment five to six times as high as it was in the sixties and twice as high as the late seventies. Even worse in the long term, the hard pound damaged the heart of Britain's export effort: our manufacturing industry. Our share of world trade dropped by over a fifth and investment in manufacturing dropped by nearly 40 per cent, not recovering for a decade. Effectively the oil income was used for consumption, so when the oil surplus dwindled, instead of having a refurbished industry, we were heavily dependent on imports; our visible trade was deep in the red; we had to borrow billions a year to keep going and the aim of full employment was further off than ever.

The figures below plot the dissipation of the oil income and the resultant unemployment.

Year	Balance of trade in oil £000s	Non-oil balance £000s	Balance of visible trade £000s	Current balance £000s
1980	308	1,049	1,357	2,795
1981	3,106	146	3,252	6,639
1982	4,638	(2,728)	1,910	4,604
1983	6,972	(8,479)	(1,507)	3,794
1984	6,933	(12,100)	(5,167)	1,955
1985	8,101	(11,229)	(3,128)	3,162
1986	4,070	(13,433)	(9,363)	(37)
1987	4,183	(15,058)	(10,904)	(3,822)
1988	2,797	(23,612)	(20,815)	(14,672)
1989	1,491	(24,593)	(23,112)	(20,312)

	Unemployment		Investment in plant and machinery in manufacturing (1990 prices)	
	000s	%	£000s	1970 = 100
1980	1,590	6.1	9,818	106
1981	2,422	9.3	8,102	87
1982	2,080	10.8	7,631	82
1983	2,988	11.5	7,697	83
1984	3,038	11.5	8,862	95
1985	3,149	11.7	10,330	111
1986	3,161	11.7	9,844	106
1987	2,827	10.4	10,258	110
1988	2,255	8.2	11,169	120
1989	1,693	6.1	11,998	124

Sources: CSO Economic Trends 1990 Nos 435 and 440; for investment, CSO Economic Trends, 1994 Annual Supplement and, for unemployment, Economist Diary 1991

Notes:

1. The non-oil balance is mainly manufacturing industry and the current balance takes into account services. Deficits are shown in brackets.

2. The high pound in the early eighties not only lost nearly a quarter of existing manufacturing production, but investment in new plant did not recover for four years, until the pound came down again and then, with the opening of the frontiers following the Single European Act in 1986, it recovered and went up to new heights – though at peak in 1989, it was no more than 24 per cent up on the 1978 level.

The Early Nineties

	Current trade balance £000s	Unemployment 000s	Investment in plant and machinery in manufacturing (1990 prices) £000s	1970 = 100
1990	(22,512)	1,799	11,495	129
1991	(19,035)	1,664	10,333	124
1992	(8,176)	2,292	9,677	104
1993	(10,311)	2,946	n.a.	

Sources: Balance of trade and unemployment, CSO Economic Trends October 1994; Investment, CSO 1994 Annual Supplement

Notes:
1. In the first four years of the nineties, Germany borrowed to pay the very heavy cost of union with the former Communist East Germany and this forced up European interest rates, curbed the growth of the single European market and finally, in September 1993, broke the European Monetary System, forcing the weakest economies, Britain (we finally fixed the pound in 1990) and Italy, out altogether. Investment, as the figures show, dropped sharply back to the level of 1978 and, as we go to press, is probably lower still.
2. Unless and until Britain is part of a stronger European Monetary Union, where the German domestic policy can no longer dominate the European economy, we are once more trapped in the vicious spiral of high trade deficits, low investment and continuing high unemployment. Those who wrap the Union Jack round the pound never say how this would help to further Britain's vital interests or how they would deal with the problem of a weak economy, heavily dependent on holding our own in international trade.

Index

INDEX

231

232